Lecture Notes in Computer S

Commenced Publication in 1973
Founding and Former Series Editors:
Gerhard Goos, Juris Hartmanis, and Jan van Lee

Thomas Gschwind   Uwe Aßmann
Oscar Nierstrasz (Eds.)

Software
Composition

4th International Workshop, SC 2005
Edinburgh, UK, April 9, 2005
Revised Selected Papers

 Springer

Volume Editors

Thomas Gschwind
IBM Research
Zurich Research Laboratory
Säumerstraße 4, 8803 Rüschlikon, Switzerland
E-mail: thomasg at ieee.org

Uwe Aßmann
Technische Universität Dresden
Fakultät Informatik
Institut für Software- und Multimediatechnik
01062 Dresden, Germany
E-mail: uwe.assmann at inf.tu-dresden.de

Oscar Nierstrasz
University of Bern
Software Composition Group
Neubrückstrasse 10, 3012 Bern, Switzerland
E-mail: oscar.nierstrasz at acm.org

Library of Congress Control Number: 2005931333

CR Subject Classification (1998): D.2, D.1.5, D.3, F.3

ISSN   0302-9743
ISBN-10   3-540-28748-5 Springer Berlin Heidelberg New York
ISBN-13   978-3-540-28748-3 Springer Berlin Heidelberg New York

Springer is a part of Springer Science+Business Media

springeronline.com

© Springer-Verlag Berlin Heidelberg 2005
Printed in Germany

Typesetting: Camera-ready by author, data conversion by Scientific Publishing Services, Chennai, India
Printed on acid-free paper   SPIN: 11550679   06/3142   5 4 3 2 1 0

Preface

Component-based software development is the next step after object-oriented programming that promises to reduce complexity and improve reusability. These advantages have also been identified by the industry, and consequently, over the past years, a large number of component-based techniques and processes have been adopted in many of these organizations. A visible result of this is the number of component models that have been developed and standardized. These models define how individual software components interact with each other and simplify the design process of software systems by allowing developers to choose from previously existing components.

The development of component models is a first step in the right direction, but there are many challenges that cannot be solved by the development of a new component model alone. Such challenges are the adaptation of components, and their development and verification.

Software Composition is the premiere workshop to advance the research in component-based software engineering and its related fields. SC 2005 was the fourth workshop in this series. As in previous years, SC 2005 was organized as an event co-located with the ETAPS conference.

This year's program consisted of a keynote on the revival of dynamic languages given by Prof. Oscar Nierstrasz and 13 technical paper presentations (9 full and 4 short papers). The technical papers were carefully selected from a total of 41 submitted papers. Each paper was thoroughly peer reviewed by at least three members of the program committee and consensus on acceptance was achieved by means of an electronic PC discussion. This LNCS volume contains the revised versions of the papers presented at SC 2005.

Finally, the organizers would like to express their gratitude to a large number of people without whom this event would not have been possible: the authors of submitted papers, the Program Committee, and the external referees for their careful reviews and active participation in the paper selection process, and Dirk Peters who managed the electronic submission and reviewing service with the fabulous Paperdyne Conference Management System. We would also like to thank Massimo Felici in his role as the ETAPS 2005 Satellite Events Chair who simplified our task considerably by scheduling our work and providing us with instructions.

June 2005

Thomas Gschwind
Uwe Aßmann
Oscar Nierstrasz
(Proceedings Editors)

Organization

This year's Software Composition Workshop (SC 2005) was held on April 9, 2005, in Edinburgh, Scotland, as a co-located event of the ETAPS conference. SC 2005 was the fourth workshop in the SC workshop series. Previous workshops were held in 2004 in Barcelona, in 2003 in Warsaw, and in 2002 in Grenoble.

Executive Committee

Program Co-chairs: Thomas Gschwind (IBM Research, Switzerland)
Uwe Aßmann (Technische Universität Dresden, Germany)

Program Committee

Antonia Bertolino (Istituto di Scienza e Tecnologia della Informazione A. Faedo, Italy)
Judith Bishop (University of Pretoria, South Africa)
Pierre Cointe (École des Mines de Nantes, France)
Flavio De Paoli (Università degli Studi di Milano Bicocca, Italy)
Susan Eisenbach (Imperial College London, UK)
Volker Gruhn (Universität Leipzig, Germany)
Arnd Poetzsch-Heffter (Technische Universität Kaiserslautern, Germany)
Paola Inverardi (Università dell'Aquila, Italy)
Mehdi Jazayeri (Technische Universität Wien, Austria)
Welf Löwe (Växjö Universitet, Sweden)
Nenad Medvidovic (University of Southern California, USA)
Oscar Nierstrasz (Universität Bern, Switzerland)
Claus Pahl (Dublin City University, Ireland)
Elke Pulvermüller (Universität Karlsruhe, Germany)
Mario Südholt (École des Mines de Nantes, France)
André van der Hoek (University of California Irvine, USA)
Wim Vanderperren (Vrije Universiteit Brussel, Belgium)

External Referees

Marco Autili
Felice Cardone
Marco Comerio

Bruno De Fraine
Antinisca Di Marco
Sebastian Fischmeister

Harald Gall
Didier Le Botlan
Jacques Malenfant
Johann Oberleitner
Franz Puntigam
Ilie Savga

Simone Semprini
Davy Suvee
Massimo Tivoli
Bart Verheecke

Table of Contents

Component Adaptation and Configuration

On the Revival of Dynamic Languages

Oscar Nierstrasz, Alexandre Bergel, Marcus Denker, Stéphane Ducasse,
Markus Gälli, and Roel Wuyts

Software Composition Group, University of Bern
www.iam.unibe.ch/~scg

Abstract. The programming languages of today are stuck in a deep rut
that has developed over the past 50 years. Although we are faced with
new challenges posed by enormous advances in hardware and internet
technology, we continue to struggle with old-fashioned languages based
on rigid, static, closed-world file-based views of programming. We argue
the need for a new class of dynamic languages that support a view of programming as constant evolution of living and open software models. Such
languages would require features such as dynamic first-class namespaces,
explicit meta-models, optional, pluggable type systems, and incremental
compilation of running software systems.

1 Introduction

It is no exaggeration to say that mainstream programming languages of today
are inherently *static*. That is to say, these languages tolerate change at compile
time, but precious little at run-time. To state the case more strongly, most
languages assume a *closed world view*: specifically, they assume that *the world
is consistent, and it will not change*.

That this assumption is patently false is obvious to anyone who has experi-
enced the development of real, large software systems. Nevertheless, it is a fact
that virtually no programming language today provides specific language mechanisms to help developers cope with the fact that the systems they work on will,
inevitably change [LB85].

As concrete examples, we can observe that it is hard to:

- modify a running system,
- make changes that impact the whole system,
- reason about consequences of change,
- introduce run-time reflection *on-demand*,
- keep code, documentation and tests synchronized.

Furthermore, we can observe that increasing trends towards open, distributed
systems, and pervasive computing make these issues even more critical. In this
paper we take the standpoint that:

*Inherently static languages will always pose an obstacle to the effective
realization of real applications with essentially dynamic requirements.*

T. Gschwind, U. Aßmann, and O. Nierstrasz (Eds.): SC 2005, LNCS 3628, pp. 1–13, 2005.

We therefore conclude that research is urgently needed to develop a new class of *dynamic languages*, *i.e.*, languages that support change at run-time. With this in mind, we outline five complementary research tracks that explore support for change in dynamic programming languages.

In Section 2 we revisit the most basic assumption behind most programming languages today: that programs live in *files*. By challenging this assumption, we argue, we can make it easier to change a running system. In Section 3 we argue that *first-class namespaces* are a fundamental concept missing from most programming languages, yet are needed to properly manage the scope of change. In Section 4 we explore the theme of type systems for dynamic languages (an apparent *non sequitur*), and in particular argue in favour of *pluggable type systems* as a means to reason about change. In Section 5 we explore the notion of *reflection on demand* as a mechanism to support and control both run-time introspection and behavioural reflection. In Section 6 we argue that *examples* integrated into the programming language and environment offer an effective way to keep code, documentation and tests in sync. We conclude in Section 7 with some remarks on ongoing and future work.

2   Living Objects

The static nature of most programming languages is immediately evident in the programming model these languages support. Programs lives in files. To change a system, we must edit these files, recompile them, and restart the system. Oh, and by the way, if the layout of any persistent data changes, we will have to have some *ad hoc* way to migrate the data. It is essentially *impossible to change a running system*. The system must be stopped and restarted for changes to take effect.

Surprisingly little effort has been invested over the years in developing languages that support run-time change to the persistent program state. Smalltalk [Gol84] and its descendants, like Self [US87], support a programming model in which all objects live in a persistent program *image*. This model of persistence, however, is rather weak, as images reside in memory, and must be explicitly saved to the file system. Although intermediate changes are logged, disasters can occur, and images may be corrupted.

Smalltalk and CLOS [Kee89, KdRB91] also support shape-changing of objects: when a class' format is changed (for example, instances are added), the memory layout of instances of this class (or its subclasses) is updated to follow suit [MLW05]. Even though this is a very rudimentary form of data migration, it is quite effective.

Considerable work was done in the mid to late 1980s on object-oriented databases and their integration with programming languages [MOP85, PS87]. This work also led to research on schema evolution [BKKK87], addressing the problem of schema changes to running systems. Considerable research has also been carried out on so-called *database programming languages* [AB87], but these languages have only had a limited impact on programming language design in general.

Aside from various technical difficulties involved in resolving the dichotomy between databases and programming languages [TN88], Bloom and Zdonik noted as early as 1987 that there are numerous cultural differences that make it difficult for programming language and database designers to see eye to eye [BZ87].

Let us imagine what a truly dynamic and persistent object system would be like. In a such a system, one would have the illusion of directly interacting with software artifacts. Software entities and their meta-representations would be causally connected, so that changes would have an immediate effect. Furthermore, the histories of changes would be first-class entities so that change itself can be manipulated. In a distributed object system, local changes may even have a global impact.

Technically, none of these issues are especially problematic. For example languages such as Smalltalk and CLOS already offer dynamic and living object facilities with causally connected meta-representations. Several pragmatic issues must be addressed, however, in order to arrive at an effectively usable dynamic and persistent object system. How, for example, do we control the scope of change in an open, distributed and causally connected system? How do we reason about the impact of possible changes? How do we limit and control the cost of reflection? And how can we keep various software artifacts synchronized with tests and documentation? These are issues that we will touch on in the following sections.

3   First-Class Namespaces

Most programming languages are static in the sense that they assume the world is consistent. They do not tolerate inconsistency. As a consequence, changes must always be made in a way that restores consistency to the world.

Reality, however, dictates that in complex systems, consistency is an illusion. For this reason, workarounds are needed to maintain this illusion, such as deprecation, or ornate naming conventions to differentiate concurrent versions of software artifacts.

There is, in fact, a well-established programming language mechanism that supports inconsistent world views, but it is in most cases unfortunately realized at best as a second class citizen. *Namespaces* are well-defined boundaries providing a set of *definitions*, *i.e.* names bound to values. Every programming language supports various forms of namespaces, be they as fine-grained as the context of a procedure or a block, or as coarse-grained as packages or modules. With the notable exception of Scheme [Dyb03], virtually no mainstream programming languages exist that have all their namespaces as first-class citizens *i.e.* that can be passed and manipulated as any other value in the language.

As it turns out, first-class namespaces can be used to great effect to form the basis of a computational model for a programming language [ALSN01]. First-class namespaces can be used to model objects, classes, metaobjects, software

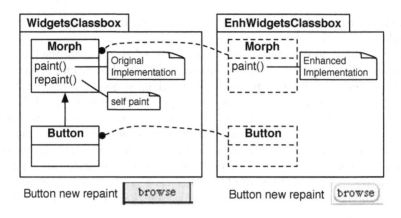

Fig. 1. Implicitly rebinding classes within classboxes.

components, modules, and a variety of compositional abstractions, such as wrappers and mixin layers [AN00, NA00, NA05]. Furthermore, namespaces lend themselves well to formal specification using standard semantic modeling techniques, which can form the basis for reasoning about language constructs [AN05].

A particularly interesting application of namespaces in the context of change is to encapsulate *class extensions*. Languages like Smalltalk [GR89] or CLOS [Kee89] have traditionally supported the ability for programmers to define a set of extensions to existing classes. Extensions typically are used to add or redefine methods in situations where subclassing is not an option. (For example, by extending the class Object, one can ensure that the extension will be available to all classes, not just those that inherit from a particular subclass.)

Classboxes are namespaces that define both classes and class extensions [BDNW05]. A classbox may import a class from another classbox, and extend it locally. The *local rebinding* feature ensures that extensions remain local to the classbox introducing the extension, and other classboxes that (transitively) import the extended classes. A method addition or redefinition can be executed only within the classbox that defines this extension and to other classboxes that import the extended class. Within a given classbox, the world is always consistent, so collaborating classes are always well-defined. But multiple classboxes can support very different views of a universe full of inconsistencies.

The following example illustrates a method extension with local rebinding. Figure 1 depicts a classbox WidgetsClassbox that defines a class Morph, which is the root of the graphic element hierarchy in the Squeak system [IKM+97], and a subclass Button. Morph contains a paint() method and a repaint() method that calls paint(). The classbox EnhWidgetsClassbox imports Morph and redefines the paint() method. It also imports the subclass Button. In the context of WidgetsClassbox, invoking the repaint() method on an instance of Button invokes the definition of paint() in Morph defined by WidgetsClassbox. Within EnhWidgetsClassbox, invoking repaint() triggers the enhanced implementation of paint() defined in EnhWidgetsClassbox. This is an illustration of the *local rebinding* facility.

Static classboxes can be used effectively to bundle a set of related class extensions that capture cross-cutting concerns, much in the way that mixin layers bundle sets of related features that can be applied in tandem [SB02]. *Dynamic* classboxes furthermore offer the possibility to dynamically apply (or disable) a set of related class extensions.

Imagine the situation in which a running system has to be upgraded *without being interrupted* and while *preserving behavior of its clients*. Dynamic classboxes offer a disciplined way out of this predicament: A patch consisting of classboxes can be dynamically applied to a running system without it being halted. Modifications, consisting of method additions and redefinitions, and encapsulated as classboxes, are locally visible to these classboxes and to new clients that rely on them. Former clients are guaranteed not to be impacted whereas new clients can rely on the new system.

Dynamic, first-class namespaces would appear to offer a number of further interesting and useful capabilities. First of all, a namespace can be used to restrict the scope of certain changes. Within a single running system, namespaces could help to indicate which clients may see a given set of changes. More interestingly, dynamic namespaces could broaden their scope at run-time, much in the way that dynamic classboxes can be applied or disabled. With dynamic namespaces, one could gradually introduce changes to a running system, extending the scope of change till it applies to all concerned clients. At any one point in time, however, there would be no need for different parts of the universe of namespaces to be mutually consistent.

4   Pluggable Types

Generally speaking, static languages have *obligatory* and static type systems, that is, they attempt to use static type information to guarantee that no dynamic type errors may occur, and *refuse* any program that cannot be type-checked. The way this is achieved *always* entails a trade-off in the sense that any static type system will prevent you from writing certain "correct" programs simply because it cannot prove that no type error exists. The art of designing a usable type system is to make sure that no "interesting" program is forbidden (or that interesting programs can always be rewritten in an easy way to make them acceptable).

Static type systems, however, are the enemy of change. Reflective code, especially in statically typed object-oriented languages, can be especially cumbersome and verbose, since workarounds are needed for any operations that will not be known till run-time. Even languages that sport state-of-the-art type systems, such as (different variants of) ML or Haskell, struggle with overloading, polymorphism and reflection in the context of type-safety [Mac93]. For example, MetaOCaml, an extension of OCaml, provides a type-safe quasi-quoting mechanism that can be used to generate type-safe code at runtime [Tah03], but has no support for reflection. Extensions of polymorphism (such as first-class poly-morphism in ML [Rus00] or in Haskell [Jon97]) exist but do not always allow for separate compilation (unless the type-preservation rules are relaxed) [KS04].

Furthermore, static type systems can produce a false sense of security. Run-time type-checks (*i.e.* "downcasts") in Java, for example, can hide a host of type-errors.

The issue of static typing is a divisive one, often splitting programmers into two camps: those who believe that dynamic languages are evil because they are "untyped" (not true — they are *dynamically* typed), and those who believe that static languages are evil because they prevent you from writing interesting programs without catching any interesting errors.

Instead of having static types hinder change, we would like to use them to support change. In particular, we want more, rather than less, expressiveness, fewer constraints, and more kinds of checks. We believe there exists a comfortable middle ground. At the center of this middle ground is a simple principle:

> *A type system should never be used to affect the operational semantics of a programming language.*

Once this principle is out of the way, we can entertain various notions of *optional type systems*, such as that of the Strongtalk language [BG93], [Str], which intro-duce static typechecking without compromising flexibility. We can even go one step further and explore the notion of multiple, *pluggable type systems* proposed by Gilad Bracha [Bra04].

Considerable research has been carried out in recent years on non-standard type systems such as (for example) alias types [SWM00], confined types [GPV01], [ZPV03], flow-sensitive type qualifiers [Fos02, FTA02], proxy inference [PSH04], scoped types [ZNV04], and demand-driven type inference with subgoal pruning [SS04].

It is clearly unrealistic to expect that static programming languages will or even could be developed to take advantage of all these new developments. A much more reasonable, and interesting alternative, is to envisage a dynamic programming language into which various non-standard type systems could be plugged. For example, a heuristics-based type inferencer can enable program understanding of dynamically typed programs [Wuy01]. Or a pluggable type-system dealing with worst-case execution times for methods or components can check runtime properties for programs intended to be run in hard real-time systems [HBW02, WDN05].

5   Reflection on Demand

Reflection enables the changing of systems without the need to rebuild or even restart them. This is an important basis for building the dynamic sytems of the future: Mobile, Ubiquitous, Always-On.

To change a running system means that we must *reify* behavioural aspects, *interact* with them to indicate the desired changes, and *reflect* changes to obtain their effects in the running system.

Reflection is a well-understood research topic with a long tradition of support in various programming languages and within various paradigms [FJ89, KdRB91] but with limited support in most static languages [Chi95]. Nevertheless, totally reflective systems suffer from many disadvantages:

- *Security:* If a language is reflective, the client that uses reflection can do anything.
- *Stability:* The effects of reflection are global: In a system with multiple clients, one client using reflection on a system service impacts all other clients.
- *Performance:* Full reflection is costly: To enable it, all behavioral aspects need to be reified in such a way that clients have the opportunity to change them.

These disadvantages all stem from the absence of a scope concept in the context of reflection. Scope is needed to:

- Separate the meta- from the base-layer.
- Define *where* and *when* reflection should be available.
- Limit the reflective interface to certain clients.
- Constrain the effects of reflection to certain clients.

Ideally, we would like to have *scoped reflection on demand*, that is to control *when* and *where* and *for whom* reflective services should be available. Such a reflective language would first of all be more secure, as untrusted clients could be given restricted reflective access. It would also be more stable, since changes made using reflection could be limited to the client that made them. Last but not least it could be made faster, since the reification would only be done for those clients that need it. Two recent research activities give us some hints how this may be achieved.

Mirrors in Self and Strongtalk provide structural reflection on demand [BU04]. In order to reflect on a particular object, a mirror object will be created at run-time. The mirror reifies the reflective services for the object under study. Thus mirrors provide a dedicated interface for the reflective services: meta- and base-layer are separated, the particular interface handed to a client can be defined by the object and it can differ between multiple clients. So mirrors provide some of the properties we need. But they have shortcomings, as the support they offer for full behavioral reflection is limited. They do not support fine-grain reflection below the method level, nor mirror-based intercession. And mirrors do not provide a way to scope the effects of reflective change.

Reflex provides fine-grained behavioural reflection for Java entities [TBN01] [TNCC03]. The entities to be reified can be selected by time (enabled/disabled by the program), or space. For spatial selection we can specify the entity (e.g., a class or an object), the operation (*e.g.* message send or a field access) or combine these to select a specific operation (*e.g.* a certain message sent to a certain object).

Reflex uses bytecode transformations for reifying Java execution entities like instance variable access, method calls, exceptions and typecasts. Java as a static system does not allow bytecode to be modified at runtime, it needs to be done statically at load-time: Only those entities selected at load time can be reflective at runtime.

Geppetto is an implementation of Reflex for Squeak that provides the same fine-grained behavioural reflection for Squeak language entities. It supports reification of variables (instance variables and temps), message sends and message receive. Like Reflex, Geppetto uses bytecode transformation, but as Squeak is a dynamic system, these modifications are done at runtime. With Geppetto we want to explore the ideas of Reflex in a dynamic language, especially how to combine Geppetto with the idea of dynamic classboxes as outlined in Section 3.

Classboxes can be used to package reflective aspects of objects. When reflection is needed, the corresponding classbox can be dynamically loaded. Only clients that need reflection will see those services. Classboxes are used to extend the system without making the effect of this extension global. In the same way, classboxes could scope the effect of reflection.

6   Example Objects

Object-oriented code can be hard to understand, extend and adapt. One source of this difficulty is the disconnect between run-time architecture and source code: whereas at run-time we have a collection of interacting objects, the source code merely presents us with a class hierarchy. As a consequence it can be hard to identify the run-time structures in the code [Nie04]. Furthermore, architectural constraints and contracts tend to be implicit in the code, so it may be hard to tell whether given changes are consistent with the existing contracts in place.

Examples are a well-established medium for communicating how things works in virtually all domains. Dictionaries like the Oxford Dictionary of Current English [Soa01] provide the reader with lots of concrete examples of current usage of a given word. Curiously the use of examples is not widespread in running software systems, though they would offer many benefits. In particular, examples are run-time entities that can be manipulated, examples document usage scenarios, examples can form the basis of executable tests, and finally examples (that fulfil their tests) are guaranteed to be in sync with the running system.

A particularly useful notion is that of *one-method commands*. These are argument-free methods that serve as examples for methods and objects, focus on some given method under test, and return an example object. One-method commands may be composed to form suites of tests.

As an example, consider the following Smalltalk method (defined on the class side of the `Account` class:

```
Account class >> deposit1000n123
  |anAccount|
  anAccount:= Account accountNumber123.
  self test: [ anAccount deposit: 100 ].
  self assert: [ anAccount balance==100 ].
  ^anAccount
```

This code is evaluated by sending the message `Account deposit1000n123`. The method makes use of another one-method command of the `Account` class, called `accountNumber123`, which presumably returns an example `Account.deposit-1000n123` then focuses on the `deposit:` method, thus providing an example usage of this method. (`self test: aBlock` performs `aBlock`, while documenting what is actually under test). A test is performed, (`self assert: ...`) and the modified example object is returned.

Here we can see how tests are composed from one-method commands, and explicitly link tests with methods under test, tests with classes under test, and tests with other tests.

Taivalsaari [Tai97] gives an overview about the philosophical differences between prototypical and class-based languages. We believe that a class-based language with a built-in facility for composing and fetching examples can help to bridge the gap between these two paradigms.

[IKM+97], attempted to bring more concreteness into the Smalltalk layer of Squeak by introducing the method `initializedInstance`. The idea there is to be able to recursively (re-)create exactly one prototypical instance for each class, resembling our idea of example objects. In Squeak 3.7 there are still only 13 implementations of `initializedInstance` so one could say that this concept of providing a single best example object for a given class did not take off.

Deursen *et al.* [Deu01] discuss several benefits and drawbacks of unit tests for program comprehension. They do not discuss how one can navigate between tests and programs but it is clear that they should be together as close as possible.

In [DMBK01] Deursen *et al.* discuss several bad smells of test code. They describe the bad smell of *eager tests* which which test several methods of an object at the same time, and are hard to comprehend. They therefore suggest to apply the extract method refactoring to separate tests into what we call one-method commands which exemplify exactly only one method. Other bad smells include "general fixture" and "test code duplication", which we suggest to clean using de- and recomposition of the test code into one-method commands.

Edwards [Edw04] coined the term "example centric programming". Based on user provided examples (which we again call one-method commands) the developer can browse abstract methods side by side with concrete calls of these methods triggered by the one-method commands. Edwards does not provide means of composing and linking these one-method commands as we do.

7   Conclusions

In many ways, we are still in the dark ages of programming language design. Consider, for example, the great innovations in programming languages over the past fifty years. To a large extent, most of these innovations were achieved in the 1950s and 1960s. It is harder and harder to identify significant contributions over the past 20 years. It is also hard to identify truly radical language designs in recent years.

One may interpret this as a sign that the state-of-the-art in programming language design is stabilizing, or even that research in programming languages is essentially dead. Another interpretation, however, is that language design is in a rut due to our fixation with a certain style of language design. We have argued in this paper that static languages have hampered innovation, and furthermore that the death of file-based languages is the first step towards a new generation of dynamic languages.

We need to come to terms with persistency, inconsistency and change in programming languages. This means that dynamic programming languages should support the notion of software as living, changing systems, they should provide support multiple and possibly inconsistent viewpoints of these systems. Static type systems still have their place, but they should serve rather than hinder expressiveness. To support dynamic change, behavioural reflection is needed, but it should be provided only on-demand, when and where it is needed. Finally, examples integrated into the language run-time can help one to document and test the software in a synchronized fashion.

Acknowledgments

We gratefully acknowledge the financial support of the Swiss National Science Foundation for the project "A Unified Approach to Composition and Extensibility" (SNF Project No. 200020-105091/1, Oct. 2004 - Sept. 2006).

References

[AB87]   Malcolm P. Atkinson and O. Peter Buneman. Types and persistence in database programming languages. *ACM Comput. Surv.*, 19(2):105–170, 1987.

[ALSN01]   Franz Achermann, Markus Lumpe, Jean-Guy Schneider, and Oscar Nierstrasz. Piccola — a small composition language. In Howard Bowman and John Derrick, editors, *Formal Methods for Distributed Processing — A Survey of Object-Oriented Approaches*, pages 403–426. Cambridge University Press, 2001.

[AN00]   Franz Achermann and Oscar Nierstrasz. Explicit Namespaces. In Jürg Gutknecht and Wolfgang Weck, editors, *Modular Programming Languages*, volume 1897 of *LNCS*, pages 77–89, Zürich, Switzerland, September 2000. Springer-Verlag.

[AN05]   Franz Achermann and Oscar Nierstrasz. A calculus for reasoning about software components. *Theoretical Computer Science*, 331(2-3):367–396, 2005.

[BDNW05]   Alexandre Bergel, Stéphane Ducasse, Oscar Nierstrasz, and Roel Wuyts. Classboxes: Controlling visibility of class extensions. *Computer Languages, Systems and Structures*, September 2005. To appear.

[BG93]   Gilad Bracha and David Griswold. Strongtalk: Typechecking Smalltalk in a production environment. In *Proceedings OOPSLA '93, ACM SIGPLAN Notices*, volume 28, pages 215–230, October 1993.

[BKKK87]   Jay Banerjee, Won Kim, H-J. Kim, and H.F. Korth. Semantics and implementation of schema evolution in object-oriented databases. In *Proceedings ACM SIGMOD '87*, volume 16, pages 311–322, December 1987.

[Bra04]   Gilad Bracha. Pluggable type systems, October 2004. OOPSLA Workshop on Revival of Dynamic Languages.

[BU04]   Gilad Bracha and David Ungar. Mirrors: design principles for meta-level facilities of object-oriented programming languages. In *Proceedings of OOPSLA '04, ACM SIGPLAN Notices*, pages 331–344, New York, NY, USA, 2004. ACM Press.

[BZ87]   Toby Bloom and Stanley B. Zdonik. Issues in the design of object-oriented database programming languages. In *Proceedings OOPSLA '87, ACM SIGPLAN Notices*, volume 22, pages 441–451, December 1987.

[Chi95]   Shigru Chiba. A metaobject protocol for C++. In *Proceedings of OOPSLA '95*, volume 30 of *ACM SIGPLAN Notices*, pages 285–299, October 1995.

[Deu01]   Arie van Deursen. Program comprehension risks and opportunities in extreme programming. In *Working Conference on Reverse Engineering*, pages 176–, 2001.

[DMBK01]   Arie van Deursen, Leon Moonen, Alex van den Bergh, and Gerard Kok. Refactoring test code. In M. Marchesi, editor, *Proceedings of the 2nd International Conference on Extreme Programming and Flexible Processes (XP2001)*, pages 92–95. University of Cagliari, 2001.

[Dyb03]   Kent Dybvig. *The Scheme Programming Language*. MIT Press, 2003.

[Edw04]   Jonathan Edwards. Example centric programming. In *OOPSLA 04: Companion to the 19th annual ACM SIGPLAN conference on Object-oriented programming systems, languages, and applications*, pages 124–124. ACM Press, 2004.

[FJ89]   Brian Foote and Ralph E. Johnson. Reflective facilities in Smalltalk-80. In *Proceedings OOPSLA '89, ACM SIGPLAN Notices*, volume 24, pages 327–336, October 1989.

[Fos02]   Jeffrey Scott Foster. *Type Qualifiers: Lightweight Specifications to Improve Software Quality*. Ph.D. thesis, University of California, Berkeley, December 2002.

[FTA02]   Jeffrey S. Foster, Tachio Terauchi, and Alex Aiken. Flow-sensitive type qualifiers. In *Proceedings of PLDI '02 Conference on Programming Language Design and Implementation*, pages 1–12. ACM Press, 2002.

[Gol84]   Adele Goldberg. *Smalltalk 80: the Interactive Programming Environment*. Addison Wesley, Reading, Mass., 1984.

[GPV01]   Christian Grothoff, Jens Palsberg, and Jan Vitek. Encapsulating objects with confined types. In *OOPSLA '01: Proceedings of the 16th ACM SIGPLAN conference on Object oriented programming, systems, languages, and applications*, pages 241–255, New York, NY, USA, 2001. ACM Press.

[GR89]   Adele Goldberg and Dave Robson. *Smalltalk-80: The Language*. Addison Wesley, 1989.

[HBW02]   E. Yu-Shing Hu, G. Bernat, and A. Wellings. A Static Timing Analysis Environment Using Java Architecture for Safety Critical Real-Time Systems. *In Proceedings of 7th IEEE International Workshop on Object-Oriented Real-Time Dependable Systems (WORDS-2002)*, pages 64–71, January 2002.

[IKM+97]   Dan Ingalls, Ted Kaehler, John Maloney, Scott Wallace, and Alan Kay. Back to the future: The story of Squeak, A practical Smalltalk written in itself. In *Proceedings OOPSLA '97, ACM SIGPLAN Notices*, pages 318–326. ACM Press, November 1997.

[Jon97]   Mark P. Jones. First-class polymorphism with type inference. In *POPL '97: Proceedings of the 24th ACM SIGPLAN-SIGACT symposium on Principles of programming languages*, pages 483–496. ACM Press, 1997.

[KdRB91]   Gregor Kiczales, Jim des Rivières, and Daniel G. Bobrow. *The Art of the Metaobject Protocol*. MIT Press, 1991.

[Kee89]   Sonia E. Keene. *Object-Oriented Programming in Common-Lisp*. Addison Wesley, 1989.

[KS04]   Andrew Kennedy and Don Syme. Transposing f to c#: Expressivity of polymorphism in an object-oriented language. *Concurrency and Computation: Practice and Experience*, 16(7), 2004.

[LB85]   Manny M. Lehman and Les Belady. *Program Evolution – Processes of Software Change*. London Academic Press, 1985.

[Mac93]   David B. MacQueen. Reflections on standard ml. In *Functional Programming, Concurrency, Simulation and Automated Reasoning*, pages 32–46. Lecture Notes in Computer Science, 1993.

[MLW05]   Eliot Miranda, David Leibs, and Roel Wuyts. Parcels: a fast and feature-rich binary deployment technology. *Computer Languages, Systems and Structures*, September 2005. To appear.

[MOP85]   David Maier, Allen Otis, and Alan Purdy. Object-oriented database development at servio logic. *IEEE Database Engineering*, 8(4):58–65, December 1985.

[NA00]   Oscar Nierstrasz and Franz Achermann. Supporting Compositional Styles for Software Evolution. In *Proceedings International Symposium on Principles of Software Evolution (ISPSE 2000)*, pages 11–19, Kanazawa, Japan, November 2000. IEEE.

[NA05]   Oscar Nierstrasz and Franz Achermann. Separating concerns with first-class namespaces. In Robert E. Filman, Tzilla Elrad, Siobhán Clarke, and sit Mehmet Ak editors, *Aspect-Oriented Software Development*, pages 243–259. Addison-Wesley, 2005.

[Nie04]   Oscar Nierstrasz. Software evolution as the key to productivity. In A. Knapp M. Wirsing and S. Balsamo, editors, *Radical Innovations of Software and Systems Engineering in the Future*, volume 2941 of *LNCS*, pages 274–282. Springer-Verlag, 2004.

[PS87]   D. Jason Penney and Jacob Stein. Class modification in the gemstone object-oriented DBMS. In *Proceedings OOPSLA '87, ACM SIGPLAN Notices*, volume 22, pages 111–117, December 1987.

[PSH04]   Polyvios Pratikakis, Jaime Spacco, and Michael Hicks. Transparent proxies for java futures. In *OOPSLA '04: Proceedings of the 19th annual ACM SIGPLAN Conference on Object-oriented programming, systems, languages, and applications*, pages 206–223, New York, NY, USA, 2004. ACM Press.

[Rus00]   Claudio V. Russo. First-class structures for standard ml. *Nordic J. of Computing*, 7(4):348–374, 2000.

[SB02]   Yannis Smaragdakis and Don Batory. Mixin layers: an object-oriented implementation technique for refinements and collaboration-based designs. *ACM TOSEM*, 11(2):215–255, April 2002.

[Soa01]   Catherine Soanes, editor. *Oxford Dictionary of Current English*. Oxford University Press, July 2001.

[SS04]   S. Alexander Spoon and Olin Shivers. Demand-driven type inference with subgoal pruning: Trading precision for scalability. In *Proceedings of ECOOP'04*, pages 51–74, 2004.

[Str]   The strongtalk type system for smalltalk. http://bracha.org/nwst.html.

[SWM00]   Frederick Smith, David Walker, and J. Gregory Morrisett. Alias types. In *ESOP '00: Proceedings of the 9th European Symposium on Programming Languages and Systems*, pages 366–381, London, UK, 2000. Springer-Verlag.

[Tah03]   Walid Taha. A gentle introduction to multi-stage programming. In *Domain-Specific Program Generation*, pages 30–50, 2003.

[Tai97]   Antero Taivalsaari. Classes versus prototypes: Some philosophical and historical observations. *Journal of Object-Oriented Programming (JOOP)*, 10(7):44–50, 1997.

[TBN01]   Éric Tanter, Noury Bouraqadi, and Jacques Noyé. Reflex — towards an open reflective extension of java. In *Proceedings of the Third International Conference on Metalevel Architectures and Separation of Crosscutting Concerns*, volume 2192 of *LNCS*, pages 25–43. Springer-Verlag, 2001.

[TN88]   Dennis Tsichritzis and Oscar Nierstrasz. Fitting round objects into square databases. In S. Gjessing and K. Nygaard, editors, *Proceedings ECOOP '88*, volume 322 of *LNCS*, pages 283–299, Oslo, April 1988. Springer-Verlag.

[TNCC03]   Éric Tanter, Jacques Noyé, Denis Caromel, and Pierre Cointe. Partial behavioral reflection: Spatial and temporal selection of reification. In *Proceedings of OOPSLA '03, ACM SIGPLAN Notices*, pages 27–46, nov 2003.

[US87]   David Ungar and Randall B. Smith. Self: The power of simplicity. In *Proceedings OOPSLA '87, ACM SIGPLAN Notices*, volume 22, pages 227–242, December 1987.

[WDN05]   Roel Wuyts, Stéphane Ducasse, and Oscar Nierstrasz. A data-centric approach to composing embedded, real-time software components. *Journal of Systems and Software — Special Issue on Automated Component-Based Software Engineering*, 74(1):25–34, 2005.

[Wuy01]   Roel Wuyts. *A Logic Meta-Programming Approach to Support the Co-Evolution of Object-Oriented Design and Implementation*. PhD thesis, Vrije Universiteit Brussel, 2001.

[ZNV04]   Tian Zhao, James Noble, and Jan Vitek. Scoped types for real-time java. In *RTSS '04: Proceedings of the 25th IEEE International Real-Time Systems Symposium (RTSS'04)*, pages 241–251, Washington, DC, USA, 2004. IEEE Computer Society.

[ZPV03]   Tian Zhao, Jens Palsber, and Jan Vite. Lightweight confinement for featherweight java. In *OOPSLA '03: Proceedings of the 18th annual ACM SIGPLAN conference on Object-oriented programing, systems, languages, and applications*, pages 135–148, New York, NY, USA, 2003. ACM Press.

Composition-Oriented Service Discovery

Antonio Brogi, Sara Corfini, and Razvan Popescu

Department of Computer Science,
University of Pisa, Italy

Abstract. Service discovery and service aggregation are two crucial issues in the emerging area of Service-oriented Computing (SoC). We propose a new technique for the discovery of (Web) services that accounts
for the need of composing several services to satisfy a client query. The
proposed algorithm makes use of OWL-S ontologies, and explicitly returns the sequence of atomic process invocations that the client must
perform in order to achieve the desired result. When no full match is
possible, the algorithm features a flexible matching by returning partial
matches and by suggesting additional inputs that would produce a full
match.

1 Introduction

Service-oriented Computing (SoC) [10] is emerging as a new, promising computing paradigm that centres on the notion of *service* as the fundamental element for
developing software applications. According to [10], services are self-describing
components that should support a rapid and low-cost composition of distributed
applications. Services are offered by service providers, which procure service
implementations and maintenance, and supply service descriptions. Service descriptions are used to advertise service capabilities, behaviour, and quality, and
should provide the basis for the discovery, binding, and composition of services.
Services possess the ability of engaging other services in order to complete complex transactions, like checking credit, ordering products, or procurement. The
platform-neutral nature of services creates the opportunity for building composite services by composing existing elementary or complex services, possibly
offered by different service providers [14].

The Web service model includes three component roles — clients, providers
and registries — where providers advertise their services to registries, and clients
query registries to discover services. In this scenario, two prominent issues involved in the development of next generation distributed software applications
can be roughly synthesised as:

(1) discovering available services that can be exploited to build a needed application, and
(2) suitably aggregating such services to achieve the desired result.

Currently, the universally accepted core standard employed for Web service
discovery is the Universal Description & Discovery Interface (UDDI [11]). UDDI

T. Gschwind, U. Aßmann, and O. Nierstrasz (Eds.): SC 2005, LNCS 3628, pp. 15–30, 2005.

supports the definition of service registries in the style of yellow pages, but unfortunately it features only keyword-based matches that often give poor performance.

Given the pivotal importance of service discovery for SoC, several attempts to improve the quality of UDDI discovery are currently being pursued. One of the major efforts in this direction is promoted by the World Wide Web Consortium (W3C) which strongly advocates the introduction of semantic information in the description of Web services [12]. Indeed, currently service description are expressed by means of the Web Services Description Language (WSDL [13]), by declaring a set of message formats and their direction (incoming/outgoing). The resulting description is purely syntactic, very much in the style of Interface Description Languages (IDLs) in component-based software engineering.

The W3C proposes a semantic-based description of Web services, based on the use of OWL-S (formerly DAML-S) ontologies [8], where each service is provided with an *advertisement* containing three descriptions: *service profile* ("what the service does"), *service model* ("how the service works"), and *service grounding* ("how to access the service"). The process of Web service discovery — often referred to as service matchmaking — then takes a query specifying inputs and outputs (IOs) of the desired service as well as a service registry consisting of (service) advertisements, and returns as output a list of matched services.

In this paper we present a new algorithm for the composition-oriented discovery of Web services. The algorithm — called SAM (for Service Aggregation Matchmaking) — can be used to match queries with service registries making use of OWL-S ontologies. SAM extends a matchmaking algorithm proposed by Bansal and Vidal in [3] by featuring a more flexible matching and, more importantly, by accounting for service compositions. Indeed, queries that cannot be satisfied by a single service might be frequently satisfied by composing several services. An immediate example of this is a client wishing to plan its holidays by booking flight tickets as well as hotel accommodation while taking into account various parameters such as weather, season prices, special offers, and so on.

The main features of the proposed algorithm can be summarised as follows:

– *Flexible matching*. The proposed algorithm (SAM) features a more flexible matching with respect to [3] as:
  • SAM performs a fine-grained matching at the level of atomic processes, or sub-services (rather than at the level of entire services as in [3]).
  • Rather than returning only full matches (when a single service can fully satisfy the client request by itself), SAM also returns (when no full match is possible) a list of *partial* matches. A partial match is a (composition of) sub-service(s) that can provide only some of the outputs requested by the client. It is important to stress that a partial match can be a valuable answer for the client, which may have over-specified its query or may decide to use the selected services even if its query will be only partially satisfied.

- When no full match is possible, SAM — besides returning partial matches — is also capable to suggest to the client additional inputs that would suffice to get a full match.
- *Composition-oriented matching.* More importantly, SAM is the first algorithm (at the best of our knowledge) to provide a composition-oriented matchmaking based on semantic descriptions of queries and services by taking into account service process models.
  - When no single service can satisfy the client query, SAM checks whether there are service compositions that can satisfy the query, possibly including multiple executions of services as well.
  - When SAM finds a match, it explicitly returns the sequence of atomic process invocations that the client must perform in order to achieve the desired result.

The rest of the paper is organised as follows. Section 2 is devoted to introduce OWL-S ontologies for service discovery, while in Section 3 we describe the new algorithm for the composition-oriented discovery of services. Finally, we draw some concluding remarks in Section 4.

2   Web Service Discovery Using OWL-S Ontologies

As the use of UDDI for service discovery often leads to inaccurate matches, increasing attention is being devoted to semantics-based techniques to improve the quality of the matchmaking process. The best known approaches use DAML-S/OWL-S [8] ontologies. OWL-S is an ontology for describing Web services and it is written in DAML+OIL. The root of the ontology is represented by the generic class Service which has three subclasses: service profile ("what the service does"), service model ("how the service works") and service grounding ("how to access the service").

The service profile provides a high-level description of a service and it consists of three types of information: a human readable description of the service, the functionalities provided by the service, and some functional attributes. Service functionalities are represented by listing the inputs required as well as the outputs produced by the service, and functional attributes specify additional information about the service such as what guarantees of response time or accuracy it provides, or the cost of the service.

The service model has a process model subclass which provides a view of a Web service in terms of process compositions. OWL-S defines three types of processes: atomic, simple and composite. An atomic process is executed in a single step (from the point of view of the client of the service). It can not be decomposed further and it has an associated grounding. Only atomic processes are allowed to have associated inputs and outputs (IOs) and they are the only processes that can be directly invoked by the client. A simple process is similar to an atomic one but it can not be invoked directly and it does not have an associated grounding. It is a simplified and abstract view of a composite process. Finally, a composite process consists of other processes, the composition being made with the following control constructs: `split`, `sequence`, `unordered`, `split+join`, `choice`, `if-then-else`, `iterate` and `repeat-until/while`.

The first matchmaking algorithms based on DAML-S/OWL-S ontologies (e.g., [9]) use the service profile. The matching based on the service profile (similar somehow to matching two black boxes) allows to match a service request asking for two outputs o_1 *and* o_2 with a service advertisement that provides *either* o_1 *or* o_2 but *not necessarily both* o_1 *and* o_2 (e.g., a `choice` process). Indeed, in order to clearly specify the behaviour of such service one would have to provide two service profiles corresponding to the two alternatives. As one may note this would lead to advertising a large number of profiles, even for non trivial services. Moreover, analysing Web services only through their service profile (i.e., their IOs), severely affects the process of discovery of service aggregations that satisfy a request. Indeed, the service profile does not describe the internal behaviour of services and hence it does not provide valuable information needed for composing services.

Bansal and Vidal present in [2,3] an improvement of the matchmaking process by using an algorithm based on the OWL-S process model. Their algorithm takes as input a query specifying the desired IOs as well as a repository of OWL-S Web services and returns one of the following degrees of match: `exact` (e.g., client asks for "DVD", provider replies with "Digital Versatile Disk"), `plug-in` (e.g., client asks for "British Music DVDs", provider replies with "Music DVDs"), `subsumes` (e.g., client asks for "Music DVDs", provider replies with "British Music DVDs"), or `failed` (e.g., client asks for "DVD", provider replies with "MC"). The algorithm takes into account the process model trees of the advertisements as well as the ontological relations between matched IOs. According to [9], a service request matches a service advertisement if the request provides all the inputs (possibly more) needed by the advertisement while the advertisement generates all the outputs (possibly more) needed by the requester. The algorithm of Bansal and Vidal stores OWL-S service advertisements as trees corresponding to their process models. Composite processes correspond to intermediary nodes while atomic processes are represented as leaves. The root of the process model corresponds to the root of the tree. The matchmaking algorithm begins at the root of the advertisement tree and recursively visits all its subtrees finishing at the leaves. For each node (e.g., `sequence`, `choice` and so on) a corresponding matching algorithm that verifies the compatibility between its IOs and the IOs of the query is employed. For example, in the case of a `sequence` process, if the outputs requested by the query can be satisfied by all its children collectively then we have a success, otherwise a failure. In the case of a `choice` process we get a success or a failure depending on whether there exists at least one child able to provide by itself all the outputs desired by the query. A detailed description of the matching algorithms corresponding to several composite processes can be found in [2].

Two of the main limitations of existing matchmaking algorithms are single service discovery and single service execution. Indeed, existing algorithms look (inside a repository) for a *single* service capable to fulfil the request. For example,

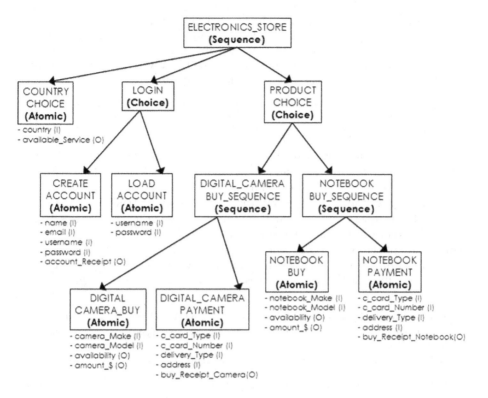

Fig. 1. Process model of an Electronics Store Service

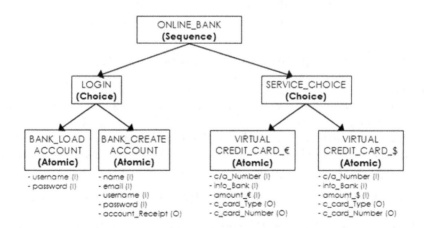

Fig. 2. Process model of an Online Bank Service

let us consider a registry containing two services: ELECTRONICS_STORE (Figure 1) and ONLINE_BANK (Figure 2). The first sells electronic items like notebooks or digital cameras. The second is able to create virtual credit cards; a client obtains a credit card number and a credit card type through a bank transfer. We suppose that all concepts contained in the OWL-S advertisements are defined in a shared ontology. Consider now the query specifying:

- inputs: `username`, `password`, `country`, `notebook_Model`, `notebook_Make`, `c/a_Number`, `info_Bank`, `delivery_Type` and `address`, and
- output: `buy_Receipt_Notebook`.

Existing matchmaking algorithms give a `failed` match because in the registry there is no service able to fulfil the request by itself. On the other hand, we can observe that the `c_card_Type` and `c_card_Number` needed as inputs by the `Notebook_Payment` atomic process of the ELECTRONICS_STORE service are not provided by the query but they can be obtained by executing the ONLINE_BANK service. In other words, while the first service cannot satisfy the query, a suitable composition of the two services can.

A second limitation of existing matchmaking algorithms is that they do not consider multiple executions of services. Consider for instance the query specifying:

- inputs: `username`, `password`, `country`, `camera_Model`, `camera_Make`, `notebook_Model`, `notebook_Make`, `delivery_Type`, `address`, `c_card_Type`, and `c_card_Number`, and
- outputs: `buy_Receipt_Notebook` and `buy_Receipt_Camera`.

We observe that while existing algorithms return a `failed` match for this query, it could be satisfied by executing *twice* the ELECTRONICS_STORE service. Indeed, the `Digital_Camera_Buy_Sequence` and `Notebook_Buy_Sequence` composite processes of the first service are children of a `choice` process and hence they cannot be both executed in a single run.

The following section is devoted to present a composition-oriented algorithm for service discovery that overcomes the above described limitations.

3   Service Aggregation Matchmaking (SAM)

The goal of the SAM algorithm is to determine whether a query can be satisfied by a (composition of) service(s), advertised in an OWL-S registry. SAM starts with a preliminary phase during which it builds a tree for each process model stored in the registry, as described by Bansal and Vidal in [3] and as we have summarised in the previous section. The SAM algorithm consists of two main parts (which will be described in the next two subsections):

1. Construction of a graph representing the dependencies among atomic processes of the services in the registry;
2. Analysis of such dependency graph to determine a service composition capable to satisfy the query (or part of it, when no service composition can fully satisfy the query).

3.1   Construction of the Dependency Graph

The graph produced during the matchmaking phase is a directed graph. It has two node types: *data* node and *process* node, the former corresponding to data (inputs or outputs) and the latter to matched processes. In SAM the match regards exclusively atomic processes, the only processes that can be directly invoked by the client. An atomic process matches if and only if:

- either all its inputs are available because they are part of the query or because they are returned as outputs by other previously matched atomic processes,
- or at least one of its outputs is part of the query or it is an input for some previously matched atomic process.

When the algorithm finds a new matched atomic process, it creates a corresponding process node and adds it to the graph. For each process node inserted in the graph, the algorithm creates and inserts (if not already present) a data node for each input and output of such process. If a data node is an input for the process node, SAM inserts a directed edge from the former to the latter. Similarly, if a data node is an output of the process node, the algorithm inserts an edge from the latter to the former. There are also two types of edges between process nodes, called *sequencing* and *excluding* constraints. If a process node P_2 is a successor of another process node P_1 as both are children of a sequence construct, the algorithm inserts an edge $P_1 \to P_2$ (*sequencing* constraint). We also say that P_1 is a predecessor of P_2. SAM introduces a bidirectional edge $P_1 \leftrightarrow P_2$ in the graph for each pair of process nodes (P_1, P_2) that are children of a choice process (*excluding* constraint).

Initially, the graph contains only the data nodes corresponding to the inputs and the outputs of the query. The matchmaking phase cycles over the registry until no more process nodes can be added to the dependency graph. The matchmaking is implemented by a recursive function Match, invoked over each service. The Match function starts its execution at the root of the advertisement tree and it is recursively invoked over children nodes. The execution finishes at leaf nodes, where Match verifies the compatibility between the inputs and the outputs of the corresponding atomic process and the data nodes currently present in the graph. According to the OWL-S specification [8], we assume that an output O_i is *compatible* with an input I_j if and only if either O_i and I_j represent the same concept (*exact match*), or O_i represents a sub-concept of I_j ("O_i plugs-in I_j", or equivalently "I_j subsumes O_i"). Match deals with different types of OWL-S nodes (sequence, choice and so on). For atomic nodes for example, Match checks whether the corresponding atomic process is already contained in the graph. If this is not the case, Match verifies the compatibility between the inputs and the outputs of the atomic node and the data nodes currently contained in the graph. If all its inputs or at least one of its outputs are contained (w.r.t. compatibility) in the graph then the atomic process is considered to be matched and added to the graph. Match then creates a new process node, new data nodes and all needed edges and constraints, and inserts them in the dependency graph. In the case of a sequence node, Match verifies if the corresponding sub-tree contains at least one matched atomic process. If so, all (matched and unmatched) atomic processes contained in the sub-tree are inserted in the dependency graph. For a `choice` node it verifies if it has at least one matched atomic process. In this case, differently from a `sequence` node, only the matched atomic process children are added to the graph.

The behaviour of the `Match` function is summarised by the following pseudo-code, where I_p and O_p denote the inputs and the outputs of P, respectively. Let also PREV_p be the set of atomic processes which must be executed before P, and CHOICE_p be the set of atomic processes which can be executed only if P is not executed.

MATCH(ServiceRegistry SR, Query Q, Graph G)
   repeat
      forall service S in SR **do** MATCH (Root(S), Q, G);
   until no process node is added to G;

MATCH(AtomicProcess P, Query Q, Graph G)
   if $(P \notin G)$ **then**
      if $(I_p \in G \vee O_p \cap G \neq \emptyset)$ **then**
         Add P to G;
         forall outputs O in O_p **do**
            if $(O \notin G)$ **then** Add O to G;
            Add (P, O) to G;
         forall inputs I in I_p **do**
            if $(I \notin G)$ **then** Add I to G;
            Add (I, P) to G;
         forall predecessors PR in PREV_p **do**
            if $(PR \in G)$ **then** Add (PR, P) to G;
         forall choice processes PC in CHOICE_p **do**
            if $(PC \in G)$ **then** Add $(P, PC) \wedge (PC, P)$ to G;

MATCH(SequenceProcess SP, Query Q, Graph G)
   forall child C in SP.children **do**
      MATCH(C, Q, G);
   if (at least one process node is added to G) **then**
      Add all atomic processes of SubTree(SP) to G;

MATCH(ChoiceProcess CP, Query Q, Graph G)
   forall child C in CP.children **do** MATCH(C, Q, G);

3.2   Analysis of the Dependency Graph

The second phase of the algorithm consists of analysing the dependency graph constructed during the first phase. This second phase consists of five steps, described next.

Step 1. Reachability of query outputs. The dependency graph includes a data node for each query input and output, regardless of whether or not these data have been matched during the first phase. SAM hence first checks whether there are query output nodes in the graph G that do not have incoming edges from process nodes. Indeed, such disconnected query outputs can not be produced as no service in the registry can generate them. If there are disconnected query outputs in the graph, the client has to choose whether the matchmaking process should nevertheless continue (by discarding such outputs from the query) or abort. In the latter case SAM terminates with a FAILURE. In the former case SAM removes the disconnected query outputs and continues with Step 2.

Step 2. **Yellow Colouring**. In this step SAM identifies — by colouring them in yellow — all processes which *may* be useful for generating the query outputs. Initially all nodes in the graph are white. The white colour is used to denote all process and data nodes that do not have yet proved to be useful for satisfying the query. SAM first colours in yellow all the query outputs. It then recursively paints in yellow all process and data nodes that are white and that have an outgoing edge leading to a yellow node. Note that excluding constraints are not taken into account here (i.e., the yellow paint does not spread over excluding constraints). The process of painting in yellow finishes when there is no other node that can be coloured. At the end of this step all yellow process nodes correspond to processes that might have to be executed in order to generate the query outputs. Dually, yellow data nodes correspond to data that "might be useful as input"/"might be generated as output" to/by yellow processes in order to generate the query outputs. All nodes that are still white at the end of this phase are not needed for fulfilling the request (and could be removed from the graph). One may note that more nodes than necessary may have been painted. The algorithm then continues with Step 3.

Step 3. **Red&Black Colouring**. The goal of this step is to identify — by painting them in red — the processes which contribute to generate the query outputs and which can be actually executed given the query inputs are provided. To describe this step it is convenient to introduce the notion of FIRABLE process. *A process node P is* FIRABLE *in a graph G if P is yellow and all its input data nodes are red and if there are predecessor processes linked through sequencing constraints then there is at least one such predecessor process node coloured in red.* The algorithm first paints in red all data nodes corresponding to query inputs. While there is at least one yellow query output node and at least one FIRABLE process, the algorithm selects a FIRABLE process for execution. If there are several FIRABLE processes linked through excluding constraints then SAM non-deterministically chooses one such FIRABLE process node and paints it in red. Every non-deterministic choice corresponds to a "fork" (split) into several instances. After painting a process in red, all its output data nodes are coloured in red and all the process nodes linked to it by excluding constraints are inhibited by painting them in black. (We do so as for example, by colouring in red a Pay_with_Credit_Card process we should inhibit another Pay_with_Cash process linked to it by an excluding constraint.) When painting in red a process node, the algorithm adds it to a PROCESS_SEQUENCE list initially empty. Each instance of this step finishes either with a SUCCESS if all query outputs became red, or with a FAILURE if there are no more FIRABLE processes but there is still at least one yellow query output. It is important to note that if there are several FIRABLE processes linked through excluding constraints then the non deterministic CHOOSE operator splits the current execution of this step into a number of instances equal to the number of FIRABLE processes, each such instance corresponding to painting in red the respective process node and further on its outputs as well as to inhibiting the processes linked to it by excluding constraints. As a result of this step we shall obtain a set of triples <SUCCESS/FAILURE, COLOURED GRAPH G, PROCESS_SEQUENCE>. Next, SAM continues with Step 4.

Step 4. **Analysis of Triples**. The algorithm further checks whether there is at least one tuple <SUCCESS, G, PROCESS_SEQUENCE>. If so, it returns to the client an ordered list of all tuples T_i where $T_i = \{$<SUCCESS, G_i, PRO-CESS_SEQUENCE$_i$>$\}$. Such list can be ordered by taking into account client's preferences (expressed together with the query). Such preferences can include minimal number of matched services, minimal PROCESS_SEQUENCE length and so on.

Now, in the case that all the triples generated by Step 3 are FAILUREs, SAM checks whether there exists a set of FAILUREs that together are able to generate all outputs requested by the query. If so, the request can be satisfied by simply considering one of the possible sequences of the FAILUREs in this set. It is important to note again that the choice of such set is made with respect to client's preferences. If such a set exists, the process finishes by returning to the client a sequence obtained by the concatenation of all PROCESS_SEQUENCEs corresponding to the considered FAILUREs in the set. In this case we have a SUCCESS obtained from the aggregation of a set of FAILUREs.

If instead there is no such set of FAILUREs that can collectively satisfy the query it means that there are query outputs that remain yellow in all graphs obtained at the end of Step 3. The algorithm then computes the intersection of the sets of all such unsatisfiable query outputs for all FAILUREs. Next, similarly to the previous case, it considers a set of FAILUREs able to collectively satisfy the producible outputs (i.e., the query outputs less the unsatisfiable ones). The algorithm further asks the client whether it wishes more information with respect to what is needed to completely satisfy the request. This information consists of the additional inputs that are needed in order to be able to unlock and to execute other processes so as to fully satisfy the request. If the client agrees then SAM continues with Step 5. Otherwise it terminates.

Step 5. **Individuating Additional Inputs**. During this last step the algorithm looks for additional inputs that need to be provided in order to have further FIRABLE processes that help generating the unsatisfiable query outputs. Hence, for each FAILURE and for each unsatisfied output, SAM looks for yellow process nodes that generate this output. The set of additional inputs needed for producing this output in the respective FAILURE comes from considering all yellow input data nodes of these processes and recursively all yellow input data nodes of the processes that should be executed before them due to sequencing constraints[1].

The following pseudo-code summarises the analysis of the dependency graph described so far.

Let $G = (N, E)$, where $E = E_{dp} \bigcup E_{pd} \bigcup E_{sc} \bigcup E_{cc}$, E_{pd} = links from process to data nodes of the form (P, D), E_{dp} = links from data to process nodes of the form (D, P), as well as sequencing

---

[1] If two or more processes generate the same output then they are taken as alternatives. The same happens for processes with more than one yellow predecessors.

constraints: $(P', P) \in E_{sc}$, and excluding constraints: $(P', P) \in E_{cc}$. Let I_p and O_p denote the inputs and the outputs of a process P respectively, and let $Q = \{I_Q, O_Q\}$ denote the query. Let also O_F be the set of data output nodes that are red in failure F.

$U = \{D \in O_Q \mid \nexists P : (P, D) \in E\}$;   //Step 1 → Reachability of Query Outputs
if $U \neq \emptyset$ then
    Query client whether to go ahead ignoring U;
    if client says yes then $O_Q = O_Q \setminus U$;
    else
        Return("Query cannot be satisfied");
Paint in white all X s.t. $X \in N$;

Paint in yellow all D s.t. $D \in O_Q$;   //Step 2 → Yellow Colouring
while $\exists X, Y : (X, Y) \in E_{dp} \cup E_{pd} \cup E_{sc} \wedge X$ white $\wedge Y$ yellow do Paint X in yellow;

Initialise ProcessSequence;   //Step 3 →Red & Black Colouring
Paint in red all D s.t. $D \in I_Q \wedge D$ yellow;
while $(Firable(G) \neq \emptyset \wedge \exists D \in O_Q : D$ yellow$)$ do
    if $\exists P' : (P'$ firable $\wedge \forall P" \in Firable(G) : (P', P") \notin E_{cc})$ then $P = P'$;
    else $P = $ choose(Firable(G));
    Paint P in red and add P to ProcessSequence;
    $\forall D : D$ yellow $\wedge (P, D) \in E_{pd}$: paint D in red;
    $\forall P' : P'$ yellow $\wedge (P, P') \in E_{cc}$: paint P' in black;
if $\exists D : D$ yellow $\wedge D \in O_Q$ then failure;
else success;

if there exists at least one success then   //Step 4 →Analysis of Triples
    Return an ordered list of (successful) results;
else
    if $\exists$ a set S of failures s.t. $\forall D \in O_Q \exists F \in S : D \in O_F$ then
        Return a concatenation of the ProcessSequences of all graphs in S;
    else
        $NonProducibleOutputs = \{D \mid D \in O_Q \wedge \forall$ failure $F : D$ yellow in $F\}$;
        $ProducibleOutputs = O_Q \setminus NonProducibleOutputs$;
        $S = \{F \mid F$ is a failure$\} \wedge \forall D \in ProducibleOutputs \exists F \in S : D \in O_F$;
        $AddI = \emptyset$;
        Query client whether it wants info on additional inputs;
        if client says yes then
            forall failure F do   // Step 5 → Individuating Additional Inputs
               forall $D \in NonProducibleOutputs$ do
                   $P = Q \in G \mid D \in O_Q$;
                   $AI = \{D \mid (D \in I_P \wedge D$ yellow$)\}$;
                   while $(\exists P' \mid (P', P) \in E_{sc})$ do
                       $AI = AI \cup \{D \mid (D \in I_{P'} \wedge D$ yellow$)\}$;
                       $P = P'$;
               $AddI = AddI \cup$ "Add inputs needed for" $+ D + $ "in" $+ F + $ ":" $+ AI$;
        Return (a concatenation of the ProcessSequences of all graphs in S, AddI);

3.3   An Example

We shall present next an example that illustrates the behaviour of SAM. Let us consider a registry of OWL-S advertisements containing only the two services – Electronics_Store and Online_Bank – described in Section 2.
Consider now the query specifying:

- inputs: username, password, country, camera_Model, camera_Make, notebook_Model, notebook_Make, c/a_Number, info_Bank, delivery_Type and address, and
- outputs: buy_Receipt_Camera and buy_Receipt_Notebook.

One may note that Bansal and Vidal's algorithm [2,3] would return a failure because there is no service in the registry able to satisfy the query by itself. More precisely, the Electronics_Store service requires c_card_Type and c_card_Number as inputs in order to be able to provide buy_Receipt_Camera and buy_Receipt_Notebook. Yet these inputs are not provided with the request but are to be obtained by executing the ONLINE_BANK service. Bansal and Vidal's algorithm fails as it is unable to find such relation between IOs of distinct services.

In its first phase SAM constructs the dependency graph (the graph in Figure 3 without colours) as the result of the matching process between the query and the registry of services advertisements. One may note the exclusion constraints between the Load_Account and Create_Account atomic processes, between the Bank_Load_Account and Bank_Create_Account, as well as between Notebook_Buy, Digital_Camera_Buy, Notebook_Payment and Digital_Camera_Payment atomic processes.

During the second phase SAM continues as follows:

1. During the first step SAM checks whether there are disconnected query outputs in the graph, yet in this example all query outputs are produced by at least an atomic process.
2. SAM continues next with the second step ("Yellow Colouring") during which it paints in yellow all data nodes corresponding to the query outputs and then it recursively paints in yellow all process and data nodes linked to other yellow nodes. At the end of this step all data nodes are painted in yellow with the exception of available_Service, account_Receipt and availability concepts.
3. During step three ("Red&Black Colouring") SAM starts by painting in red all yellow data nodes corresponding to the query inputs. At this point the only FIRABLE processes are Country_Choice and Bank_Load_Account as all their data inputs are red and they have no predecessors. Let us consider that SAM chooses to execute the Country_Choice process. By doing so, it paints it in red and it adds it to the PROCESS_SEQUENCE list. Moreover, the Load_Account process becomes FIRABLE as its (unique) predecessor is now red. By further assuming that SAM selects the Load_Account process for execution, it paints it in red and then it inhibits the Create_Account process by painting it in black. In our case, the algorithm continues until there are no more FIRABLE processes available. One may note that there is a moment in which both Digital_Camera_Buy and Notebook_Buy are FIRABLE. At that point SAM splits the execution in two instances: the first one paints in red the Digital_Camera_Buy process and it paints in black the Notebook_Buy and Notebook_Payment processes, while the second paints in red the Notebook_Buy process and it paints in black the Digital_Camera_Buy and Digital_Camera_Payment processes. At the end of step three of the algorithm both instances return a FAILURE as they were unable to generate (i.e., to paint in red) all the requested outputs — the first one produces the buy_Receipt_Camera but not the buy_Receipt_Notebook while the second one produces the buy_Receipt_Notebook but not the buy_Receipt_Camera. The PROCESS_SEQUENCE list resulting from the first instance is hence [Country_Choice, Load_Account,Bank_Load_Account, Digital_Camera_Buy,

Virtual_Credit_Card_$, Digital_Camera_Payment][2]. The second instance produces the following PROCESS_SEQUENCE list: [Country_Choice, Load_Account, Bank_Load_Account, Notebook_Buy, Virtual_Credit_Card_$, Notebook_Payment].

4. SAM continues with step four of the algorithm ("Analysis of Triples"). Due to the fact that both instances of the previous step return a FAILURE, it checks whether their union is able to generate all the requested outputs. Consequently, SAM obtains a SUCCESS from the aggregation of the PROCESS_SEQUENCEs corresponding to the two FAILUREs. SAM finishes by returning to the client the following PROCESS_SEQUENCE: [[Country_Choice, Load_Account, Bank_Load_Account, Digital_Camera_Buy, Virtual_Credit_Card_$, Digital_Camera_Payment], [Country_Choice, Load_Account, Bank_Load_Account, Digital_Notebook_Buy, Virtual_Credit_Card_$, Notebook_Payment]].

5. For our scenario, the last step of the algorithm is not executed as the request has been fulfilled.

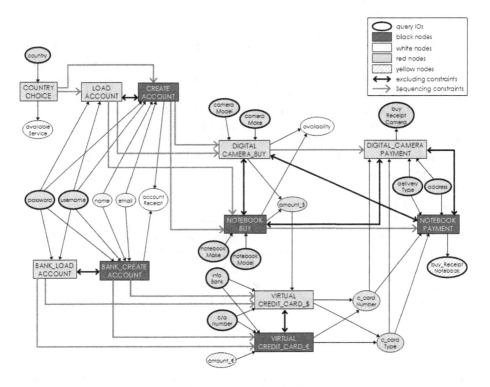

Fig. 3. Coloured graph for the first query

---

[2] The corresponding coloured graph is shown in Figure 3.

Consider next the query specifying:

- inputs: username, password, camera_Model, camera_Make, notebook_Model, note-book_Make, c/a_Number, info_Bank, delivery_Type and address, and
- outputs: buy_Receipt_Camera and buy_Receipt_Notebook.

The algorithm proceeds similarly to the first considered case. The graph produced at the end of the matchmaking phase is the same as the one produced for the previous example and all query outputs are produced by at least an atomic process. During the second step, SAM paints in yellow all data nodes with the exception of available_Service, account_Receipt and availability as in the previous example. At the beginning of the "Red&Black Colouring" phase only the Bank_Load_Account process is FIRABLE and hence it is coloured in red and added to the PROCESS_SEQUENCE list, while the Bank_Create_-Account process is painted in black. This step ends with a FAILURE as there are yellow query outputs but there are no FIRABLE processes. SAM continues then with the "Analysis of Triples" phase but is unable to find a set of FAILUREs that collectively are able to provide the buy_Receipt_Camera and buy_Receipt_Notebook outputs. Next, SAM queries the client whether it wants more information about the generated process sequence and about how it is possible to fully satisfy the query. Assuming that it agrees, SAM continues with step five ("Individuating Additional Inputs") when it looks for each unsatisfied output for yellow process nodes that generate this output. In our case, Digital_Camera_Payment and Notebook_Payment are the atomic process that can generate the buy_Receipt_Camera and buy_Receipt_Notebook outputs respectively. Yet, their execution is conditioned by the execution of their predecessors and moreover, both processes need c_Card_Number and c_Card_Type to be provided as inputs. A possible list of such additional inputs returned by SAM is: {country, c_Card_Number, c_Card_Type}. Indeed, all inputs needed for the execution of their predecessor processes are contained in the query with the exception of country.

It is worth noting that SAM is able to solve both queries presented in Section 2. SAM responds to the first query with the following PROCESS_SEQUENCE: [Country_Choice, Load_Account, Bank_Load_Account, Notebook_Buy, Virtual-_Credit_Card_$, Notebook_Payment]. To the second query, SAM responds with: [[Country_Choice, Load_Account, Digital_Camera_Buy, Digital_Camera_Payment], [Country_Choice, Load_Account, Notebook_Buy, Notebook_Payment]].

4   Concluding Remarks

We have presented a new algorithm — called SAM (for Service Aggregation Matchmaking) — for the composition-oriented discovery of Web services. As already mentioned in Section 1, the main novel features of SAM are:

(1) to perform a fine-grained matching (at the level of atomic processes of services rather than at the level of entire services),

(2) to feature a flexible matching by returning partial matches and by suggesting additional inputs (when some query output cannot be produced by the services in the registry),

(3) to discover service compositions capable of satisfying a query, when no single service can satisfy it. In such cases SAM also explicitly returns the sequence of atomic process invocations that the client must perform in order to achieve the desired result.

The first semantics-based algorithm for Web service discovery using DAML-S ontologies was developed by Paolucci et al. [9]. Their algorithm performs a matching between service requests and service advertisements described as DAML-S service profiles. An assessment of the deployment of this algorithm to a UDDI registry was recently reported in [6], where WSDL service descriptions were enriched with semantics descriptions in the style of DAML-S service profiles. As we already noted in Section 2, the algorithm described in [9] is however limited to discovering a single service, and it does not address the issue of discovering service compositions. An algorithm for service discovery using service compositions was recently presented by Aversano et al. [1]. Their algorithm analyses DAML-S service profiles (as [9]) and it is also capable of performing a cross ontology matching (for service descriptions using different ontologies) as well as of matching service compositions (when no single service can fulfil the client request). Comparing SAM with [1], one may note that SAM analyses the process model of services to perform a finer-grained matchmaking, at the level of atomic processes inside services rather than at the level of entire services. Moreover, when no service composition can satisfy the query, SAM is also capable of suggesting additional inputs that would suffice to get a full match.

The first service discovery algorithm based on the analysis of DAML-S process models of services was proposed by Bansal and Vidal [3]. As we already discussed in Section 2, SAM extends [3] by considering both compositions and multiple executions of services. A preliminary version of SAM was presented in [5], where a first, limited form of service composition discovery was described. The current version of SAM described in this paper substantially extends [5] by introducing the dependency graph and its analysis, by providing a list of atomic process invocations, and by suggesting additional inputs when needed.

A semi-automatic approach to composite service discovery was recently presented by Liang et al. [7]. An interesting feature of it is the employment of constraint matching over a service dependency graph, where constraints may specify data dependencies as well as non-functional properties of services (such as Quality Of Service). Their approach is however based on UDDI registries, and hence the accuracy of the discovery is limited due to the absence of semantic information.

Our plans for future work include assessing SAM by experimenting it on large numbers of queries and service advertisements. While we have tested our Java implementation of SAM on several examples, an obstacle to running massive experiments is the lack of available OWL-S descriptions of services (only a few are publicly available in the W3C Web site). A promising approach to ease the generation of OWL-S descriptions of services may be to publicly deploy (to UDDI registries) supporting tools that facilitate such descriptions, as done for instance by Kawamura et al. [6] to promote the generation of DAML-S service profiles. Another direction for future work is to extend the matching featured by SAM in order to deal with other attributes of services (including extra-functional ones) and the use of different ontologies. Our long-term goal is to develop a well-founded methodology to support the discovery, aggregation, and —when necessary— adaption [4] of services.

References

1. L. Aversano, G. Canfora, and A. Ciampi. An algorithm for web service discovery through their composition. In L. Zhang, editor, *IEEE International Conference on Web Services (ICWS'04)*, pages 332–341. IEEE Computer Society, 2004.
2. S. Bansal. *Matchmaking of Web Services Based on the DAML-S Service Model, Master Thesis.* University of South Carolina, 2002.
3. S. Bansal and J. Vidal. Matchmaking of Web Services Based on the DAML-S Service Model. In T. Sandholm and M. Yokoo, editors, *Second International Joint Conference on Autonomous Agents (AAMAS'03)*, pages 926–927. ACM Press, 2003.
4. A. Bracciali, A. Brogi, and C. Canal. A formal approach to component adaptation. *Journal of Systems and Software*, 3:45–54, 2005.
5. A. Brogi, S. Corfini, and R. Popescu. Flexible Matchmaking of Web Services Using DAML-S Ontologies. In *IBM Research Report. ICSOC 2004 Proceedings – Short Papers*, November 2004.
6. T. Kawamura, J. D. Blasio, T. Hasegawa, M. Paolucci, and K. Sycara. Public Deployment of Semantic Service Matchmaking with UDDI Business Registry. In S. McIlraith and D. Plexousakis, editors, *Third International Semantic Web Conference (ISWC'04)*, LNCS 3298, pages 752–766. Springer-Verlag, 2004.
7. Q. Liang, L. N. Chakarapani, S. Y. W. Su, R. N. Chikkamagalur, and H. Lam. A Semi-Automatic Approach to Composite Web Services Discovery, Description and Invocation. *International Journal of Web Services Research*, 1(4):64–89, 2004.
8. OWL-S Coalition. OWL-S 1.1 release. http://www.daml.org/services/owl-s/1.1/
9. M. Paolucci, T. Kawamura, T. Payne, and K. Sycara. Semantic Matchmaking of Web Services Capabilities. In I. Horrocks and J. Hendler, editors, *First International Semantic Web Conference on The Semantic Web, LNCS 2342*, pages 333–347. Springer-Verlag, 2002.
10. M. Papazoglou and D. G. (editors). Service-oriented computing. *Communications of the ACM*, 46(10):25–28, 2003.
11. UDDI. The UDDI Technical White Paper. 2000. http://www.uddi.org/.
12. W3C. Semantic Web Services Interest Group Charter. http://w3c.org/2003/10/swsig-charter.
13. W3C. Web Service Description Language (WSDL) 1.1. World Wide Web Consortium (2001), http://www.w3.org/TR/wsdl.
14. J. Yang. Web service componentization. *Communications of the ACM*, 46(10):35–40, 2003.

Ad Hoc Composition of User Tasks in Pervasive Computing Environments

Sonia Ben Mokhtar, Nikolaos Georgantas, and Valérie Issarny

INRIA Rocquencourt,
78153 Le Chesnay, France
{Sonia.Ben_Mokhtar,Nikolaos.Georgantas,Valerie.Issarny}@inria.fr
http://www-rocq.inria.fr/arles/

Abstract. Due to the large success of wireless networks and portable devices, the pervasive computing paradigm is becoming a reality. One of the most challenging objectives to be achieved in pervasive computing environments is to allow a user to perform a task by composing on the fly the environment's service and resource components. However, existing approaches commonly assume that networked components have been developed to integrate in terms of interfaces and conversations, which restricts the user's ability to fully exploit the diversity of the pervasive computing components. In order to overcome this constraint, we propose a solution for ad hoc composition of pervasive computing components, based on the Web services and Semantic Web paradigms. The main feature of our solution is the ability to integrate on the fly a number of Web services' conversation fragments to reconstruct a conversation enabling the target user task.

1 Introduction

The paradigm of pervasive computing has opened new perspectives to the enactment of human everyday activities related to accessing information and computation. Pervasive computing enables user-centric retrieval and consumption of information, compared to the conventional computer-centric approach. Systemically, this is realized as a synergistic combination of intelligent human-machine interfaces and ubiquitous computing and networking. The ubiquitous property implies a useful, pleasant and unobtrusive presence of the system everywhere around us.

A pervasive computing environment is populated with networked, both computing and input/output devices providing the environment's components. Within this environment, users perform tasks which integrate the functionalities offered by the environment's components. A pervasive computing environment is characterized by a number of features, such as: (i) the highly dynamic character of the computing and networking environment due to the intense use of the wireless medium and the mobility of users; (ii) the resource constraints of mobile devices, in terms of CPU, memory, storage, display capabilities, battery power and bandwidth; and (iii) the high heterogeneity of integrated technologies in terms of networks, devices and software infrastructures. In such an environment, satisfying the functional requirements of user tasks becomes extremely hard. Specifically, the integration of the environment's components to support a user task shall: (i) be dynamic, according to available components at the specific time and place;

T. Gschwind, U. Aßmann, and O. Nierstrasz (Eds.): SC 2005, LNCS 3628, pp. 31–46, 2005.

(ii) satisfy the functional requirements in an effective way within the bounds posed by the resource constraints of mobile devices; and (iii) accommodate the heterogeneity of technologies. However, existing approaches assume that pervasive computing components have been developed to integrate. This means that components being integrated shall perfectly match with the task specification in terms of supported interfaces and conversations.

Our aim is to allow a user who carries an abstract task description on his/her device, i.e., a description without any reference to existing component instances, to perform this task by integrating on the fly the environment's components that are available around him/her, without any preliminary knowledge about these components. This is what we call "ad hoc composition of user tasks". This requires building upon an architectural style that deals with the heterogeneity of pervasive computing components.

Service Oriented Architecture (SOA) is an architectural style that offers solutions to the interoperability problem among distributed applications. In the SOA approach, software resources that are available on the network are abstracted as services. These services are described in a declarative manner that is independent from their implementation; they are loosely coupled, and communicate using standard protocols. This architectural style is most convenient to the pervasive computing environment, as it enables homogeneous use of the heterogeneous software components that populate the pervasive computing environments.

Web services is one of the realizations of the SOA architectural style. Web services introduces loosely coupled services that communicate using the standard technologies that made the success of the Web. More precisely, a Web service is a software component that is developed using any programmation language and deployed on any platform, and that is accessible via the Web. It exposes an XML interface that describes its public operations and its access details; this interface is specified using the Web Services Description Language (WSDL)[1]. A Web service communicates using the Simple Object Access Protocol (SOAP)[2] on top of Internet protocols (HTTP, SMTP). Furthermore, Web services have already been used in pervasive computing environments [13] and have proved to be efficient when deployed on mobile, resource-constrained devices. All these features make Web services an excellent candidate to support application-level interoperability in pervasive computing environments. Thus, by representing each pervasive computing component as a Web service, the problem of dynamic integration of components can be treated as a problem of dynamic composition of Web services.

Dynamic composition of Web services involves automating the discovery and selection of services, ensuring semantic and data-type compatibility [16], but also automating service invocation. The automation of service discovery and selection can be achieved only if service descriptions are machine-interpretable. A key issue is that the two main standards for describing and publishing Web services (WSDL and UDDI[3]) are mainly syntactic. Thus, to discover and select services a strong matching (i.e. a syntactic comparison) have to be made between the required functionalities and the ad-

---

[1] WSDL: Web Services Description Language. http://www.w3c.org/TR/wsdl

[2] SOAP: Simple Object Access Protocol. http://www.w3c.org/TR/SOAP

[3] UDDI: Universal Description, Discovery, and Integration of Business for the Web. http://www.uddi.org

vertised ones. The semantic representation of service descriptions' content will allow machines to understand and process this content, and to support dynamic discovery and integration. Thus, a number of research efforts have been made to apply to Web services the solutions that have been proposed by the Semantic Web community for semantically annotating Web pages. This leads the emergence of semantic Web services. In this area, Ontology Web Language for Services (OWL-S)[4] is one of the most promising languages for describing semantic Web services.

On the other hand, the automation of service invocation involves the use of conversation languages (e.g., WSCI [27], WS-CDL[26], WSCL[28]) to describe the external behavior of the service rather than describing only the service operations as supported by WSDL. This conversation description prescribes how to interact with the service so that it behaves in a specific desired manner.

Our work presented in this paper is a part of the effort of the IST Amigo project[5] that investigates solutions to realize the full potential of home networking to improve people's lives. In this paper, we present a solution to the ad hoc composition of user tasks from available pervasive computing components. Both the user task and the environment's components are represented as semantic Web services described using OWL-S. The main feature of OWL-S that we exploit, is the ability to describe semantic conversations. More precisely, OWL-S allows the description of the external behavior of a Web service by using a semantic model, in which each operation involved is described semantically in terms of inputs/outputs. The difference between the user task description and the environments' services descriptions, is that the task description is abstract and does not contain any concrete reference to existing Web services.

Our solution introduces a matching algorithm that attempts to reconstruct the abstract task process description by integrating fragments from the environments' services process descriptions. The result obtained is a concrete task description that contains references to available environments' services and that is executable by invoking those services.

The remainder of the paper is structured as follows. First, we present the general context of our work (Section 2). We then present our approach to the ad hoc composition of Web services (Section 3). Further, we review related research efforts in the area of matching algorithms (Section 4). Finally, we conclude with a summary of our contribution and discuss our future work (Section 5).

2   Background

2.1   Service Description

Web services can be described using three description levels that are : (i) the interface-level; (ii) the process-level; and (iii) the binding-level. The interface-level description contains the signatures of the service operations. The process-level description is the specification of the external behavior of the service, which is also called the service's

---

[4] OWL-S: Semantic Markup for Web Service. http://www.daml.org/services/owl-s
[5] Amigo: ambient   intelligence   for   the   networked   home   environment. http://www.extra.research.philips.com/euprojects/amigo/

conversation. Finally, the binding-level description contains the low level information necessary to communicate with the service, including protocols, addressing and message formats.

WSDL describes services using the interface-level description and the binding-level description. While these two levels are sufficient when the service has a simple behavior (i.e., invocation of a single operation), it remains insufficient when the service has a complex behavior. In this case, the key issue is that we do not have any indication about when and which service operations have to be invoked in order to lead the service to behave as we want. Moreover, for dynamic service invocation, this has to be automated. Thus, by having a conversation description, a requester dynamically can derive the sequence of information to exchange with the service, which in turn correspond to the interaction protocol of the service [22]. This is what makes the process-level description an important requirement to achieve dynamic service composition.

2.2 Semantic Web Services

Semantic Web services is a research area at the intersection of two important research domains that concern Web technologies : the Semantic Web and Web services. The Semantic Web aims at describing the static information provided by Web pages in a non-ambiguous manner, in order to allow machines to understand and process their content [3]. Web services standards, such as WSDL and UDDI, use XML structures to describe Web services functionalities and their exchanged data. However, these structures are syntactic which makes it impossible for a machine to automatically understand Web services descriptions. A semantic Web service is then a Web service described using a well defined semantic language, which provides the service with a non-ambiguous interface, facilitating the automation of certain tasks, such as discovery, invocation and composition.

There are two main approaches to semantically describe Web services. The first approach adds semantics on top of WSDL. The second approach uses ontologies[6] that have been developed specifically to describe Web services.

A number of research efforts have been undertaken in order to bring semantics to WSDL [25,7,11,21,1]. These introduce different models to semantically annotate WSDL descriptions, and some of them propose solutions for mapping XSD structures to ontologies and/or classify services into categories. However, as they are build upon WSDL, these models lack in describing Web services' conversation, which is an important requirement to achieve dynamic service composition.

2.3 OWL-S

OWL-S (previously DAML-S), is a Web service ontology based on the Ontology Web Language (OWL)[7], used to describe Web services properties and capabilities. Using OWL-S a service description is composed of three parts : the service profile, the process model and the service grounding.

---

[6] Ontologies describe structured vocabularies, containing useful concepts for a community who wants to organize and exchange information in a non-ambiguous manner.

[7] OWL: Web Ontology Language. http://www.w3.org/TR/owl-ref/

The benefit of using OWL-S rather than another approach to semantically describe Web services is that OWL-S offers a generic model to describe Web services. This model is easily extensible and allows the different levels of service description that we have identified earlier. Furthermore, OWL-S brings semantics to the conversation description, and thus allows flexible conversation matching.

OWL-S Service Profile. The service profile gives a high level description of a service and its provider. It is generally used for service publication and discovery. The service profile is composed of three parts: (i) an informal description of the service oriented to a human user; (ii) a description of the service's capabilities, in terms of Inputs, Outputs, Pre-conditions and Effects (IOPE); and (iii) a set of attributes describing complementary information about the service.

OWL-S Process Model. The process model is a representation of the external behavior of the service as a process. This description contains a specification of a set of sub-processes that are coordinated by a set of control constructs (e.g., Sequence or Parallel constructs); these sub-processes are atomic or composite. The atomic processes correspond to WSDL operations. The composite processes are decomposable into other atomic or composite processes by using a control construct.

OWL-S Service Grounding. The service grounding specifies the information that is necessary for the service invocation, such as the protocol, message formats, serialization, transport and addressing information. It is a mapping between the abstract description of the service and the concrete information necessary to interact with the service. The OWL-S service grounding is based on WSDL.

3 Ad Hoc Composition of Semantic Web Services

Ad hoc composition of Web services translates into the integration on the fly of a set of services to perform a user task. Our objective is to allow a user entering into a pervasive computing environment, in which services and resources publish an OWL-S description, to perform a task. A description of this task is available on the user's device as an abstract OWL-S conversation. In order to select the set of services that are suitable to be integrated to perform the user's task, and to integrate this set of services, a matching algorithm is needed. In our approach, we propose a matching algorithm that enables reconstructing the task's conversation using fragments from the conversations of the environment's services. Towards this goal, we first introduce formal modeling of the conversations of both the environment's services and the task as finite state processes (FSP). Other approaches for formalizing Web services conversation and composition have been proposed in the literature, generally based on process algebras (e.g. π-calculus, CCS)[8,15,6], or Petri nets[24,19,17]. FSP is used as a textual notation for concisely describing and reasoning about concurrent programs, such as workflows of Web service compositions[10]. These processes can be represented graphically using finite state automata.

In the following, we describe our dynamic composition approach. First, we present the notion of abstract task (Section 3.1). Then, we present our model to map OWL-S conversations to finite state automata (Section 3.2). Finally, we describe our matching algorithm (Section 3.3).

3.1 Abstract Task Description

While Web services of the pervasive computing environment are described as OWL-S processes with a WSDL grounding, the user task is described as an abstract OWL-S process without any reference to existing services. An abstract OWL-S process involves abstract atomic and composite processes.

An abstract atomic process is defined as an elementary entity that has a set of inputs/outputs. Those inputs/outputs are specified with logical names. They carry semantic definitions, and have to be matched to inputs/outputs of a concrete OWL-S atomic process contained in the description of an environment's service. An abstract composite process is composed of a set of abstract, either composite or atomic, processes, and uses a control construct from those offered by the OWL-S process model. These control constructs are: Sequence, Split, Split + Join, Choice, Unordered, If-Then-Else, Repeat-While, and Repeat-Until.

In addition to the description of the task's conversation, we allow the definition of a set of atomic conversations, that are fragments of the task conversation that must be executed by a single Web service.

3.2 Modeling OWL-S Processes as Finite State Automata

Formally, an automaton is represented by the 5-tuple $< Q, \sum, \delta, S_0, F >$ [12], where:

- Q is a finite set of states.
- $\sum$ is a finite set of symbols that define the alphabet of the language the automaton accepts. ϵ is the empty symbol.
- δ is the transition function, that is $\delta : Q \times \sum \rightarrow Q$
- S_0 is the start state, that is, the state in which the automaton is when no input has been processed yet (Obviously, $S_0 \in Q$).
- F a subset of Q (i.e. $F \subset Q$), called final states.

In our modeling approach, the symbols correspond to the atomic processes involved in the conversation. The initial state corresponds to the root composite process, and a transition between two states is performed when an atomic process is executed.

Each process, either atomic or composite, that is involved in the OWL-S conversation, is mapped to an automaton and linked together with the other ones in order to build the conversation automaton. This is achieved following the OWL-S process description and the mapping rules shown in Figure 1. In this Figure we can see that an atomic process ap is modeled as an automaton $< Q, \sum, \delta, S_0, F >$, where :

- $Q = \{S_0, S_1\}$;
- $\sum = \{ap\}$;
- $\delta(S_0, ap) = S_1$;
- S_0 is the start state ;
- $F = \{S_1\}$.

A composite process C that involves a set of processes $P_1, P_2, ..., P_n$,represented by the automata $< Q_1, \sum_1, \delta_1, S_{0,1}, F_1 >, < Q_2, \sum_2, \delta_2, S_{0,2}, F_2 >, ..., < Q_n, \sum_n, \delta_n, S_{0,n}, F_n >$, respectively, is represented by the automaton $< Q, \sum, \delta, S_0, F >$ according to the control construct it uses, as follows.

- If C=Repeat-While(P_1)[8]
  - $Q = Q_1$;
  - $\sum = \sum_1$;
  - $\delta : Q_1 \times \sum_1 \to Q_1$
    $(x, y) \mapsto \delta(x, y) = \delta_1(x, y) when (x, y) \in Q_1 \times \sum_1$ and $\delta(x, y) = S_0$ when $x \in F_1$ and $y = \epsilon$;
  - $S_0 = S_{0,1}$;
  - $F = F_1 \cup \{S_0\}$.
- If C=Choice($P_1, P_2, ..., P_n$), then:
  - $Q = (\bigcup Q_i) \cup S_{Init}$ (S_{Init} is a new start state);
  - $\sum = \bigcup \sum_i$;
  - $\delta : \bigcup(Q_i \times \sum_i) \to \bigcup Q_i$
    $(x, y) \mapsto \delta(x, y) = \delta_i(x, y) when (x, y) \in Q_i \times \sum_i$ and $\delta(x, y) = S_{0,i}$ when $x = S_{Init}$ and $y = \epsilon$;
  - $S_0 = S_{Init}$;
  - $F = \bigcup F_i$.
- If C=Sequence($P_1, P_2, ..., P_n$) then:
  - $Q = \bigcup Q_i$;
  - $\sum = \bigcup \sum_i$;
  - $\delta : \bigcup(Q_i \times \sum_i) \to \bigcup Q_i$
    $(x, y) \mapsto \delta(x, y) = \delta_i(x, y) when (x, y) \in Q_i \times \sum_i$ and $\delta(x, y) = S_{0,i+1}$ when $x \in F_i$ $(i \neq n)$ and $y = \epsilon$;
  - $S_0 = S_{0,1}$;
  - $F = F_n$.
- If C= Split(P_1, P_2) then C is treated as Choice(Sequence(P_1, P_2), Sequence (P_2, P_1)), as we process parallelism as non determinism. The Split+Join and the Unordered constructs are treated as the Split construct.
- If C=If-Then-Else(P_1, P_2) then C is treated as Choice(P_1, P_2).

The conditions involved in the constructs Repeat-While, Repeat-Until and If-Then-Else are not visible in our automata model. However, these conditions will be taken into consideration during the matching process. The OWL class Condition that defines those conditions, is actually a placeholder for further work, and will be defined as a class of logical expressions. Thus, we consider that during our matching algorithm a comparison between those logical expression will be made. More information about this comparison will be given in future work.

---

[8] If C=Repeat-Until(P_1) then it is treated as the Repeat-While(P_1) but with removing the initial state from the set of final states. The only difference between the Repeat-While construct and the Repeat-Until construct is that the process being repeated is executed at least once in the case of the Repeat-Until construct.

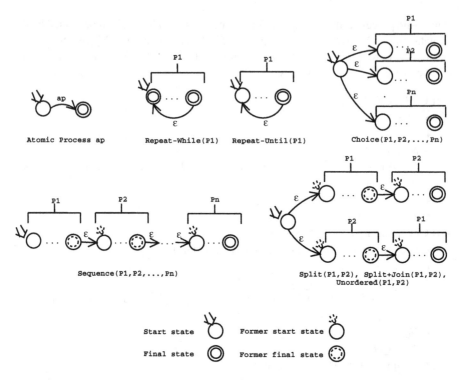

Fig. 1. Modeling OWL-S processes as finite state automata

3.3 Matching Algorithm

One of the most important features of a dynamic service composition approach is the matching algorithm being used. Following the definition given by Trastour et al. in [23], the matching is the process by which parties that are interested in having exchange of economic value are put in contact with potential counterparts. The matching process is carried out by matching together features that are required by one party and provided by another. Thus, the matching allows the selection of the most suitable services to respond to the users' requirements. In our approach, matching depends on two important features : (i) the services' advertisements; and (ii) the task's description. A service advertisement is composed of the information published by the service provider. This description could be quite simple, for example, a set of keywords describing the service, or more complex, describing for example the service's operations, conversation, functional and non-functional capabilities. This description could further be syntactic (by using XML-based standards for Web services' description) or semantic (by using semantic Web languages). In our approach, services are advertised by means of their provided behavior, i.e., conversation, while the user task is described by the behavior it requires from services.

The matching algorithm we propose aims at reconstructing the task's behavior by using fragments of the services behaviors. This algorithm is performed in two steps:

(i) semantic operation matching, and (ii) conversation matching, which are detailed bellow. Semantic operation matching aims at selecting a set of services that may be integrated to compose the target task. Our selection criterion is the provision by the service of at least one semantically equivalent operation from those that are involved in the task. Conversation matching then compares the structure of the task's conversation with those of selected services and attempts to compose fragments from the services' conversations to reconstruct the task's conversation.

Semantic Operation Matching. The objective of the semantic matching step is to compare semantically described operations involved in the task's conversation with those involved in the services' conversations. This kind of matching is more powerful and more flexible than syntactic matching, as it allows the use of inference rules enabled by ontologies to compare elements, rather than comparing syntactically their names.

To perform semantic operation matching, we build upon the matching algorithm proposed by Paolucci et al. in [18,22]. This algorithm is used to match a requested service with a set of advertised ones. The requested service has a set of provided inputs in_{Req}, and a set of expected outputs out_{Req}, whereas each advertised service has a set of expected inputs in_{Ad} and a set of provided outputs out_{Ad}. In our case, we propose to use this matching algorithm to compare atomic processes, i.e., operations, rather that high-level Web services' capabilities. This matching algorithm defines four levels of matching.

- Exact : if $out_{Req} = out_{Ad}$ or out_{Req} is a direct subclass of out_{Ad}
- Plug in : if out_{Ad} subsumes[9] out_{Req}, in other words, out_{Ad} could be used in the place of out_{Req}
- Subsumes : if out_{Req} subsumes out_{Ad}, in this case, the service does not completely fulfill the request. Thus, another service may be needed to satisfy the rest of the expected data.
- Fail : failure occurs when no subsumption relation between advertisement and request is identified.

This matching algorithm also applies between the inputs of the request and the inputs of the advertisement. A match between an advertisement and a request is recognized when all outputs of the request are matched against all outputs of the advertisement; and all the inputs of the advertisement are matched against all the inputs of the request.

Furthermore, we propose to use the two first levels of matching : Exact and Plug in matches, as we consider that a subsumes match cannot guarantee that the required functionality will be provided by the advertised service[16]. Furthermore, as we match operations we don't want to split them between two or more services.

The matching process we are building upon is a complex mechanism that may lead to costly computations. However, the algorithm uses a set of strategies that rapidly prune advertisements that are guaranteed not to match the request[18]. For example, if one of the out_{Req} cannot be matched by any of the out_{Ad} the match directly fails. Furthermore, the fact that we use only the first two levels of matching considerably reduces the cost of the matching.

---

[9] Subsumption means the fact to incorporate something under a more general category.

The main logic of our semantic operation matching algorithm is that Process model descriptions of services are parsed, and once all inputs/outputs of a task's operation are matched against all inputs/outputs of a service's operation the service is recorded. More precisely, all the operations of this service that are semantically equivalent to task's operations are recorded. This allows the selection of a set of services that offer semantically equivalent operations with those of the user's task. The conversations offered by those selected services are then used to reconstruct the task's conversation.

Conversation Matching. The objective of the conversation matching is to compare the structure of the task's process with the structure of the selected services processes, in terms of control constructs involved. In this algorithm, we use the automaton model describing each service that has been selected and the one describing the user task. The first step is to connect the selected services' automata to form a global automaton. This is achieved by adding a new initial state and an ϵ-transition from this state to each of the initial states of the selected services. Other ϵ-transitions are also added to link each final state of the selected services with the new initial state.

```
Check(TaskState, EnvState){
   if(TaskState is a final state and EnvState is a final state)
      success;
   else{
      if(EnvState.followingSymbols don't include TaskState.followingSymbols )
         fail;
      else{
         forall Symbol in TaskState.followingSymbols, state1 in EnvState.nextState(Symbol),
                state2 in TaskState.nextState(Symbol){
            Check(state1,state2);
   }}}}
```

Fig. 2. Main logic of the conversation matching algorithm

The next step of our conversation matching algorithm is to parse each state of the task's automaton by starting with the initial state and following the automaton transitions. Simultaneously, a parsing of the global automaton is done in order to find at each step of the parsing process, an equivalent state to the current one in the task. An equivalence is detected between a task's automaton state and a global automaton state, when for each input symbol of the former there is at least a semantically equivalent input symbol[10] of the latter. Each state of the task's automaton is parsed just once. We have implemented this algorithm in a recursive form. This algorithm checks whether we can find a sub-automaton in the global automaton that behaves like the task's automaton. The main logic of this algorithm is described in Figure 2. This algorithm gives a list of sub-automata of the global automaton that behave like the task automaton. Figure 3 shows an example of the conversation matching algorithm. In this figure the abstract task automaton (on the left higher corner) that involves the operations op1, op2, op3 and op4 is going to be matched against the global automaton (on the right) which connects together the automata of the services S1, S2, S3, S4 and S5. The operations involved in the task have already been matched semantically against the services' operations during the semantic operation matching step. Thus, in the global automaton we have just

---

[10] We remind that equivalence relationship between symbols is a semantic equivalence that have already been checked during the semantic matching step.

represented a selected set of operations that are semantically equivalent to the task's operations. After browsing simultaneously the two automata as specified in the algorithm, the sub-automaton of the global automaton represented in the left lower corner of the figure is found. This automaton behaves exactly as the task's automaton.

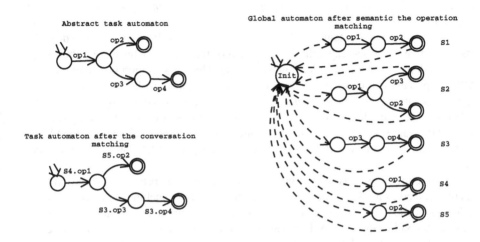

Fig. 3. An example of the conversation matching

Once the list of sub-automata that behave like the task automaton is produced, a last step consist in checking whether the atomic conversation constraints, have been respected in each sub-automaton. As the global automaton is modeled as a union of the selected services automata, it is easy to check whether an atomic conversation fragment, that is, a set of transitions, is provided by a single service. Indeed, it is sufficient to verify that for each transition set that corresponds to an atomic conversation there is no ε-transition going to the initial state before this conversation is finished. ε-transitions that connect final states to the initial state of the global automaton mark the end of a service conversation and the passing to a new one. After rejecting those sub-automata that don't verify the atomic conversation constraints, we select arbitrarily one of the remainders, as they all behave as the user task. Using the sub automaton that has been selected, an executable description of the user task that includes references to existing environment's services is generated, and sent to an execution engine that executes this description by invoking the appropriate service operations.

An example: a video application In this section we show a simple example of how our matching algorithm could be used to match conversations. This example is inspired from one of the Amigo's scenarios.

"...Robert, (Maria's and Jerry's son) is waiting for his best friend to play video games. Robert's friend arrives bringing his new portable DVD player. He proposes to watch a film rather than playing games, and asks Robert if he has any new films in his home databases. In order to use his friend's DVD player, Robert has asked the system to

consider this device as a guest device and to authorize it to use the home's services. This player is quite complex as it takes into consideration some user's contextual and access rights information. The former is used to display the video streams according to the user's physical environment and preferences (for example by adapting the luminosity and the sound volume), while the latter is used to check whether the user is authorized to visualize a specific stream (for example some violent films may be unsuitable for children)..."

This DVD player contains a video application that uses Web ontologies to describe its offered and required capabilities. The conversation that is published by this application is depicted in figure 4 (left higher corner). This conversation is described as an OWL-S process that contains concrete offered operations (uncolored) and abstract required operations (in gray) that have to be bound to environment's operations. On the other hand Robert's home environment contains a number of services among which a Digital Resource Database service and a Context manager service; both publish OWL-S conversations as shown in the same figure (on the right and left lower corner respectively).

At execution time this device will discover the missing abstract conversation fragment involved in its description. The semantic operation matching step will allow the selection of the two previous services as they contain operations that match the operations of the video application. For example, using the ontology fragment described in figure 5 the operation GetFilm of the video application will be matched against the operation GetDigitalResource of the Digital Resource Database service. More precisely, an exact match is recognized between the output of both operations as they are both instances of the concept Stream. On the other hand, a Plug In match is recognized between the inputs of both operations as the concept DigitalResource subsumes the concept VideoResource. The second step of the matching algorithm is the conversation matching. In this step our algorithm attempts to reconstruct the abstract conversation of the video application by using the conversations of the selected services. The selected fragments after matching are shown in figure 4.

4   Related Work on Matching Algorithms

We can classify the related work on service matching algorithms in two categories: interface-level matching algorithms and process-level matching algorithms. In the first category of matching algorithms, services are generally advertised as a set of provided outputs and required inputs. These inputs/outputs constitute the service's interface. On the other hand, the request is specified as a set of required outputs and provided inputs. A match between an advertisement and a request consists in matching all outputs of the request against all outputs of the advertisement and all inputs of the advertisement against all inputs of the request. An approach for matching semantic Web services at the interface level has been proposed by Paolucci et al. in [18,22]. We have employed this algorithm to semantically match operations as described in Section 3.3. This algorithm is one of the most used approaches in the literature. Because of its simplicity and efficiency, a number of research efforts such as [9,16,23,14,20], have elaborated matching algorithms that are mainly based on this algorithm. In the second category of matching

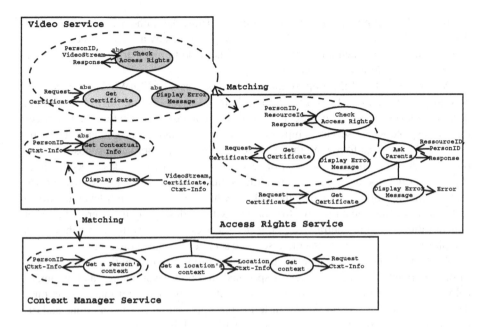

Fig. 4. An example : a video application

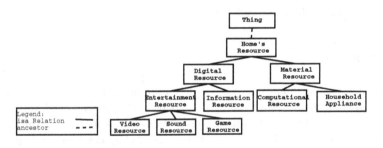

Fig. 5. A fragment of a Home Networking Ontology

algorithms, authors argue that the conversation description is richer than the interface description, as it provides more information about the service's behavior, thus, leading to a more precise matching [2]. Furthermore, we argue that to obtain valid results when dynamically executing a service that publishes a conversation, it is important to follow the sequence of operations to invoke, as specified in the conversation description, until the latter finishes. Consequently, when composing Web services that expose complex behaviors, it is important to have solutions for dynamically integrating conversations. A number of research efforts have been conducted in the area of process-level matching [4,25,16]. For example, Klein et al. in [4] propose to describe services as processes, and define a request language named PQL (Process Query Language). This language allows to find in a process database those processes that contain a fragment that responds to the request. While this approach proposes a new process query language to search for a process, there is no process integration effort. Thus, the authors implicitly assume that the user's request is quite simple and can be performed by a single process. On the contrary, in our approach a composition effort is made to reconstruct a complex task process by integrating the services' processes.

Aggarwal et al. in [25] propose to describe a task as a BPEL4WS[5] process. This description may contain both references to known services (static links) and abstract descriptions of services to be integrated (service templates). At execution time, services that correspond to the service templates are discovered and the task is carried out by invoking the services following the process workflow. This approach proposes a composition scheme by integrating a set of services to reconstruct a task's process. However, the services being integrated are rather simple. Indeed, each service is described using a semantic model defined by the authors, which specifies the high-level functional and non-functional capabilities of the service, without describing its external behavior (conversation). On the contrary, we consider services as entities that can behave in a complex manner, and we try to compose these services to realize the user task.

Another process-level matching algorithm is proposed by Majithia et al. in [16]. In this approach, the user's request is specified in a high-level manner and automatically mapped to an abstract workflow. Then, service instances that matches the ones described in the abstract workflow, in terms on inputs outputs pre-conditions and effects, are discovered in the network, and a concrete workflow description is constituted. As we have noticed in the previous approach, the service composition scheme that is proposed in this approach does not involve any process integration, as the Web services are only described at the interface level.

5   Conclusion

In the pervasive computing vision the user has a central position. This vision involves that everywhere around us, the environment is populated with networked, both computing and input/output devices that provide the environment's components. Our objective has been to allow a user entering to a pervasive computing environment to perform a task, abstractly described on his/her device, by integrating on the fly the environment's components. A key feature of pervasive computing components is their heterogeneity. Most existing solutions poorly deal with heterogeneity since they assume that components being integrated have been developed to conform syntactically in terms of interfaces and conversations.

Our solution building on semantic Web services offers much more flexibility by enabling semantic matching of interfaces and ad hoc reconstruction of the user task's conversation from service's conversations. Our solution is achieved in two steps. In the first step, we perform a semantic matching of interfaces that leads to the selection of the set of services that may be useful during the integration. In the second step, we perform a conversation matching starting from the set of previously selected services, thus obtaining a conversation composition that behaves as the task's conversation. Our matching is based on a mapping of OWL-S conversations to finite state automata. This mapping facilitates the conversation integration process, as it transform this problem to an automaton equivalence issue.

The main feature of our solution is the ability to compose Web services that expose complex behaviors to realize a user's task that itself has a complex behavior. Existing approaches in process-level matching generally consider either that the services or the task have a simple behavior, thus leading to simple integration solutions. In our case, we assume complex behaviors for both services and task and we propose a matching algorithm that attempts to reconstruct the task's behavior using fragments of the services behaviors. In order to deal with such a high level of dynamicity our solution uses some costly mechanisms such as semantic reasoning. Thus, we intend to implement our approach and to evaluate it in terms of efficiency and performance. We have already implemented the conversation matching algorithm based on automata analysis; the next step is to augment this algorithm with the semantic matching.

References

1. Patil A., Oundhakar S., and Sheth A. Semantic annotation of web services. Technical report, LSDIS Lab, Department of Computer Science, University of Georgia, March 2003.
2. Sharad Bansal and Jose M. Vidal. Matchmaking of web services based on the daml-s service model. In *Proceedings of the second international joint conference on Autonomous agents and multiagent systems*, pages 926–927. ACM Press, 2003.
3. Tim Berners-Lee, James Hendler, and Ora Lassila. The semantic web. *Scientific American*, May 2001.
4. Klein M. Bernstein A. Towards high-precision service retrieval. In Ian Horrocks and James Hendler, editors, *Proceedings of The First International Semantic Web Conference(ISWC), 2002*, number 2342 in Lecture Notes in Computer Science. Springer-Verlag, 2342 2002.
5. BPEL4WS. *Business Process Execution Language for Web Services (BPEL4WS) 1.1*. IBM , Microsoft , BEA, 1.1 edition, 2003. http://www-106.ibm.com/developerworks/library/ws-bpel/.
6. Antonio Brogi, Carlos Canal, Ernesto Pimentel, and Antonio Vallecillo. Formalizing web services choreographies. In *Proceedings of the First International Workshop on Web Services and Formal Methods, Pisa, Italy*, February 2004.
7. Andreas Eberhart. Ad-hoc of invocation semantic web services. In *IEEE International Conference on Web Services (San Diego, California ICWS 2004)*, pages 116–124, June 2004.
8. Valrie Issarny Ferda Tartanoglu. Specifying web services recovery support with conversations. In *In Proceedings of the 38th Hawaii International Conference on System Sciences (HICSS-38) , January 2005*.
9. J. G. Pereira Filho and M. van Sinderen. Web service architectures - semantics and context-awareness issues in web services platforms. Technical report, Telematica Instituut, 2003.
10. Howard Foster, Sebastian Uchitel, Jeff Magee, and Jeff Kramer. Model-based verification of web service compositions. In *IEEE International Conference on Automated Software Engineering*, 2003.
11. Andreas Heß and Nicholas Kushmerick. Machine learning for annotating semantic web services. In *AAAI Spring Symposium on Semantic Web Services*, Palo Alto, California, USA, 2004.
12. John E. Hopcroft, Rajeev Motwani, and Jeffrey D. Ullman. *Introduction to Automata Theory, Languages, and Computation(2nd Edition)*. Addison-Wesley, 2000.
13. Valerie Issarny, Daniele Sacchetti, Ferda Tartanoglu, Francoise Sailhan, Rafik Chibout, Nicole Levy, and Angel Talamona. Developing ambient intelligence systems: A solution based on web services. *Journal of Automated Software Engineering*, 2004.

14. Gonzalez-Castillo Javier, Trastour David, and Bartolini Claudio. Description logics for matchmaking of services. In *Proceedings of the of the KI-2001, Workshop on Applications of Description Logics Vienna, Austria*, September 2001.
15. M. Koshkina and F. van Breugel. Verification of business processes for web services. Technical report, York University, 2003.
16. Shalil Majithia, David W. Walker, and W. A. Gray. A framework for automated service composition in service-oriented architecture. In *1st European Semantic Web Symposium*, 2004.
17. Srini Narayanan and Sheila A. McIlraith. Simulation, verification and automated composition of web services. In *Proceedings of the eleventh international conference on World Wide Web*, pages 77–88. ACM Press, 2002.
18. Massimo Paolucci, Takahiro Kawamura, Terry R. Payne, and Katia Sycara. Semantic matching of Web services capabilities. *Lecture Notes in Computer Science*, 2342:333–??, 2002.
19. Hamadi Rachid and Benatallah Boualem. A petri net-based model for web service composition. In Klaus-Dieter Schewe and Xiaofang Zhou, editors, *Fourteenth Australasian Database Conference (ADC2003)*, volume 17 of *Conferences in Research and Practice in Information Technology*, pages 191–200, Adelaide, Australia, 2003. ACS.
20. P.D.; Guizzardi G.; Ferreira Pires L.; Pereira Filho J.G. van Sinderen M Rios, D.; Costa. Using ontologies for modeling context-aware service platforms. In *OOPSLA 2003 Workshop on Ontologies to Complement Software Architectures*. Anaheim, CA, USA, 2003.
21. Kaarthik Sivashanmugam, Kunal Verma, Amit P. Sheth, and John A. Miller. Adding semantics to web services standards. In *Proceedings of the International Conference on Web Services, ICWS '03, 2003, Las Vegas, Nevada, USA*, pages 395–401, June 2003.
22. Katia Sycara, Massimo Paolucci, Anupriya Ankolekar, and Naveen Srinivasan. Automated discovery, interaction and composition of semantic web services. *Web Semantics: Science, Services and Agents on the World Wide Web*, 1(1):27–46, 2003.
23. David Trastour, Claudio Bartolini, and Javier Gonzalez-Castillo. A semantic web approach to service description for matchmaking of services. In *The first Semantic Web Working Symposium, Stanford University, California, USA, July 30 - August 1, 2001SWWS*, pages 447–461, 2001.
24. W.M.P. van der Aalst and A.H.M. ter Hofstede. Yawl: Yet another workflow language. *Accepted for publication in Information Systems*, 2004.
25. Rohit Aggarwaland Kunal Verma, John Miller, and Willie Milnor. Dynamic web service composition in meteor-s. Technical report, LSDIS Lab, Computer Science Dept., UGA, 2004.
26. WS-CDL. *Web Services Choreography Description Language Version 1.0*. W3C, 1.0 edition, 2004. http://www.w3.org/TR/2004/WD-ws-cdl-10-20040427/.
27. WSCI. *Web Service Choreography Interface (WSCI) 1.0*. BEA Systems, Intalio, SAP AG , Sun Microsystems, 1.0 edition, 2002. http://www.w3.org/TR/wsci/.
28. WSCL. *Web Services Conversation Language (WSCL) 1.0*. Hewlett-Packard Company, 1.0 edition, 2002. http://www.w3.org/TR/2002/NOTE-wscl10-20020314/.

Improving Composition Support with Lightweight Metadata-Based Extensions of Component Models

Johann Oberleitner and Michael Fischer

Vienna University of Technology, Vienna A-1040, Austria
joe@infosys.tuwien.ac.at
http://www.infosys.tuwien.ac.at/Staff/joe/index.html

Abstract. Software systems that rely on the component paradigm build new components by assembling existing prefabricated components. Most currently available IDEs support graphical components such as .NET Controls or JavaBeans for building GUI applications. Even though all those IDEs support arrangement and layout of those desktop components, composition support is rather limited. None of the most important composition environments support built-in validation of composition for .NET components or JavaBeans no further than type checking.

Our approach addresses these problems with lightweight extensions of existing component models with metadata attributes. We enhance the built-in composition facilities of the component model and the composition environment to exploit those metadata attributes. As we show the metadata attributes may be used to support required interfaces, constraint checks for method invocation or if all participants in a component collaboration satisify a certain protocol.

1 Introduction

Prefabricated software components are known to improve the quality of software construction and reduction of the development costs [1]. Component models [2] define the structure, components adhere to and how they can interoperate. Instead of implementing every functionality from scratch new features are built by assembling existing components.

Different component models have been introduced for different purposes, ranging from desktop component models to distributed component models. Most development environments focus primarily on desktop component models that are intended to be used in the development of client applications with graphical user interfaces. Hence, most today's utilized platforms, such as Java and .NET include simple component models for building desktop applications such as JavaBeans [3] or components for .NET [4]. Components that adhere to these component models usually represent graphical widgets.

In graphical composition environments developers may create component instances and put them in composite components, visualized in graphical design

T. Gschwind, U. Aßmann, and O. Nierstrasz (Eds.): SC 2005, LNCS 3628, pp. 47–56, 2005.

windows, browse and configure component instance properties such as fonts or colors, and create event listeners.

Inventors of component models wanted a fast adoption of those models, hence the requirements on components are rather small. The only requirement imposed on a Java class to become a JavaBean is to provide a default constructor. Similarly, .NET introduces a component model primarily targeted for GUI components. The single requirement for a .NET class to be used in standard .NET composition environments is that this class inherits from the `Component` class of the `System.ComponentModel` namespace.

Unfortunately, these simple component models and composition environments only support simple instantiation and creation features. For instance, in Visual Studio .NET 2003 it is possible to configure the property value of a component with the instance of any other component created in the composition environment. However, there are no standardized checks if such compositions are valid or required. Furthermore, there are no generic ways to use proxies or adaptors for such compositions.

New composition environments and component models have been introduced that provide validity checks at design time or the generation of adapters [5]. The flexibility of this introduction comes with the cost that these composition environments are not seamlessly integrated in the IDEs, making the adoption of those component models difficult if not impossible. Furthermore, these component models require rather large runtime environments.

We focus on this problem and introduce lightweight extensions of the existing desktop component models. Primarily, we rely on two different functionalities. First, we define metadata to describe additional information such as validity requirements or if a component's properties are required to be set to let the component work. Components are enriched by this metadata. Since the use of this metadata can be ignored by a composition environment all components that use this metadata can still be used in composition environments unaware of it. Second, we use the extension mechanisms provided by standard composition environments to build extensions for the composition environment to enforce the composition conditions described by the metadata. These extension mechanisms are defined by the component models but can optionally be used by components and composition environments.

We have designed and implemented our approach for the desktop component model of the .NET framework and Microsoft Visual Studio .NET 2003 as the appropriate composition environment. We show three examples for extending composition capabilities:

- introduction of required interfaces,
- use of OCL constraints [6] for methods and classes, and
- use of protocols for verifying component collaborations.

Although our implementation focuses on .NET the metadata annotation feature of JDK 1.5 allows that large parts of the approach can be ported to Java and JavaBeans, too.

The structure of this paper is as follows. Section 2 discusses existing techniques we build on. In Section 3 metadata attributes for enhancing composition facilities of components are introduced. Section 4 further extends these facilities with support for composition environments. We discuss related work in Section 5 and our future plans in Section 6. We draw our conclusions in Section 7.

2 Background

This section introduces the .NET metadata facility the .NET component model frequently uses and our approach is based on.

2.1 Metadata Facilities

Metadata attributes are used to attach additional static information to programming entities such as classes, fields, or methods. The compiler stores the attributes in the executable files and DLLs. The runtime environment provides read access to the attributes with reflection mechanisms.

For space reasons we cannot discuss in detail the .NET metadata facility. Instead we refer to Figure 1 that shows the assignment of metadata attributes to methods with edged braces and on an intuitive understanding of the reader. A complete discussion of .NET metadata can be found in [7] and our webpage [8].

2.2 Desktop Component Models

Instances of desktop components are instantiated in graphical design environments and may be configured with property sheets. A property is exposed by a component by accessor methods that allow read and write access to a logical property of the component instance. Components often support emission of events that are delivered to handler methods.

2.3 Component Model Support for Composition Environments

The .NET component model is supported by the formular designer included in Microsoft Visual Studio .NET and any other .NET based IDE. These composition environments support instantiation of components and in case of graphical components also positioning and resizing of the components in graphical windows. Configuration property-sheets are created dynamically based on component's reflection features.

3 Attributes for Components and Composition

In this section we introduce three different kinds of attributes that aid the composition process. All three attributes represent assumptions that have to be satisfied by components to provide a correct application. We support two different approaches for the enforcement of these assumptions. The manual approach relies on manual calls to helper methods for checking if the assumptions are satisfied. The compositional approach introduced in the next section relies on either the composition methods provided by the composition environment or by code injected by the environment to check the assumptions.

3.1   Required Interfaces

Most component models define a notion of *provided interfaces*. Furthermore, some component models introduce a notion of *required interfaces*.

For marking some properties as required we introduce the *required* attribute implemented by the class `RequiredAttribute`. It can be applied to properties to signal that these properties must be set to let the component work. It is also possible to attach multiple required attributes to require that a property supports all those interfaces. An example of the required attribute can be seen in Figure 1. Furthermore, for property arrays and collections we support a minimum and a maximum number of instances that must be set for the property.

In addition to required interfaces represented as properties we also support events to become marked as required. Instead of components that implement the required interfaces now event listeners have to be set.

A programmatic check of all required properties is done manually by calling a helper method to detect if all required interfaces are set. The implementation of this checker uses reflection on the component instance, iterates over all properties and verifies those that have a *required* attribute attached to it. The result of the check can be visualized in the composition environment already at design time in overwriting the `OnPaint` method (see Figure ref:RequiredUsage.

3.2   OCL Constraints

The application of pre- and postcondition in programming is widely accepted. Unfortunately, only few programming languages such as Eiffel [9] have built-in support for constraints. We propose two attributes that store the precondition and the postcondition of methods with `PreAttribute` and `PostAttribute`, respectively. We use the Object Constraint Language (OCL) for formulating the constraint expressions since it can be parsed easily, can be learned quite fast, and is simple to understand. Figure 2 shows a component that attaches pre- and postcondition to a withdraw method of an account class.

In addition to pre- and postcondition, the `InvariantAttribute` stores invariant conditions for classes and interfaces. We have faced one problem in using these attributes. The OCL constraints are provided as string parameters for the attribute classes. Unfortunately, is is not possible to execute the attribute constructor at compile time to verify if the expression is a syntactic valid OCL expression.

At the bottom of figure 2 we show how OCL constraints can be verified by calling a static method of the `OCLCheck` class we have implemented.

```
public interface IMyInterfaceA { public void MethodA(); }

public interface IMyInterfaceB { public void MethodB(); }

public class Test : Control
{
   private IMyRequiredInterface required;

   [Required(typeof(IMyInterfaceA))]
   [Required(typeof(IMyInterfaceB))]
   public IMyInterfaceA RequiredProperty
   { get { return this.required; }
     set { this.required = value; }
   }

   // paint method checks all required properties
   public override void OnPaint(PaintEventArgs e)
   {
      if (!RequiredHelper.CheckAllRequiredProps(this))
          { /* paint error message */ }
      else { /* normal drawing code */ }
   }

}
```

Fig. 1. Required attribute

```
public class Account
{
   int balance;

   [Pre("amount >= 0 and self.balance >= amount")]
   [Post("self.balance = self.balance@pre - amount")]
   public void Withdraw(int amount)
   {
      this.balance -= amount;
   }
}
// check code
OCLCheck.PreconditionCheck(this, "Withdraw", increment);
```

Fig. 2. OCL attribute specification

3.3   Collaboration Protocols

In many scenarios it is not possible to call methods or query and update properties from arbitrary component states. For instance, to operate on a file it must have been opened before. Hence, it is necessary that components interact by following a certain protocol [10,11]. Protocols define a predefined order in which methods and properties may be accessed, i.e. protocols define state machines for ordering method invocations.

We use various attributes to assign a state machine to an interface. One or multiple *Protocol* attributes declare all protocols an interface participates in. Besides the name of the protocol it also takes an array of state names of the state machine, and the initial state. Other interfaces that act in this protocol are marked with *Collaborator* attributes that are initialized with the protocol name and the type of the participating interface.

For each method *Transition* attributes are used to declare allowed state transitions associated with the invocations.. Each transition attribute is initialized with the name of the source state and the target state.

Figure 3 shows an example of two interfaces that share the access on a particular resource. These interfaces can be used in the same class or in two different classes. However, the semantics remains the same. Before the reader can access the data the state machine has to be in the open state.

```
[ Protocol("Interaction", new string[]{"Closed","Open"},
          Initial="Closed")]
[ Collaborator(typeof(IReader))]
public interface IProvider
{
   [Transition("Closed", "Open")] void Open();

   [Transition("Open", "Closed")] void Close();
}

[ Protocol("Interaction", new string[]{"Closed", "Open"},
          Initial="Closed")]
[ Collaborator(typeof(IProvider))]
public interface IReader
{
   [Transition("Open", "Open")] object Read();
}

// check code
StateMachine.Check(this, "Read");
```

Fig. 3. Protocol specification

We have provided a helper class that verifies if a method invocation starts from the appropriate state. When applying the checks manually this code has to be inserted at the beginning of a method.

4   Tool Support and Automatic Adaptor Generation

This section describes how the composition process can be improved by the attributes defined before.

Without any tool support constraints defined with the attributes described before can only be verified manually with invocation of checking methods and are neither verified nor enforced automatically. However, with the use of adaptors based on these attributes we can automatically enforce verification of those constraints. The .NET component model in connection with design environments such as Visual Studio .NET allow almost seamless use of those attributes.

4.1   Composition Support

The .NET component model defines some metadata attributes for layouting and arrangement of .NET widgets and components. Some of these attributes are used in conjunction with the .NET propertysheet used by Microsoft's Visual Studio .NET and other IDEs. The *Editor* metadata attribute allows developers to assign user defined editors to classes and interfaces but also to properties. These editors are automatically used by the propertysheet in Visual Studio .NETs designer and allows modification of those properties. When a developer selects a cell in the propertysheet the environment detects if an editor attribute is attached to the datatype or the property.

We have implemented such an editor that may be attached to properties that use the *required* attribute. This editor provides the developers with a list of component instances which components match all *required* interfaces for the particular property.

After the selection of one of the proposed component instances Visual Studio automatically generates the correct instance assignment in the constructor of the class that hosts the instances. In case of a property with a multiplicity larger than one, either arrays or collections are used. The same editor class is used but it does not provide a combobox but a dialog to select the component instances.

When the editor has finished Visual Studio generates code fragments that reflect the choice the user makes in the editor in the constructor of the component instance owner's class. We have implemented a code serializer that generates an appropriate source code fragment for initializing the required component compositions. The code serializer generates the appropriate initialization statements for arrays and collections and inserts it into the predefined code generation stream provided by .NET.

4.2   Verification Adaptors

For automatic evaluation of constraints described with the attributes defined above we generate adaptors that include verification code. These adaptors include checks if required properties are bound, if method arguments satisify preconditions or method results satisfy postconditions, and if a protocol sequence is still satisifed. The adaptors just include code sequences described above.

The verification adaptors are set in the initialization code of the component constructor when an editor has been used. We generate adaptor initialization code instead of field assignments. Figure 4 shows an example for such a code fragment. However, a serious limitation of our automatic approach is that we cannot change method call statements where the interface used has not been set via properties. Instead of the field assignment the code serializer initializes an adaptor interface and uses the original value as argument.

```
...  // code inside InitializeComponents
// this.RequiredProperty = required1;

// new code
this.RequiredProperty = new ConstraintAdaptor_IReq(required1);
```

Fig. 4. Adaptor Initialization

The adaptors are generated on demand. Here we use another .NET feature for dynamically creating or loading assemblies.

5   Related Work

The use of metadata beyond type information is frequently used within some component models. Enterprise JavaBeans [12] rely on metadata stored in deployment descriptors to configure components for different installation systems. JavaBeans [3] provides and uses descriptor classes to store additional information about components. For instance, this information can be used to support custom editors similar to .NET's type editors we have used. In .NET metadata attributes are used for instance configuration which we have used and extended. Further attributes are used for remoting and distribution purposes. Another area where metadata attributes are heavily used in .NET are system interoperability. .NET predefines some attributes for importing methods from native DLLs and allows to modify method calling conventions and argument conversion.

The notion of a required interfaces is well-known for several years [1]. However, component models that support required interfaces are usually not supported by any standard development environment. Our extension can be considered lightweight since it can be used without any modification in all .NET IDEs that support the metadata attributes Microsoft has predefined with .NET. Even, if these attributes are not supported the components are still functional. Validation, however, must be done manually.

The first general purpose object-oriented programming language that supports constraints is Eiffel [9] with its support for Design-by-Contract [13]. For Java different approaches implement pre- and postconditions such as JML [14] or iContract. Since Java did not support metadata these approaches primarily use JavaDoc comments to store the constraints. We expect that some of these approaches will adopt the new metadata notation of JDK 1.5. Using .NET attributes for constraints has already been described before in [15].

6 Future Work

We plan to introduce additional metadata attributes and further support for composition environments. The .NET component model supports the implementation of so-called designers, graphical editors for components useable directly in the composition environment's assembly window. When layouting graphical components on the standard containers such as panels or forms provided by .NET no visualization of the compositions is shown. We plan to extend the containers to draw graphical representations for the compositions of components.

We also plan to port the attributes to Java with JDK 1.5. The attributes and the classes for enforcing the constraints described with the attributes can easily be ported to Java despite the differences of the platforms. However, porting the support for composition environments such as the Component Workbench [5] or Eclipse requires more effort.

Since not everything can be done with checking the validity of component composition attributes at design time we plan to build a simple verifier that takes a root component as input and traverses recursively all child components and checks if all constraints are fulfilled.

7 Conclusions

In this paper we have shown how a simple widely used component model can be extended with metadata attributes specifically introduced for composition. These metadata attributes improve readability and act as additional documentation of components. Furthermore the attributes store additional semantic information beyond the capabilities of the programming languages and component models used. This semantic information may be used to realize simple semantic checks without preventing the use of the components in standardized environments.

We introduced attributes to describe required interfaces that are mandatory to be set before a component instance may be used. We also introduced attributes for describing constraints with OCL. Furthermore, we presented attributes for component collaboration.

The validation of these attributes may be done programmatically in the components or the components' clients refering to small helper classes that implement the validation semantics.

References

1. Szyperski, C.: Component Software: Beyond Object-Oriented Programming. Addison-Wesley (1998)
2. Heineman, G.T., Councill, W.T., eds.: Component-Based Software Engineering: Putting the Pieces Together. Addison-Wesley (2001)
3. Hamilton, G., ed.: JavaBeans. Sun Microsystems, http://java.sun.com/beans/ (1997)

4. Griffiths, I., Adams, M.: .NET Windows Forms in a Nutshell. O'Reilly (2003)
5. Johann, O., Gschwind, T.: Composing distributed components with the component workbench. In: Proceedings of the 3rd International Workshop on Software Engineering and Middleware 2002 (SEM 2002). (2002)
6. Warmer, J., Kleppe, A.: The Object Constraint Language: Getting your models ready for MDA. Addison-Wesley (2003)
7. Richter, J.: Applied Microsoft .NET Framework Programming. Microsoft Press (2002)
8. Johann, O.: Webpage: .NET Metadata Facilities (2005) http://www.infosys.tuwien.ac.at/Staff/joe/dotnet-metadata.html.
9. Meyer, B.: Object Oriented Software Construction. Prentice Hall (1997)
10. Yellin, D.M., Strom, R.E.: Interfaces, protocols, and the semi-automatic construction of software adaptors. In: OOPSLA '94: Proceedings of the ninth annual conference on Object-oriented programming systems, language, and applications, ACM Press (1994) 176–190
11. Yellin, D.M., Strom, R.E.: Protocol specifications and component adaptors. ACM Trans. Program. Lang. Syst. **19** (1997) 292–333
12. DeMichiel, L.G., Yalcinalp, L.Ü., Krishnan, S.: Enterprise JavaBeans Specification, Version 2.0. Sun Microsystems. (2001) Proposed Final Draft 2.
13. Meyer, B.: Applying Design by Contract. IEEE Computer **25** (1992) 40–51
14. Cheon, Y., Leavens, G.T.: A runtime assertion checker for the Java Modeling Language (JML). In: International Conference on Software Engineering Research and Practice (SERP '02), CSREA Press (2002) 322–328
15. Sjörgen, A. In: A Method for Support for Design By Contract on the .NET platform. Artech House Publishers (2002) 12–20

Directory Support for Large-Scale, Automated Service Composition

Walter Binder, Ion Constantinescu, and Boi Faltings

Ecole Polytechnique Fédérale de Lausanne (EPFL),
Artificial Intelligence Laboratory,
CH-1015 Lausanne, Switzerland
`firstname.lastname@epfl.ch`

Abstract. In an open environment populated by large numbers of services, automated service composition is a major challenge. In such a setting the efficient interaction of directory-based service discovery with different service composition algorithms is crucial. In this paper we present a directory with dedicated features for service composition. In order to optimize the interaction of the directory with different service composition algorithms exploiting application-specific heuristics, the directory supports user-defined selection and ranking functions written in a declarative query language. Inside the directory queries are transformed in order to enable a best-first search for matching directory entries, efficiently pruning the search space.[1]

Keywords: Service discovery and composition, Service directories, Query language and query processing.

1 Introduction

There is a good body of work which addresses the service composition problem by applying planning techniques based either on theorem proving (e.g., Golog [6]) or on hierarchical task planning (e.g., SHOP-2 [7]). All these approaches assume that the relevant service descriptions are initially loaded into the reasoning engine and that no discovery is performed during composition. However, due to the large number of services and to the loose coupling between service providers and consumers, services are indexed in directories. Consequently, planning algorithms have to be adapted to a situation where planning operators are not known a priori, but have to be retrieved through queries to these directories.

Our approach to automated service composition is based on matching input and output parameters of services using type information in order to constrain the ways how services may be composed. Our composition algorithm allows for *partially matching* types and handles them by computing and introducing *switches* in the composi-

---

[1] The work presented in this paper was partly carried out in the framework of the EPFL Center for Global Computing and supported by the Swiss National Funding Agency OFES as part of the European projects KnowledgeWeb (FP6-507482) and DIP (FP6-507483).

T. Gschwind, U. Aßmann, and O. Nierstrasz (Eds.): SC 2005, LNCS 3628, pp. 57–66, 2005.

tion plan. Experimental results show that using partial matches significantly decreases the failure rate compared with a composition algorithm that supports only complete matches [4].

We have developed a directory service with specific features to ease service composition. Queries may not only search for complete matches, but may also retrieve *partially matching* directory entries. As the number of (partially) matching entries may be large, the directory supports *incremental retrieval* of the results of a query. This is achieved through *sessions*, during which a client issues queries and retrieves the results in chunks of limited size [2].

As in a large-scale directory the number of (partially) matching results for a query may be very high, it is crucial to order the result set within the directory according to heuristics and to transfer first the better matches to the client. If the heuristics work well, only a small part of the possibly large result set has to be transferred, thus saving network bandwidth and boosting the performance of a directory client that executes a service composition algorithm (the results are returned incrementally, once a result fulfills the client's requirements, no further results need to be transmitted). However, the heuristics depend on the concrete composition algorithm. For each service composition algorithm (e.g., forward chaining, backward chaining, etc.), a different heuristic may be better adapted. Because research on service composition is still in the beginning and the directory cannot anticipate the needs of all possible service composition algorithms, our directory supports *user-defined selection and ranking heuristics* expressed in a *declarative query language*. The support for application-specific heuristics significantly increases the flexibility of our directory, as the client is able to tailor the processing of directory queries. For efficient execution, the queries are *dynamically transformed and compiled* by the directory.

As the main contributions of this paper, we show how our directory supports user-defined selection and ranking heuristics. We present a dedicated query language and explain how queries are processed by the directory. In a first step, the directory transforms queries in order to better exploit the internal directory organization during the search. This allows a best-first search that generates the result set in a lazy way, reducing response time and workload within the directory. In a second step, the query is compiled in order to speed up the directory search. Compared with previous work [2,1], the novel, original contributions of this paper are the declarative directory query language and the transformation mechanism to make better use of the internal directory structure. These techniques, which have not been applied in the context of service directories before, provide a flexible and efficient mechanism for query processing.

This paper is structured as follows: Section 2 gives an overview of our service description formalism and of the internal index structure of our directory. In Section 3 we present a simple, functional query language which allows to express application-specific selection and ranking heuristics. Section 4 explains the processing of directory queries and introduces query transformations that enable a best-first search with early pruning. In Section 5 we discuss how user-defined queries are compiled and integrated into the directory. Section 6 discusses a sample query and shows its transformation. Finally, Section 7 concludes this paper.

2   Service Descriptions and Directory Index

Service descriptions are a key element for service discovery and service composition and should enable automated interactions between applications. In this paper we partially build on existing formalisms, such as WSDL (http://www.w3.org/TR/wsdl) and OWL-S (http://www.daml.org/services/owl-s/), by considering a simple table-based formalism where each service is described by a set of tuples mapping service parameters (unique names of inputs or outputs) to parameter types (the spaces of possible values for a given parameter). We require that parameter types are not empty, i.e., there must be at least one allowed value for each parameter. Parameter types can be expressed either as sets of intervals of basic data types (e.g., date/time, integers, floating-points) or as classes of individuals. Class parameter types can be defined in a descriptive language such as OWL (http://www.w3.org/2004/OWL/). From the descriptions we derive a directed graph (DG) of simple is-a relations either directly (for basic data types) or by using a description logic classifier (for concepts). For efficiency reasons, we represent the DG numerically. We assume that each class is represented as a set of intervals. We encode each parent-child relation by sub-dividing each of the intervals of the parent. In the case of multiple parents, the child class is represented by the union of the sub-intervals resulting from the encoding of each of the parent-child relations. Since for a given domain we can have several parameters represented by intervals, the space of all possible parameter values can be represented as a rectangular hyperspace with a dimension for each parameter. For details, see [3].

The need for efficient discovery and matchmaking leads to a need for search structures and indexes for directories. We consider numerically encoded service descriptions as multidimensional data and use techniques related to the indexing of such kind of information in the directory. Our directory index is based on the Generalized Search Tree (GiST), proposed as a unifying framework by Hellerstein [5]. The design principle of GiST arises from the observation that search trees used in databases are balanced trees with a high fanout in which the internal nodes are used as a directory and the leaf nodes point to the actual data.

Each leaf node in the GiST of our directory holds references to all service descriptions with a certain input/output behaviour. The required inputs of the service and the provided outputs (sets of parameter names with associated types) are stored in the leaf node. For inner nodes of the tree, the union of all inputs/outputs found in the subtree is stored. More precisely, each inner node I on the path to a leaf node L contains all input/output parameters stored in L. The type associated with a parameter in I subsumes the type of the parameter in L. That is, for an inner node, the input/output parameters indicate which concrete parameters may be found in a leaf node of the subtree. If a parameter is not present in an inner node, it will not be present in any leaf node of the subtree.

3   Directory Query Language

As directory queries may retrieve large numbers of matching entries (especially when partial matches are taken into consideration), our directory supports sessions in order to incrementally access the results of a query [2]. By default, the order in which matching service descriptions are returned depends on the actual structure of the directory index (the GiST structure discussed before). However, depending on the service composition algorithm, ordering the results of a query according to certain heuristics may significantly improve the performance of service composition. In order to avoid the transfer of a large number of service descriptions, the pruning, ranking, and sorting according to application-dependent heuristics should occur directly within the directory. As for each service composition algorithm a different pruning and ranking heuristic may be better suited, our directory allows its clients to define custom selection and ranking functions which are used to select and sort the results of a query.

A directory query consists of a set of provided inputs and required outputs (both sets contain tuples of parameter name and associated type), as well as a custom selection and ranking function. The selection and ranking function is written in the simple, high-level, functional query language $DirQL_{SE}$ (<u>Dir</u>ectory <u>Q</u>uery <u>L</u>anguage with <u>Se</u>t <u>E</u>xpressions). An (informal) EBNF grammar for $DirQL_{SE}$ is given in Table 1. The non-terminal *constant*, which is not shown in the grammar, represents a non-negative numeric constant (integer or decimal number). The syntax of $DirQL_{SE}$ has some similarities with LISP.[2] We have designed the language considering the following requirements:

- Simplicity: $DirQL_{SE}$ offers only a minimal set of constructs, but it is expressive enough to write relevant selection and ranking heuristics.
- Declarative: $DirQL_{SE}$ is a functional language and does not support destructive assignment. The absence of side-effects eases program transformations.
- Safety: As the directory executes user-defined code, $DirQL_{SE}$ expressions must not interfere with internals of the directory. Moreover, the resource consumption (e.g., CPU, memory) needed for the execution of $DirQL_{SE}$ expressions is bounded in order to prevent denial-of-service attacks: $DirQL_{SE}$ supports neither recursion nor loops, and queries can be executed without dynamic memory allocation.
- Efficient directory search: $DirQL_{SE}$ has been designed to enable an efficient best-first search in the directory GiST. Code transformations automatically generate selection and ranking functions for the inner nodes of the GiST (see Section 4).
- Efficient compilation: Due to the simplicity of the language, $DirQL_{SE}$ expressions can be efficiently compiled to increase performance (see Section 5).

A $DirQL_{SE}$ expression defines custom selection and ranking heuristics. The evaluation of a $DirQL_{SE}$ expression is based on the 4 sets qin (available inputs specified in the query), qout (required outputs specified in the query), sin (required inputs of a certain service S), and sout (provided outputs of a certain service S). Each element in each of these sets represents a query/service parameter identified by its unique name within the set and has an associated type (encoded as a set of numeric intervals).

A $DirQL_{SE}$ expression may involve some simple arithmetic. The result of a numeric $DirQL_{SE}$ expression is always non-negative. The '−' operator returns 0 if the

---

[2] In order to simplify the presentation, in this paper the operators 'and', 'or', '<', '>', '<=', '>=', '=', '+', '*', '−', 'min', and 'max' are binary, whereas in the implementation they may take an arbitrary number arguments, similar to the definition of these operations in LISP.

Table 1. A grammar for $DirQL_{SE}$

```
dirqlExpr   : selectExpr | rankExpr | selectExpr rankExpr ;
selectExpr  : 'select' booleanExpr ;
rankExpr    : 'order' 'by' ('asc' | 'desc') numExpr ;
booleanExpr : '(' ('and' | 'or') booleanExpr booleanExpr ')'
            | '(' 'not' booleanExpr ')'
            | '(' ('<' | '>' | '<=' | '>=' | '=') numExpr numExpr ')' ;
numExpr     : constant
            | '(' ('+' | '*' | '-' | '/') numExpr numExpr ')'
            | '(' ('min' | 'max') numExpr numExpr ')'
            | '(' 'if' booleanExpr numExpr numExpr ')'
            | setExpr ;
setExpr     : '(' 'union' querySet serviceSet ')'
            | '(' 'intersection' querySet serviceSet typeTest ')'
            | '(' 'minus' querySet serviceSet typeTest ')'
            | '(' 'minus' serviceSet querySet typeTest ')'
            | '(' 'size' (querySet | serviceSet) ')' ;
querySet    : 'qin' | 'qout' ;
serviceSet  : 'sin' | 'sout' ;
typeTest    : 'FALSE' | 'EQUAL' | 'S_CONTAINS_Q' | 'Q_CONTAINS_S' | 'OVERLAP' | 'TRUE' ;
```

second argument is bigger than the first one. The $DirQL_{SE}$ programmer may use the 'if' conditional to ensure that the first argument of '-' is bigger or equal than the second one. For division, the second operand (divisor) has to evaluate to a constant for a given query. That is, it is a numeric expression with only numeric constants, as well as size(qin) and size(qout) at the leaves. Before a query is executed, the directory ensures that the $DirQL_{SE}$ expression will not cause a division by zero. For this purpose, all subexpressions are examined. The reason for these restrictions will be explained in the following section.

A $DirQL_{SE}$ query may comprise a selection and a ranking expression. Service descriptions (inputs/outputs defined by sin/sout) for which the selection expression evaluates to *false* are not returned to the client (pruning). The ranking expression defines the custom ranking heuristics. For a certain service description, the ranking expression computes a non-negative value. The directory will return service descriptions in ascending or descending order, as specified by the ranking expression.

The selection and ranking expressions may make use of several set operations. size returns the cardinality of any of the sets qin, qout, sin, or sout. The operations union, intersection, and minus take as arguments a query set (qin or qout) as well as a service set (sin or sout). For union and intersection, the query set has to be provided as the first argument. All set operations return the cardinality of the resulting set.

union: Cardinality of the union of the argument sets. Type information is irrelevant for this operation.

intersection: Cardinality of the intersection of the argument sets. For a parameter to be counted in the result, it has to have the same name in both argument sets and the type test (third argument) has to succeed.

minus: Cardinality of the set minus of the argument sets (first argument set minus second argument set). For a parameter to be counted in the result, it has to occur in the first argument set and, either there is no parameter with the same name in the second set, or in the case of parameters with the same name, the type test has to fail.

The type of parameters cannot be directly accessed, only the operations intersection and minus make use of the type information. For these operations, a type test is applied to parameters that have the same name in the given query and service set. The following type tests are supported (T_S denotes the type of a common parameter in the service set, while T_Q is the type of the parameter in the query set): FALSE (always fails), EQUAL (succeeds if $T_S = T_Q$), S_CONTAINS_Q (succeeds if T_S subsumes T_Q), Q_CONTAINS_S (succeeds if T_Q subsumes T_S), OVERLAP (succeeds if there is an overlap between T_S and T_Q, i.e., if a common subtype of T_S and T_Q exists), and TRUE (always succeeds).

4   Efficient Directory Search

Processing a user query requires traversing the GiST structure of the directory starting from the root node. The given $DirQL_{SE}$ expression is applied to leaf nodes of the directory tree, which correspond to concrete service descriptions (i.e., sin and sout represent the exact input/output parameters of a service description). For an inner node I of the GiST, sin and sout are supersets of the input/output parameters found in any node of the subtree whose root is I. The type of each parameter in I is a supertype of the parameter found in any node (which has a parameter with the same name) in the subtree. Therefore, the user-defined selection and ranking function cannot be directly applied to inner nodes.

In order to prune the search (as close as possible to the root of the GiST) and to implement a best-first search strategy which expands the most promising branch in the tree first, appropriate selection (pruning) and ranking functions are needed for the inner nodes of the GiST. In our approach, the client defines only the selection and ranking function for leaf nodes (i.e., to be invoked for concrete service descriptions), while the corresponding functions for inner nodes are automatically generated by the directory. The directory uses a set of simple transformation rules that enable a very efficient generation of the selection and ranking functions for inner nodes (the execution time of the transformation algorithm is linear with the size of the query).

If the client desires ranking in ascending order, the generated ranking function for inner nodes computes a lower bound of the ranking value in any node of the subtree; for ranking in descending order, it calculates an upper bound. While the query is being processed, the visited nodes are maintained in a heap or priority queue, where the node with the most promising heuristic value comes first. Always the first node is expanded; if it is a leaf node, it is returned to the client. Further nodes are expanded only if the client needs more results. This technique is essential to reduce the processing time in the directory until the the first result is returned, i.e., it reduces the response time. Furthermore, thanks to the incremental retrieval of results, the client may close the result set when no further results are needed. In this case, the directory does not spend resources to compute the whole result set. Consequently, this approach reduces the workload in the directory and increases its scalability. In order to protect the directory from attacks, queries may be terminated if the size of the internal heap or priority queue or the number of retrieved results exceed a certain threshold defined by the directory service provider.

Table 2 shows the transformation operators $\uparrow$ and $\downarrow$ which allow to generate the code for calculating upper and lower bounds in inner nodes of the GiST. The variables a and

Table 2. Transformation operators $\uparrow$, $\downarrow$, $\oplus$, and $\ominus$ for the generation of inner node code

$\uparrow constant$	$\longrightarrow constant$	$\downarrow constant$	$\longrightarrow constant$
$\uparrow (+\ a\ b)$	$\longrightarrow (+\ \uparrow a\ \uparrow b)$	$\downarrow (+\ a\ b)$	$\longrightarrow (+\ \downarrow a\ \downarrow b)$
$\uparrow (*\ a\ b)$	$\longrightarrow (*\ \uparrow a\ \uparrow b)$	$\downarrow (*\ a\ b)$	$\longrightarrow (*\ \downarrow a\ \downarrow b)$
$\uparrow (-\ a\ b)$	$\longrightarrow (-\ \uparrow a\ \downarrow b)$	$\downarrow (-\ a\ b)$	$\longrightarrow (-\ \downarrow a\ \uparrow b)$
$\uparrow (/\ a\ c)$	$\longrightarrow (/\ \uparrow a\ c)$	$\downarrow (/\ a\ c)$	$\longrightarrow (/\ \downarrow a\ c)$
$\uparrow (min\ a\ b)$	$\longrightarrow (min\ \uparrow a\ \uparrow b)$	$\downarrow (min\ a\ b)$	$\longrightarrow (min\ \downarrow a\ \downarrow b)$
$\uparrow (max\ a\ b)$	$\longrightarrow (max\ \uparrow a\ \uparrow b)$	$\downarrow (max\ a\ b)$	$\longrightarrow (max\ \downarrow a\ \downarrow b)$
$\uparrow (if\ x\ a\ b)$	$\longrightarrow (max\ \uparrow a\ \uparrow b)$	$\downarrow (if\ x\ a\ b)$	$\longrightarrow (min\ \downarrow a\ \downarrow b)$
$\uparrow (union\ q\ s)$	$\longrightarrow (union\ q\ s)$	$\downarrow (union\ q\ s)$	$\longrightarrow (size\ q)$
$\uparrow (intersection\ q\ s\ t)$	$\longrightarrow (intersection\ q\ s\ \oplus t)$	$\downarrow (intersection\ q\ s\ t)$	$\longrightarrow 0$
$\uparrow (minus\ q\ s\ t)$	$\longrightarrow (size\ q)$	$\downarrow (minus\ q\ s\ t)$	$\longrightarrow (minus\ q\ s\ \oplus t)$
$\uparrow (minus\ s\ q\ t)$	$\longrightarrow (minus\ s\ q\ \ominus t)$	$\downarrow (minus\ s\ q\ t)$	$\longrightarrow 0$
$\uparrow (size\ q)$	$\longrightarrow (size\ q)$	$\downarrow (size\ q)$	$\longrightarrow (size\ q)$
$\uparrow (size\ s)$	$\longrightarrow (size\ s)$	$\downarrow (size\ s)$	$\longrightarrow 0$
$\oplus TRUE$	$\longrightarrow TRUE$	$\ominus TRUE$	$\longrightarrow TRUE$
$\oplus OVERLAP$	$\longrightarrow OVERLAP$	$\ominus OVERLAP$	$\longrightarrow FALSE$
$\oplus Q\_CONTAINS\_S$	$\longrightarrow OVERLAP$	$\ominus Q\_CONTAINS\_S$	$\longrightarrow Q\_CONTAINS\_S$
$\oplus S\_CONTAINS\_Q$	$\longrightarrow S\_CONTAINS\_Q$	$\ominus S\_CONTAINS\_Q$	$\longrightarrow FALSE$
$\oplus EQUAL$	$\longrightarrow S\_CONTAINS\_Q$	$\ominus EQUAL$	$\longrightarrow FALSE$
$\oplus FALSE$	$\longrightarrow FALSE$	$\ominus FALSE$	$\longrightarrow FALSE$

b are arbitrary numeric expressions, c is a numeric expression that is guaranteed to be constant throughout a query, x is a boolean expression, q may be qin or qout, s may be sin or sout, and t is a type test. The operator $\oplus$ relaxes certain type tests, the operator $\ominus$ constrains them. For a $DirQL_{SE}$ ranking expression 'order by asc E', the code for inner node ranking is 'order by asc $\downarrow E$'; for a ranking expression 'order by desc E', the inner node ranking code is 'order by desc $\uparrow E$'.

If I is an inner node on the path to the leaf node L and E is a $DirQL_{SE}$ ranking expression, $\uparrow E$ (resp. $\downarrow E$) applied to I has to compute an upper (resp. lower) bound for E applied to L. While a formal proof of the correctness of the transformation rules in Table 2 had to be omitted due to space limitations, we exemplarily explain 2 rules in an informal way:

First we consider computing an upper bound for $E = (intersection\ q\ s\ t)$. In an inner node I the service set s_I is a superset of s_L in a leaf node, while the query set q remains constant. Moreover, the type of each parameter in s_L is subsumed by the type of the parameter with the same name in s_I. Not considering the parameter types, applying E to I would compute an upper bound for E applied to L, as intuitively the intersection of q with the bigger set s_I will not be smaller than the intersection of q with s_L. Taking parameter types into consideration, we must ensure that whenever a type test succeeds for L, it will also succeed for I. That is, if a common parameter is counted in the intersection in L, it must be also counted in the intersection in I. As it can be seen in Table 2, $\oplus t$ will succeed in I, if t succeeds in L (remember that parameter types are guaranteed to be non-empty). For instance, if the type of a parameter in s_L is subsumed by the type of the parameter with the same name in q (Q_CONTAINS_S succeeds for that parameter in L), the type of the corresponding parameter in s_I (which subsumes the type in s_L) will overlap with the parameter type in q. If the types in s_L and q are equal, the type in s_I will subsume the type in q.

Table 3. Transformation operator $\updownarrow$ for the generation of code in inner nodes of the GiST

$\updownarrow (and\ x\ y)\ \longrightarrow\ (and\ \updownarrow x\ \updownarrow y)$	$\updownarrow (or\ x\ y)\ \longrightarrow\ (or\ \updownarrow x\ \updownarrow y)$
$\updownarrow (<\ a\ b)\ \longrightarrow\ (<\downarrow a\ \uparrow b)$	$\updownarrow (<=\ a\ b)\ \longrightarrow\ (<=\downarrow a\ \uparrow b)$
$\updownarrow (>\ a\ b)\ \longrightarrow\ (>\uparrow a\ \downarrow b)$	$\updownarrow (>=\ a\ b)\ \longrightarrow\ (>=\uparrow a\ \downarrow b)$

As a second example we want to compute an upper bound for $E = (minus\ s\ q\ t)$. Without considering parameter types, applying E to I would give an upper bound for E applied to L, as s_I is a superset of s_L. In contrast to intersection, a common parameter is counted in the result if the type test fails. That is, if the type test fails in L, it has also to fail in I. As shown in table Table 2, $\ominus t$ will fail in I, if t fails in L. For example, if the type of a parameter in q does not subsume the type of the parameter with the same name in s_L (Q_CONTAINS_S fails for that parameter in L), it will also not subsume the type of that parameter in s_I (which subsumes the type of the parameter in s_L). If the type test is TRUE, it will never fail, neither in L nor in I. In all other cases, no matter whether the type test fails in L or not, it will fail in I (because $\ominus t$ will be FALSE). Hence, '$\uparrow(minus\ s\ q\ t)$' may result in '$(minus\ s\ q\ FALSE)$', which is equivalent to '$(size\ s)$'.

Considering the upper bound operator $\uparrow$, the reason why we require the divisor of '$/$' to evaluate to a constant becomes apparent: If c was not constant, for division the operator $\uparrow$ would have been defined as '$\uparrow(/\ a\ c)\ \longrightarrow\ (/\ \uparrow a\ \downarrow c)$'. Hence, even if the ranking expression provided by the client did not divide by zero ($c > 0$), the automatically generated code for computing an upper bound in inner nodes might possibly result in a division by zero ($\downarrow c = 0$). For this reason, c must depend neither on sin nor on sout.

In order to automatically generate the code for inner node selection (pruning), we define the transformation operator $\updownarrow$ for boolean expressions (see Table 3). If E is $true$ for a leaf node L, $\updownarrow E$ has to be $true$ for all nodes on the path to L. In other words, if $\updownarrow E$ is $false$ for an inner node, it must be guaranteed that E will be $false$ for each leaf in the subtree. This condition ensures that during the search an inner node may be discarded (pruning) only if it is sure that all leaves in the subtree are to be discarded, too. For a $DirQL_{SE}$ selection expression 'select E', the code for inner node selection is 'select $\updownarrow E$'. In Table 3 a and b are numeric expressions, while x and y are boolean expressions. Again, due to space limitations, a formal proof of these rules cannot be included in this paper.

The alert reader may have noticed that the operators 'not' and '=' have been omitted in Table 3. The reason for this omission is that initially we transform all boolean expressions in the query according to De Morgan's theorem, moving negations towards the leaves, removing double negations, and changing the comparators if needed. The resulting expressions are free of negations. Moreover, an expression of the form $(=\ a\ b)$ is transformed to the equivalent expression $(and\ (<=\ a\ b)\ (<=\ b\ a))$.

5   Efficient Query Execution

As the custom selection and ranking functions may be invoked very often, interpretation would cause high overhead. Thus, the directory includes a fast compiler for

$DirQL_{SE}$ expressions. Because our extensible directory is entirely programmed in Java, the $DirQL_{SE}$ compiler directly generates JVM bytecode which is linked into the same JVM that executes the core functionality of the directory. The compiler uses the Bytecode Engineering Library BCEL (http://jakarta.apache.org/bcel/) to manipulate JVM bytecode.

Compiling and integrating user-defined code into the directory leverages state-of-the-art optimizations in recent JVM implementations. Many modern JVMs first interpret bytecode to gather execution statistics. If code is executed frequently enough, it is compiled to optimized native code for fast execution. In this way, frequently used selection and ranking functions are executed as efficiently as algorithms directly built into the directory. Due to space limitations, details concerning the compilation of $DirQL_{SE}$ expressions had to be omitted.

As service composition clients may use the same selection and ranking function for multiple queries, our directory keeps them in a cache. This cache maps a hashcode of the $DirQL_{SE}$ expression to a structure containing the $DirQL_{SE}$ expression as well as the loaded class. In case of a cache hit the user-defined code is compared with the cache entry, and if it matches, the function in the cache is reused, avoiding compilation and linking. This approach mitigates the overhead of query compilation.

6   Example Query for Service Composition

In this section we show the transformation of a simple selection and ranking function for service composition based on forward chaining [4].

For forward chaining with complete type matches (see Table 4 (a)), we want that all inputs required by the service are provided by the query (and the service has to be able to handle the parameter types of the provided inputs, i.e., the types in the query have to be more specific than in the service). Moreover, we require that the service provides new outputs which are not already available as query inputs. The results are sorted in ascending order according to the remaining outputs that are required by the query, but not provided by the service (services that provide more of the required outputs come first). In order to support partial type matches [4], only S_CONTAINS_Q has to be replaced with OVERLAP in the first line of the selection expression in Table 4 (a).

The code for inner nodes is generated according to the transformation scheme presented in Section 4, as illustrated in Table 4 (b). Note that after applying the transforma-

Table 4. Selection and ranking function for service composition using forward chaining

```
select (and (<= (minus sin  qin S_CONTAINS_Q) 0)
            (>  (minus sout qin Q_CONTAINS_S) 0))
order by asc (minus qout sout Q_CONTAINS_S)
```

(a) User-defined selection and ranking function.

```
select (> (minus sout qin Q_CONTAINS_S) 0)
order by asc (minus qout sout OVERLAP)
```

(b) Generated code for inner nodes.

tion rules, the resulting expressions have been simplified according to simple algebraic rules, such as '$(<= 0 \ 0) = true$', '$(and \ true \ X) = X$', etc.

7 Conclusion

In this paper we presented a service directory with special support for service composition: Indexing techniques allowing the efficient retrieval of (partially) matching services, incremental data retrieval, as well as user-defined selection and ranking functions that enable the dynamic installation of application-specific heuristics within the directory. In order to efficiently support different service composition algorithms, it is important not to hard-code such heuristics in the directory, but to enable the dynamic installation of specific pruning and ranking heuristics. The selection and ranking functions are written in a simple, declarative language. Thanks to the support of application-specific heuristics, the most promising results from a directory query are returned first, which helps to reduce the number of transferred results and to save network bandwidth. Moreover, the result set is generated lazily, reducing response time and the workload in the directory. For efficient execution, the directory transforms and compiles user-defined selection and ranking functions.

References

1. W. Binder, I. Constantinescu, and B. Faltings. A directory for web service integration supporting custom query pruning and ranking. In *European Conference on Web Services (ECOWS-2004)*, pages 87–101, Erfurt, Germany, Sept. 2004.
2. I. Constantinescu, W. Binder, and B. Faltings. Directory services for incremental service integration. In *First European Semantic Web Symposium (ESWS-2004)*, pages 254–268, Heraklion, Greece, May 2004.
3. I. Constantinescu and B. Faltings. Efficient matchmaking and directory services. In *The 2003 IEEE/WIC International Conference on Web Intelligence*, pages 75–81, 2003.
4. I. Constantinescu, B. Faltings, and W. Binder. Large scale, type-compatible service composition. In *IEEE International Conference on Web Services (ICWS-2004)*, pages 506–513, San Diego, CA, USA, July 2004.
5. J. M. Hellerstein, J. F. Naughton, and A. Pfeffer. Generalized search trees for database systems. In U. Dayal, P. M. D. Gray, and S. Nishio, editors, *Proc. 21st Int. Conf. Very Large Data Bases, VLDB*, pages 562–573. Morgan Kaufmann, 11–15 1995.
6. S. A. McIlraith and T. C. Son. Adapting Golog for composition of semantic web services. In D. Fensel, F. Giunchiglia, D. McGuinness, and M.-A. Williams, editors, *Proceedings of the 8th International Conference on Principles and Knowledge Representation and Reasoning (KR-02)*, pages 482–496, San Francisco, CA, Apr. 22–25 2002. Morgan Kaufmann Publishers.
7. D. Wu, B. Parsia, E. Sirin, J. Hendler, and D. Nau. Automating DAML-S web services composition using SHOP2. In *Proceedings of 2nd International Semantic Web Conference (ISWC-2003)*, 2003.

Analysis of Compositional Conflicts in Component-Based Systems

Andreas Leicher, Susanne Busse, and Jörn Guy Süß

Technische Universität Berlin, Germany
{aleicher, sbusse, jgsuess}@cs.tu-berlin.de

Abstract. Today, incompatibilities in component specifications make their composition hard to handle in practical terms. Incompatibilities can be classified into three conflict categories: type conflicts, behavioral conflicts, and property conflicts. This paper describes a framework for the identification of compositional conflicts in component-based systems that analyses conflicts of all three categories. Furthermore, the conflict analysis framework can be integrated into the software development process and handles component transformations between different abstraction levels.

1 Introduction

Component composition is an important objective of software engineering. It promises component reuse and therefore a productivity gain, because of shorter time-to-market and improved quality. Unfortunately, composition is difficult to achieve in practical terms, because of technological incompatibilities and diverging component specifications.

Incompatibilities can be classified into three categories: type conflicts, behavioral conflicts, and property conflicts. Property conflicts refer to mismatches between communication mechanisms and technological characteristics of components and connectors. Thereby, properties describe structural and behavioral constraints from a different - a more abstract - viewpoint. Properties provide several advantages: they can be used to transform conceptual models into specific representations covering particular communication requirements, they enable one to gain more information regarding incompletely specified components, and they can be analyzed regarding compositional conflicts.

Our objective is to identify conflicts that impede component composition. Therefore, we defined and implemented a rule-based framework that uses the concepts of Architecture Description Languages (ADLs), but captures conflicts of all three categories mentioned above. Conflict identification is directly integrated in the software development process. Components of interest are small to medium-sized components of current middleware technologies.

The framework addresses the following problems that hinder analysis of conflicts and composition of middleware components:

- Handling of components specified in different standards and technologies,
- Abstraction from technology specific representations,

T. Gschwind, U. Aßmann, and O. Nierstrasz (Eds.): SC 2005, LNCS 3628, pp. 67–82, 2005.

- Conflict Identification,
- Refinement of canonic components into particular technology representations,
- Integration of the framework into the software development process.

This paper gives an overview on our framework (Chapter 3) and discusses the conflict analysis and model refinement in detail (Chapter 4). To show the usage of our framework, we take a scenario of composing a Java Bean and an Enterprise JavaBeans (EJB) component of a federated information system. Chapter 4.1 describes this scenario in more detail. Finally, Chapter 5 concludes with the discussion of our approach.

2   Related Work

A yet unresolved problem of Software Architecture concerns component composition. A composition requires checking for compliance of structural and behavioral specifications as well as of architectural properties.

In the last years, several ADLs [1,2,3,4] were proposed to handle structure and behavior of architectural elements. They define type systems to handle structural aspects of composition and use formalisms such as Process Algebra [5,6] to identify and overcome interaction mismatches.

However, despite these formalisms 'architectural mismatches' [7] still exist. According to Garlan, they are caused by divergent architectural properties. Today, several taxonomies [8,9,10,11] categorize architectural properties and several approaches aim to automatically discover mismatches based on conflicting characteristics [12,13,14,15,16]. Most of these approaches concentrate on architectural mismatches and do not handle structural and behavioral specifications. Therefore, they need to be expensively combined with heterogeneous tools to generate a connector.

We propose to combine all three specifications with a single ontology-based framework. In contrary to Pahl [17], who encodes behavior in description logic, we use external tools to check compliance. We use Triple [18] for the framework. It is designed to naturally integrate different formalisms. Furthermore, architectural descriptions are combined with principles of Model-Driven Development [19,20], enabling a transformation of architectural components into source code in future.

3   Overview on the Analysis Framework

3.1   Canonical Component Model

A problem that hinders conflict analysis is caused by different manifestations of components. For example, entities such as programs, middleware containers, Java classes, Enterprise JavaBeans, Haskell functions can be interpreted as components. Each of these provides different structures, requirements, syntax etc.

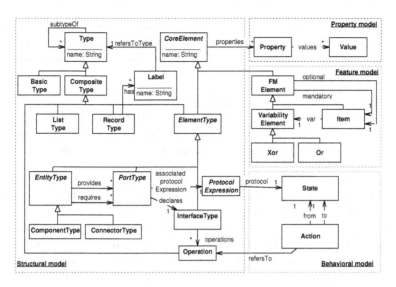

Fig. 1. Platform Independent Models of the Framework

Thus, we cannot directly compare their features and therefore not decide, if a composition fails due to unanticipated conflicts.

Our approach follows the idea of software architecture and ADLs by providing a canonical component structure that is able to represent each component of interest. The term 'canonical structure' implies a technology (platform) independent representation[1], which is restricted to elements that are common among all of the above entities.

The canonical component model consists of three main parts (see Figure 1): a structural, a behavioral, and a property (feature) model. The structural model consists of elements that are found in most ADLs: components, connectors and interfaces as well as their relationships and subordinate elements such as operations.

The behavioral model restricts components and connectors by means of pre- and post-conditions as well as by protocols (order of method invocations). This allows one to verify behavioral equivalence of components by using appropriate tools such as model checkers and theorem provers. As there exist a number of formal specification languages that can be used for behavioral specification, the framework can be customized for a particular language of choice. The framework, furthermore, provides a labeled transition system for protocol specification. This enables 'simulation' and 'bisimulation' analysis.

The property model defines a kind of ontology to cope with differences between communication mechanisms and underlying technologies. To organize the space of communication properties, we decided to reuse the existing taxonomy by Medvidovic/Mehta [9,16,8], as it provides the most fine grained properties

---

[1] In the context of the Model Driven Architecture (MDA), these representations are platform independent models.

in comparison to other approaches. This taxonomy is designed on a platform independent level, whereas we aim to analyse platform specific connectors for middleware systems of interest. Therefore, we modified the original taxonomy in the following way:

- Platform specific properties that describe communication in Java, Jini, J2EE and .Net were analyzed [21] and added to the taxonomy. Figure 3 shows for example a part of a feature model consisting of communication properties relevant for Java procedure calls. Figure 2 shows part of the feature model of a SessionBean[2].
- Mandatory and Optional features are distinguished. Mandatory features refer to structures and behavior that must be present, whereas for optional features there is a choice for implementation.
- The original Connector Taxonomy of Medvidovic/Mehta consists of eight connector types, which as they claim, are sufficient to express most of the connectors which can be found in present systems. These connector types were removed from the taxonomy. Instead features are annotated to port types ('PortType') from the structural model.
- Name clashes that occur due to the removed connector types were resolved.

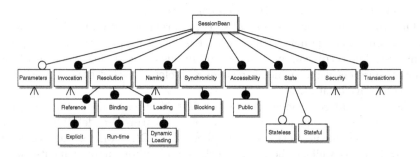

Fig. 2. Example of a Feature Model describing the Communication Properties of SessionBeans

We express this taxonomy with a Feature Model. Feature models originate in the area of product lines and domain analysis ([22]). They were introduced in Feature Oriented Domain Analysis (FODA) [23]. A feature model consists of a tree of hierarchical organized features of domain entities whereby special elements express variability. Feature models are adequate to model communication, because of the following two reasons:

1. They distinguish between optional and mandatory features. This differentiation is required for conflict analysis to deal with 'unknown' values. This issue is explained in section 4.4.

---

[2] As we attach the properties to 'PortTypes', we can use the properties with Connectors and Components.

2. At the same time feature models can be used for parameterized model transformations. They can be used to generate platform specific component and
   connector descriptions from a platform independent representation. Each
   feature triggers the generation of particular structure and behavior. Section
   3.3 provides an overview of parameterized transformations.

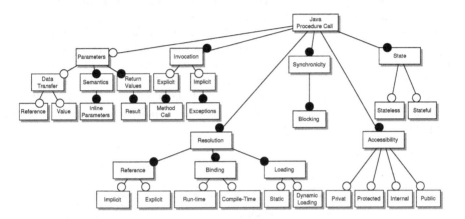

Fig. 3. Example of a Feature Model describing a Java Procedure Call: filled circles
represent mandatory features, empty circles represent optional features. The Planner-
Type component uses a restricted version of this Feature Model, where the features
'Implicit', 'Compile-Time', and 'Static' are declared mandatory.

3.2 Conflict Analysis Process

Software development is often supported by modeling tools such as Rational
Rose or TogetherJ. Most of these development tools are based on UML. As we
believe that component analysis and composition is extremely helpful within
software development, we strive to support a UML representation of canonical
components and their compositions. We provide UML Profiles that represent
canonical components as well as platform specific components in UML. Consequently, a developer can use a UML tool to work with the framework. Figure 4
shows an overview of the overall process. Execution proceeds as follows: Within
a UML tool - in this case Poseidon UML - we create a component model[3] (1).
We know that it can be extremely difficult to obtain the necessary information
for the UML specification in case that binary artifacts are to be integrated. Usually, reengineering techniques such as static or dynamic code analysis need to
be applied to extract as most information as possible. Often tools are used to
support the reengineering task and to create documentation and an architectural description. However, we do not consider these activities in this work, but
assume that the components are already specified in UML.

---

[3] In principle, this can be done either with UML 1.x or 2.0. However, most existing
   tools support only UML 1.x so that we use a profile to describe components.

Starting from the UML specification, components are annotated with the property information available. This includes properties describing the required communication and technologies as well as other properties that are known to the developer (see Figure 5 for an example). Then we submit the model to the Model Reasoner Service embedded in the Evolution and Validation Environment (EVE)[4] [24] (2). The service extracts the annotations in the model and attaches itself to the Analytical Data on Artifacts and Models (ADAM) repository. The service extracts the addressed part of the knowledge base (i.e. communication properties described by a feature model) (3/4) and passes it to the reasoner, combined with the information extracted from the model (5). The reasoner calculates the match/conflict and returns its characteristics to the service (6). The service embeds the resulting information in the model, attached to the association (7). If the result is a conflict, a conflict description is generated. If the result is a match, the service can fill in implied property information for each component, if desired by the user.

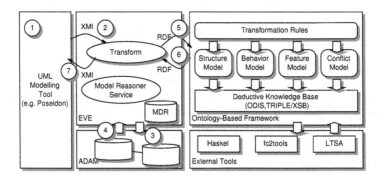

Fig. 4. The Framework Architecture

3.3 Component Abstraction and Refinement

We utilize the idea of Model-Driven Development [19] to abstract components into the canonical component model. The first step in the abstraction process involves creating a platform specific model of component artifacts, e.g. EJB jars → EJB Platform Specific Model (PSM) models. This can be done by using proprietary tools. Then transformation rules can be used to further abstract these representations into a platform independent model.

Unfortunately, existing software development tools (such as Rose, ArgoUML etc.) do not distinguish between Platform Independent Models (PIMs) and PSMs. They only provide fixed mappings between models and source code. These mappings are often defined as a one-to-one relationship (they generate code artifacts from UML classes). More sophisticated one-to-many mappings, which are necessary for a model-driven development, are normally not addressed. Thus, it

---

[4] EVE is a framework to support tool independent manipulation of UML models.

is necessary to provide PIM-to-PSM mappings that can be customized in particular situations and that can be applied to several technologies. In this refinement process, certain constructs can be mapped into different elements of a particular platform. For example, a 'set type' can be represented in different languages, e.g. Java, and for each language the set can be transformed into several concepts, e.g. a Collection class or a Vector class.

We use parameterized mapping rules describing exactly, which representation has to be generated. Parameterized transformation can also be based on more complex issues. We already demonstrated a transformation of Enterprise JavaBeans based on optimization issues [25]. The choices of a developer result in transformations based on J2EE patterns.

3.4   Framework Architecture

The framework's architecture (shown in Figure 4) is based on a deductive knowledge base (XSB) that provides the reasoning capabilities. The models and their associated rules are realized based on Triple [18], which is an 'RDF-aware' extension of F-Logic [26]. Type and behavioral conflicts are checked with external tools (Haskell, LTSA, FDR, fc2tools, Aldebaran).

As our mapping rules in Chapter 4 are specified in Triple we give a briefly introduction: Triple was proposed by Decker et. al. in [18]. Triple is a language designed to provide a reasoning service for the semantic web. Triple facts are very similar to Resource Description Framework (RDF) statements. Triple supports object-oriented features and distinguishes between instance data and schema information (types/classes). Triple states facts as tuples (S,P,O,C): S for subject, the entity to be described. P is a predicate that states the relation of interest, O stands for an Object, which is either a Literal or another tuple. C describes the context within which the tuple is valid. The 'context' is a new construct that allows specifying views of an object in different contexts. This feature is extremely helpful because it divides up fact bases into chunks that can be used as separate units.

An RDF statement can be formalized in Triple as

```
subject[predicate->object]@context.
```

Constraints for building such statements are formulated with the special schema-vocabulary (RDFS) which essentially enables the definition of binary relation signatures [27].

```
class1 [ rdfs:subClassOf -> class2 ].
prop   [ rdfs:domain -> class2; rdfs:range -> class1 ].
```

A TRIPLE-mapping is defined through a parameterized context. For example, the clause

```
forall X  @inv(X) {
    forall U,V  V[requiredBy->U] <- U[requires->V]@X.
}
```

simply defines a mapping 'inv' which filters and inverts the association 'requires'. The source model of the mapping is the set of all statements in context X. For each instantiation of the rule body with a statement of the source model a statement according to the rule head will be produced. The target model contains these statements which are in the context $inv(X)$. For example, the query

```
forall s,p,o s[p->o]@inv(componentStructure12).
```

transforms the source model with context 'componentStructure12' to the target model with context 'inv(componentStructure12)'.

4   Conflict Analysis

Conflicts are differences between component descriptions that hinder a direct integration. A sound integration requires the identification of all conflicts between two or more components. Unfortunately, this is often a problem, because of missing specification, lack of formal methods and unknown communication properties of the components and the underlying technology.

We base conflict identification on several relationships. These cover structural and behavioral conflicts and furthermore address communicational properties of components. We describe these relationships in the following sections based on a simple example.

4.1   Example

Our running example comes from federated information systems, particularly mediator-based information systems. A mediator is a kind of middleware that performs queries against heterogeneous distributed data sources ([28]). If a client queries a mediator, the mediator first calculates which data sources are capable to answer the query or part of it (Planner component). Then, it queries these sources, integrates the answers and delivers the result back to the client.

The Planner calculates its plans based on specified interfaces of the data sources. These interface descriptions are called Query Capabilities(QC). A query capability, shown at the bottom of Figure 5, consists of parameters that a data source can process as well as of result attributes returned by the data source. Query capabilities are managed by another component of the mediator: the QCManager. The Planner uses QCs, obtained by the QCManager, to decide which data sources have to be queried.

Figure 5 shows a UML representation of both components. The QCManager component is a Commercials Off-The-Shelf (COTS). It is implemented as a SessionBean. In our scenario, we want to call this component from our Planner component. However, the Planner component is implemented as a JavaBean and has slightly different requirements as provided by the QCManager. Figure 6 shows the representation of both components within our framework. This representation shows the protocols associated to both components as well as the root of the attached communication properties.

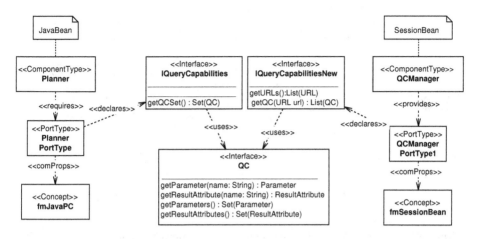

Fig. 5. Component Comparison Example: The Figure shows the UML representation of the PlannerType and the QCManagerType component. PlannerType is a JavaBean component. Its port is linked with communication properties ('comProps') required by the component. QCManagerType is a SessionBean and therefore associated with communication properties required by Session EJBs.

4.2   Structural Conflicts

Structural compliance between components can be reduced to the problem of deciding if a 'subtype' relationship between the provided and required interfaces of components hold. Before, name conflicts between identical but differently named elements need to be resolved by specifying correspondences that relate these elements.

For the 'subtype' relationship, we define several subtype rules for the complex types (component, connector, interface, operation, etc.) that are needed for conflict analysis. We assume that all elements (instances) in the framework are correctly typed and that additional relationships between basic types (such as Integers, Strings) and for newly introduced complex types are given as needed. The subtype rules correspond to standard rules found in literature of type theory such as by [29].

Two component types C_1 and C_2 can be composed, if the following predicate - written $C_1\ 'compS'\ C_2$ - holds:

$$\exists i_1 \in C_1.requires.declares, i_2 \in C_2.provides.declares \cdot i_1 \preceq i_2$$

where i_1, i_2 are interface types and $\preceq$ denotes a subtype relationship based on a 'minimal' type system, which consists only of the types that are needed to decide for conflicts between components.

Example. In the example, both interfaces are not in a subtype relationship. The interfaces 'IQueryCapabilities' and 'IQueryCapabilitiesNew' have operations, where the signatures of the operations do not match ($IQueryCapabilities \npreceq$

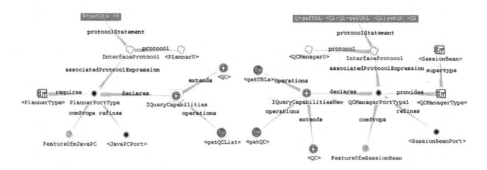

Fig. 6. Components as rendered by the Framework

IQueryCapabilitiesNew). Consequently, the framework generates a respective type conflict.

4.3   Behavioral Conflicts

Structural compatibility does not guarantee a seamless integration of commercials off-the-shelf. It misses the behavioral requirements and obligations of components such as pre- and post-conditions, invariants, communication protocols (call order of method invocations) etc. Without exact behavioral specifications, mismatched behavior can only be identified by high effort in the integration process.

In the context of this paper, we only consider process graphs. To decide compatibility, we compare the process graphs (transition systems) of two components. Component composition requires a simulation of the process graphs of both components. We define a simulation as a relation R on the nodes of two graphs g and h, which express the behavior of two components as follows:

1. The roots of g and h are related by R,
2. If $R(r, s)$ and $r \xrightarrow{a} r'$, then there exists a node s' such that $s \xrightarrow{a} s'$ and $R(r', s')$

We define additional simulation relationships including silent actions. All definitions correspond to the certain kinds of bisimulation relationships as defined by Gabbeek [30].

Two components C_1 and C_2 are compatible regarding their protocols - written C_1 '*compB*' C_2 if there is a simulation relationship $C_1 \subseteq C_2$ between these components[5].

Example. In the example, two process algebra expressions are attached to the components. The first expression is attached to the requires port of the 'Planner' component: $R = getQCList \rightarrow R$, whereas the second expression is bound

---

[5] As we base compatibility checks on model checkers, we are restricted by the abilities of these tools to solve the given protocols.

to the provides port of 'QCManager': $Q = getURL \rightarrow Q_1; Q_1 = getURL \rightarrow Q_1 | getQC \rightarrow Q_1$. Analyzing both graphs the framework first generates Naming-Conflicts, because both graphs consist of different actions labels. Consequently, there is no simulation relationship between the associated LTS. It is allowed to define correspondences between actions. However, the correspondence between the action labels $getQCList \sim getQC$ does not create a simulation. The correspondence $getQCList \sim getURL$ would result in a simulation, but is semantically invalid. The obvious correspondence $getQCList \sim getURL \rightarrow getQC$) cannot be defined because it requires an intermediate component that accepts the $getQC$ call and forwards the sequence of both actions $getURL$ and $getQC$.

4.4 Property Conflicts

We assume that the connector taxonomy as well as the taxonomy for technology related features contain all relevant properties for communication. Component comparison is based on the comparison of annotated features.Two entities are compatible, if all features annotated to the ports of the entities are compatible. For example, in Figure 5 $PlannerType$ and $QCManagerType$ would be compatible - $PlannerType$ 'compP' $QCManagerType$, if their feature models $fmJavaPC$ and $fmSessionBean$ are compatible.

As communication properties are expressed by a feature model, there are three cases a conflict identification has to take into account: a feature is mandatory, i.e. it needs to be present for a successful communication, a feature is optional, i.e. it may be used in a communication, or a feature is not present in a feature model, i.e. it is not supported.

Two components are compatible, only if they are annotated with the same mandatory features and the attributes of each feature are also compatible. The relationship 'compP' yields true between two components C_1 and C_2 if the following proposition holds:

$$
\begin{aligned}
&\forall n \in \{C_1.r.comProps \cup C_1.r.techProps\} \\
&isMandatoryFeature(n) \rightarrow \\
&\exists m \in \{C_2.q.comProps \cup C_2.q.techProps\}\cdot \\
&n.fname = m.fname\wedge \\
&isMandatoryFeature(m)
\end{aligned}
\tag{1}
$$

The symbols 'r' and 'q' refer to provides and requires relationships of components and connectors. Mismatches are generated for all other cases. The matrix, shown in Table 1 shows the generated mismatches for all value combinations. We distinguish between failures and warnings. Warnings are generated if optional features are involved. We interpret optional features as 'unknown' values for two reasons: Firstly, a component composition requires that the required features are all known. We cannot compose components for which we are not sure if a particular property such as transactions are required or not. Secondly, a composition of two components results in a connector generation that fits the requirements of

Table 1. Compatibility Matrix between two Components

Component vs. Component	mandatory	optional	unsupported
mandatory	√	w	f
optional	w	w	w
unsupported	f	w	√
w = warning f = failure			

involved components. Such a connector generation is not possible if the features are not clearly defined, i.e. there shouldn't be any free variation points in the associated features.

Example. The analysis of the example components yields several conflicts, a part of them are shown in Figure 7. The main reasons for the 15 failures of Figure 7 can be interpreted as follows:

- Transactions are unsupported by the Planner component but required by the QCManagerComponent.
- The Planner component requires a static binding, whereas the QCManager-Component as a distributed component requires a dynamic binding and furthermore requires a initialization of the communication based on a Naming service (JNDI).
- The QCManager requires security handling.

Query result	
s_	o_
FailureFeature32Resources	Mandatory feature of server unsupported by client.
FailureFeature31Single	Mandatory feature of server unsupported by client.
FailureFeature34Awareness	Mandatory feature of server unsupported by client.
FailureFeature36New	Mandatory feature of server unsupported by client.
FailureFeature33Distributed	Mandatory feature of server unsupported by client.
FailureFeature38Security	Mandatory feature of server unsupported by client.
FailureFeature22Hierarchical	Mandatory feature of server unsupported by client.
FailureFeature30Nesting	Mandatory feature of server unsupported by client.
FailureFeature54Runtime	Mandatory feature of server unsupported by client.
FailureFeature21Structurebased	Mandatory feature of server unsupported by client.
FailureFeature52ImplicitRef	Mandatory feature of server unsupported by client.
FailureFeature29Transactions	Mandatory feature of server unsupported by client.
FailureFeature20Naming	Mandatory feature of server unsupported by client.
FailureFeature25ExplicitRef	Mandatory feature of client unsupported by server.
FailureFeature27Compiletime	Mandatory feature of client unsupported by server.

Fig. 7. Property Conflicts - failures

4.5   Conflict Generation

Conflicts are generated in two steps: Firstly, mismatches are identified by predicates that are based on the proposed relationships, and secondly conflict statements are generated based on the identified violations. Examples of both rules are shown below.

```
forall ?c,?d,?p failureMandatory(?c,?d,?f)
<-
getComFeatures(?d,?f) and
?f[sys:directType->core:MandatoryFeature;
    core:fname->?n]@@ and
notInClientRole(?f) and
hasOnlyMandatoryParentFeatures(?f) and
hasNoVariablityElementsAsParent(?f) and
isFeatureNotBound(?c,?n).
```

```
forall A,B @failure(A,B) {
    forall ?x, ?p, ?ns
    ?ns:?x[sys:directType->core:FeatureConflict;
        core:concerns->A; core:relates->B;
        core:concernsFeature->?ns:?p;
        core:cause->'Mandatory feature of client
                unsupported by server.']
    <-
        failureUnsupported(A,B,?ns:?p) and
        concatConflict(?x,?p,'Failure').

    forall ?x, ?p, ?ns
    ?ns:?x[sys:directType->core:FeatureConflict;
        core:concerns->A; core:relates->B;
        core:concernsFeature->?ns:?p;
        core:cause->'Mandatory feature of server
                unsupported by client.']
    <-
        failureMandatory(A,B,?ns:?p) and
        concatConflict(?x,?p,'Failure').
}
```

The left predicate finds all mandatory features f that are annotated to an element d, which is either a component type or a connector type, that are not bound by element c. The identified features must be mandatory, relative to the root of the feature model annotated by d: There must not be any optional feature or variability element in the path from the root to f. This is one of the rules used to find feature conflicts. A complete set of rules can be found in the technical report to the framework [31].

The right rule generates conflict statements. The rule is included in a parameterized mapping with parameters A and B. A and B are for example the two component types introduced above. In the framework a complete set of rules for each case shown in table 1 are implemented.

5   Conclusion

This paper presented a framework for the identification of compositional conflicts in component-based systems. Within the framework, conflict identification is based on the analysis of structural and behavioral aspects of component descriptions. It also takes property-based descriptions of communicational requirements and technological aspects into account. Analysis identifies mismatched behavior by evaluating customizable relationships in each context. Examples of predefined relationships are subtypes, simulation and bisimulation as well as a property-based relationships.

At present, property-based conflict identification is often underestimated. Only a few approaches exist covering property-based description and analysis, such as the connector taxonomy of Mehta/Medvidovic or architectural styles proposed by Allan/Shaw. A property-based analysis has several advantages: Firstly, properties can be used to transform conceptual models into specific representations covering particular communication requirements. Secondly, they enable one to gain more information regarding incompletely specified components. Both advantages are extremely important for analyzing components in the context of modern software development.

A property-based transformation paves the way for design reuse. It becomes possible to reuse a conceptual model for different technologies. One can create a EJB model or a CORBA model or a model for another language from a single conceptual model. Regarding communication properties, different kinds of communication can be generated for a conceptual model. For example, one can create an EJB component accepting synchronous communication, e.g. a SessionBean or asynchronous communication, e.g. a MessageBean from a single conceptual component.

We believe that the framework can also be used to semi-automatically generate connectors. Currently, we focus on generating the protocol specifications of connectors. Based on correspondences between the actions of two or more process graphs, we derive the behavior description of a connector by utilizing the algorithm proposed by Inverardi [32]. Furthermore, we gain additional requirements for the connector by investigating the communication properties of components. In the example, an additional initialization action needs to be added to the connector process, because EJBs require to obtain instances via a naming server. Other properties, such as the transaction feature of the QCManager component can be used to generate the deployment descriptor of that component, when generating the artifact.

References

1. Garlan, D., Monroe, R.T., Wile, D.: Acme: Architectural description of component-based systems. In Leavens, G.T., Sitaraman, M., eds.: Foundations of Component-Based Systems. Cambridge University Press (2000) 47–68
2. Magee, J., Dulay, N., Kramer, J.: Regis: A constructive development environment for distributed programs. Distributed Systems Engineering 1 (1994) 304–312
3. Magee, J., Dulay, N., Eisenbach, S., Kramer, J.: Specifying Distributed Software Architectures. In Schafer, W., Botella, P., eds.: Proc. 5th European Software Engineering Conf. (ESEC 95). Volume 989., Sitges, Spain, Springer-Verlag, Berlin (1995) 137–153
4. Luckham, D.C., Kenney, J.L., Augustin, L.M., Vera, J., Bryan, D., Mann, W.: Specification and analysis of system architecture using rapide. IEEE Transactions on Software Engineering 21 (1995) 336–355
5. Magee, J., Kramer, J.: Concurrency, State Models & Java Programs. John Wiley & Sons (1999)
6. Hoare, C.: Communicating Sequential Processes. Prentice Hall PTR (1985)
7. Garlan, D., Allen, R., Ockerbloom, J.: Architectural mismatch, or, why it's hard to build systems out of existing parts. In: Proceedings of the 17th International Conference on Software Engineering, Seattle, Washington (1995) 179–185
8. Mehta, N.R., Medvidovic, N., Phadke, S.: Towards a taxonomy of software connectors. In: Proceedings of the 22nd international conference on Software engineering, ACM Press (2000) 178–187
9. Mehta, N.R.: Software connectors: A taxonomy approach. In: Workshop on Evaluating Software Architectural Solutions 2000, Institute for Software Research University of California, Irvine (2000) http://www.isr.uci.edu/events/wesas2000/position-papers/mehta.pdf.

10. Shaw, M., Clements, P.C.: A field guide to boxology: Preliminary classification of architectural styles for software systems. In: Proceedings of the 21st International Computer Software and Applications Conference, IEEE Computer Society (1997) 6–13
11. Davis, L., Gamble, R., Payton, J.: The impact of component architectures on interoperability. Journal of Systems and Software **61** (2002) 31–45 based on the Technical Report UTULSA-MCS-99-30.
12. Davis, L., Flagg, D., Gamble, R., Karatas, C.: Classifying interoperability conflicts. In H. Erdogmus, T.W., ed.: COTS-Based Software Systems: Second International Conference, ICCBSS 2003 Ottawa, Canada. Number 2580 in LNCS, SPRINGER (2003) 62–71
13. Allen, R., Garlan, D.: A formal basis for architectural connection. ACM Transactions on Software Engineering and Methodology (TOSEM) **6** (1997) 213–249
14. Kelkar, A., Gamble, R.: Understanding the architectural characteristics behind middleware choices. In: 1st International Conference in Information Reuse and Integration, 1999. (1999)
15. Yakimovich, D., Bieman, J.M., Basili, V.R.: Software architecture classification for estimating the cost of cots integration. In: Proceedings of the 21st international conference on Software engineering, IEEE Computer Society Press (1999) 296–302
16. Mehta, N.R., Medvidovic, N.: Understanding software connector compatibilites using a connector taxonomy. In: In Proceedings of First Workshop on Software Design and Architecture (SoDA02), Bangalore, India. (2002)
17. Pahl, C.: An ontology for software component matching. In Pezze, M., ed.: 6th International Conference, FASE 2003, Held as Part of the Joint European Conferences on Theory and Practice of Software, ETAPS 2003, Warsaw, Poland. Number 2621 in LNCS (2003)
18. Sintek, M., Decker, S.: TRIPLE - A Query, Inference, and Transformation Language for the Semantic Web. In: Proceedings of International Semantic Web Conference ISWC 2002, Lecture Notes in Computer Science, Bd. 2342, Springer (2002)
19. Mellor, S.J., Clark, A.N., Futagami, T.: Model-driven development. IEEE Software **20** (2003) 14–18
20. Miller, J., Mukerji, J.: MDA Guide Version 1.0. Web www.omg.org (2003) Document Number omg/2003-05-01.
21. Gädicke, J.: Metadatengestützte analyse der kommunikationsfähigkeit von enterprise java beans und .net. Master's thesis, TU Berlin (2004) german.
22. Czarnecki, K., Eisenecker, U.: Generative Programming - Methods, Tools, and Applications. Addison-Wesley (2000)
23. Kang, K., Cohen, S., Hess, J., Novak, W., Peterson, A.: Feature-Oriented Domain Analysis (FODA) Feasibility Study. Technical Report CMU/SEI-90-TR-21, Software Engineering Institute, Carnegie Mellon University (1990)
24. Süß, J.G., Leicher, A., Weber, H., Kutsche, R.D.: Model-centric engineering with the evolution and validation en vironment. In Stevens, P., Whittle, J., Booch, G., eds.: UML 2003 - The Unified Modeling Language: Modeling Lan guages and Applications, 6th International Conference, San Francisco, CA, USA. Volume 2863 of LNCS., Springer (2003) 31 – 43
25. Billig, A., Busse, S., Leicher, A., Süß, J.G.: Platform independent model transformation based on triple. In Jacobsen, H.A., ed.: Proceedings of Middleware 04, ACM/IFIP/USENIX International Middleware Conference. Number 3231 in LNCS (2004)
26. Kifer, M., Lausen, G., Wu, J.: Logical foundations of object-oriented and frame-based languages. Journal of the ACM **42** (1995) 741–843

27. W3C: RDF Vocabulary Description Language 1.0: RDF Schema. (2003) URL: http://www.w3.org/TR/rdf-schema/.
28. Wiederhold, G.: Mediators in the Architecture of Future Information Systems. In Huhns, M.N., Singh, M.P., eds.: Readings in Agents. Morgan Kaufmann, San Francisco, CA, USA (1997) 185 – 196
29. Pierce, B.C.: Types and programming languages. MIT Press (2002) ISBN 0-262-16209-1.
30. van Glabbeek, R.J., Weijland, W.P.: Branching time and abstraction in bisimulation semantics. J. ACM **43** (1996) 555–600
31. Leicher, A.: A framework for identifying compositional conflicts in component-based systems. Technical Report 2004-23, TU Berlin (2004) (to appear).
32. Inverardi, P., Tivoli, M.: Software architecture for correct components assembly. In Bernardo, M., Inverardi, P., eds.: Formal Methods for Software Architectures, Third International School on Formal Methods for the Design of Computer, Communication and Software Systems: Software Architectures, SFM 2003, Bertinoro, Italy. Volume 2804 of LNCS Tutorial., Springer-Verlag Berlin Heidelberg (2003)

A Lambda Calculus with Forms

Markus Lumpe

Department of Computer Science,
Iowa State University,
Ames, IA 50011, USA
lumpe@cs.iastate.edu

Abstract. The need to use position-dependent parameters often hampers the definition of flexible, extensible, and reusable abstractions for software composition. This observation has led us to explore the concept of *forms*, which are first-class extensible records and that, in combination with a small set of purely asymmetric operators, provide a core language to address this issue. One interesting application of forms is the definition of contractual specifications to ensure that a component can be safely combined with other components or deployed in a new context. In fact, contractual specifications explicitly and formally state *what* a component offers without entering into the details of *how*. In this paper, we develop a formal form-based framework for the definition of contractual specifications. More precisely, we study a substitution-free variant of the lambda-calculus, called $\lambda\mathcal{F}$, where names are replaced with forms and parameter passing is modeled using explicit contexts and show how the $\lambda\mathcal{F}$-calculus can be used to define syntactic contractual specifications.

1 Introduction

Modern software systems are constantly growing in complexity and size. Moreover, in order to timely adapt to changing requirements those systems have to be designed in a way that software evolution becomes feasible. The component-oriented software development approach targets exactly this aspect and has become the most promising software development technology today [19,23,28].

A successful component-based software development approach, however, not only needs to provide abstractions to represent different component models and composition techniques, but must also provide a systematic method for constructing large software systems [4,16]. In particular, we need a specially-designed *composition language* that allows for building applications as compositions of reusable software components [24]. This language, which should be extensible, has to provide abstractions to instantiate, coordinate, and compose components that are generally developed in different implementation language. Furthermore, to guarantee flexible, reliable, and verifiable software composition, such a composition language has to be based on a suitable formal foundation [8,14,20,24]. A precise semantics is essential if we are to deal with multiple architectural styles and component models within a common, unifying framework.

T. Gschwind, U. Aßmann, and O. Nierstrasz (Eds.): SC 2005, LNCS 3628, pp. 83–98, 2005.

There are several plausible candidates (e.g., λ-calculus, π-calculus, or variants of them) that can serve as a computational model for component-based software development. Unfortunately, they often hamper the definition of general purpose compositional abstractions, as they impose dependence on position and arity of parameters [9,25]. For example, in the standard λ-calculus the functions λ(x, y).x and λ(y, x).y are equivalent, but λ(x, y).x and λ(y, x).x are different, as position matters in λ-calculus. Moreover, if we use de Bruijn indices [11], then names disappear totally, as arguments to functions are uniquely identified by their positions. Thus, if we abstract from position and use instead the parameter names as keys functions like $\lambda\langle$x, y$\rangle$.x and $\lambda\langle$y, x$\rangle$.x become indistinguishable.

This observation has led us to explore the concept of *forms* [13,15,24]. Forms are first-class extensible records that define mappings from labels to values, which, in combination with a small set of purely asymmetric operators, provide a core language to define extensible, flexible, and robust compositional abstractions. Programmatically, forms are both compile-time and run-time entities. As compile-time entities, forms can be used to denote components, component interfaces, and component composition. At run-time, on the other hand, forms provide uniform and language-neutral access to component services and support runtime composition on demand.

Originally, forms were an integral part of the $\pi\mathcal{L}$-calculus [13], a conservative extension of the π-calculus, that already provides better support for modeling concurrent component-oriented abstractions [13,24]. However, forms are not bound to a particular computational model. They are an environment-independent framework that has to be combined with a concrete target system like the λ-calculus or the π-calculus.

In this paper, we study a substitution-free variant of the λ-calculus, called $\lambda\mathcal{F}$, where names are replaced with forms and parameter passing is modeled using explicit contexts. Explicit contexts mimic λ-calculus substitutions. However, unlike λ-calculus in which substitutions are meta-level operations [1], explicit contexts have a syntactic representation to record named parameter bindings.

The design of the $\lambda\mathcal{F}$-calculus is greatly influenced by Dami's λN-calculus [9,10] that is also a calculus in which parameters are identified by names rather than positions. However, there are two significant differences. First, in the λN-calculus an application is split into two different parts: an expression a(1 = b), called *bind expression*, passes the value b under the name 1 to a; an expression a!, called *close expression*, ends a sequence of bind expressions and forces the evaluation of a. A shortcoming of this approach is that binding expressions cannot be pooled into an additional structure or used to encode monadic communication patterns, which occur in rendezvous-based protocols like HTTP. For example, the λN-term a(1 = b)(m = c)! denotes an expression a! in which the parameters 1 and m are bound to their corresponding values b and c. Moreover, a(1 = b)(m = c) actually stands for two distinct closures a(1 = b) and ((a(1 = b))(m = c)), each requiring a separate interaction with the environment. In $\lambda\mathcal{F}$, on the other hand, we write a $\langle\rangle\langle$1 = b$\rangle\langle$m = c$\rangle$ instead of a(1 = b)(m = c)!. Here, the form $\langle\rangle\langle 1 = b\rangle\langle m = c\rangle$ is a structured argument that can be consumed in one interaction.

Secondly, rather than using an informal meta-level operation to substitute formal parameters with actual ones, we use *explicit contexts* [1,3]. These explicit contexts have a syntactic representation based on forms. In practice, contexts explicitly record named parameter bindings and provide an environment to resolve the occurrences of free variables in a $\lambda\mathcal{F}$-term. For example, the term a[b] denotes an expression a, which is evaluated with respect to the context [b]. That is, all occurrences of free variables in a are resolved using form b. Thus, the context [b] expresses the requirements posed by the free variables of a on the environment [18]. In other words, if we *close* the component a by composing it with a concrete environment or component b, then a[b] denotes a composite component, where the services *provided* by b are used to satisfy the required services of a.

On the other hand, explicit contexts also allow for the definition of (syntactic) *contractual specification* [5]. Contractual specifications are used to ensure that a component can safely be combined with other components or deployed in a new context. Ideally, all conditions of a contract should be stated explicitly and formally as part of an interface specification [26]. The information contained in a contract should tells us *what* a component offers without entering into the details of *how* it is implemented. For example, let T, S be form-based type expressions. We write $T[S]$ to express that we can close T by composing it with S. However, since this composition denotes a contractual specification, we must check now that the services *provided* by S satisfy the required type of T.

The remainder of this paper is organized as follows: In Section 2, we present the $\lambda\mathcal{F}$-calculus. We proceed by using $\lambda\mathcal{F}$ to specify syntactic contracts in Section 3. We conclude with a summary of related and future work in Section 4.

2   The $\lambda\mathcal{F}$-Calculus

The primary objective of the definition of the $\lambda\mathcal{F}$-calculus is to study the effect of replacing variables by forms in λ-calculus. So, we maintain a clear separation between the syntactic categories of *forms* and $\lambda\mathcal{F}$-*terms*. The linkage between expressions of both categories is modeled through a refined characterization of the set of values.

Next, the question arises how to handle best *substitution*? In the classical λ-calculus we write a{b/x} to denote the term a where all free occurrences of b have been replaced with x. However, substitution in λ-calculus is a very expensive term-rewriting operation, which actually does not belong to the calculus [1]. We address this issue by using *explicit contexts* [1,3], which have a form-based syntactic representation. Explicit contexts are used for both forms and $\lambda\mathcal{F}$-terms and they provide, therefore, a uniform way to resolve occurrences of free variables.

We presuppose a countably infinite set, $\mathcal{L}$, of *labels*, and let l, m, n range over labels. We also presuppose a countably infinite set, $\mathcal{V}$, of *abstract values*, and let a, b, c range over abstract values. We think of an abstract value as a representation of any programming value like integers, objects, types, and even forms. However, we do not require any particular property except that equality and inequality be defined for elements of $\mathcal{V}$. We use F, G, H to range over the set of forms, and M, N to range over the set of $\lambda\mathcal{F}$-terms. The syntax of the $\lambda\mathcal{F}$-calculus is given in Figure 1.

$F, G, H ::= \langle \rangle$	*empty form*		$V ::= \mathcal{E}$	*empty value*
$\mid X$	*form variable*		$\mid a$	*abstract value*
$\mid F\langle l = V \rangle$	*binding extension*		$\mid M$	$\lambda\mathcal{F} - value$
$\mid F \cdot G$	*form extension*			
$\mid F \backslash G$	*form restriction*		$M, N ::= F$	*form*
$\mid F \to l$	*form dereference*		$\mid M.l$	*projection*
$\mid F[G]$	*form context*		$\mid \lambda(X)\ M$	*abstraction*
			$\mid M\ N$	*application*
			$\mid M[F]$	$\lambda\mathcal{F} - context$

Fig. 1. Syntax of the $\lambda\mathcal{F}$-Calculus

Forms are used to denote both components and component composition. The services that a component offers are specified as *binding extensions*. A binding extension, written $\langle l = s \rangle$, denotes a component's capability to perform a service s that is published under the name l. For example, we write $F.a$ to invoke the service that is bound by label a in component F.

The expressive power of forms is due to the two asymmetric operators: *form extension* and *form restriction*. Form extension, written $F \cdot G$, allows one to add or redefine a set of services simultaneously, whereas form restriction, written $F\backslash G$, can be seen as a dual operation that denotes a form, which is restricted to all bindings of F that do not occur in G. In combination, these operators provide the main building block in a fundamental concept for defining adaptable, extensible, and more robust software abstractions [13,16,24]. For example, suppose we want to compose two components F and G, but we want to give a specific service of F bound by label m precedence over a service bound by the same label m in G. This operation represents a *compositional style* [2] that defines a *conditional update*, which can be specified using both form extension and form restriction: $F \cdot (G\backslash\langle\rangle\langle m = F.m\rangle)$. Depending on the actual services defined by the components F and G, we can distinguish three different situations covered by $F \cdot (G\backslash\langle\rangle\langle m = F.m\rangle)$:

- If the label m occurs neither in F nor G, then the label m does not occur in the composition of F and G.
- If the label m does not occur in F, but in G, then G's binding for label m occurs in the composition of F and G.
- If the label m occurs in F, then F's binding for label m occurs in the composition of F and G.

Forms can also occur as values in binding extensions. These forms are called *nested forms* and they facilitate the specification of structured component interfaces. To extract a nested form bound by a label 1 in a form F, we use F → 1. Note, however, that if the binding involving label 1 does not actually map a nested form, then the result of F → 1 is ⟨⟩ – the *empty form*. The reason for this is that we want to distinguish between components, which offer a set of services, and component services themselves.

A *form context* F[G] denotes a closed form expression that is derived from F by using G as an environment to look up what would otherwise be free variables in F. We use form dereference to perform the lookup operation. That is, a free variable is reinterpreted as label. For example, if X is a free variable in F and [G] is a context, then the meaning of X in F is determined by the result of evaluating G → X. In the case that G does not define a binding for X, the result is ⟨⟩, which effectively removes the set of provided services associated with X from F. This allows for an approach in which a sender and a receiver can communicate open form expressions. The receiver of this open form expression can use its local context to close (i.e., configure) the received form expression according to a site-specific protocol, but may also chose to ignore it (e.g., the configuration of a Web-browser to run an application associated with a specific MIME-type).

Forms and *projections* replace variables in λℱ. A form stands for an *explicit namespace* [3] or module [12], which can comprise an arbitrary number of provided services. The form itself can contain free variables, which will be resolved in the deployment environment or evaluation context. In other words, free variables in a form expression allow for a computational model with *late binding*.

With projections we recover variable references of λ-calculus. We require, however, that the subject of a projection denote a form. For example, the meaning of F.1 is the value bound by label 1 in form F. A projection a.1, where a is not a form yields ℰ, which means "no value".

Both *abstraction* and *application* correspond to the notions used in λ-calculus. As in λ-calculus, the X in λ(X) a stands for the parameter. But unlike λ-calculus, we do not use substitution to replace free occurrences of this name in the body of an abstraction. Parameter passing is modeled by explicit contexts.

A λℱ-context is the counterpart of a form-context. A λℱ-*context* denotes a lookup environment for free variables in a λℱ-term. Moreover, λℱ-contexts provide a convenient mechanism to retain the bindings of free variables in the body of a function. For example, let λ(X) a be a function and [F] be a creation context for it. Then we can use [F] to build a *closure* of λ(X) a. A closure is a package mechanism to record the bindings of free variables of a function at the time it was created. That is, the closure of λ(X) a is λ(X) (a[F]).

As a first example, consider the Church encoding of Booleans. In the standard λ-calculus Booleans are encoded using position-dependent parameters:

$$\text{True} = \lambda\text{true}.\lambda\text{false}.\text{true}$$

$$\text{False} = \lambda\text{true}.\lambda\text{false}.\text{false}$$

$$\text{Not} = \lambda\text{arg}.\lambda\text{true}.\lambda\text{false}.\text{arg false true}$$

These encodings have the desired property that the application (Not True) yields False. But they lack extensibility, that is, the possibility to add new functionality without effecting the previous behavior of the encodings [9]. On the other hand, the encodings in $\lambda\mathcal{F}$ are extensible, as we eliminate position dependency:

$$\text{True} = \lambda(\text{X}) \ \text{X.true}$$

$$\text{False} = \lambda(\text{X}) \ \text{X.false}$$

$$\text{Not} = \lambda(\text{B}) \ \lambda(\text{V}) \ \text{B} \ \text{V}\langle\text{true} = \text{V.false}\rangle\langle\text{false} = \text{V.true}\rangle$$

These encodings are equivalent to there λ-calculus counterparts. However, all functions are now characterized by the arguments they are effectively using and not by the ones they declare. The application (Not True) yields:

$$\text{Not True} = \lambda(\text{V}) \ \text{B} \ \text{V}\langle\text{true} = \text{V.false}\rangle\langle\text{false} = \text{V.true}\rangle \ [\langle\rangle\langle\text{B} = \text{True}\rangle]$$

which is equivalent to False, as illustrated in the following:

$$\text{False} \ \langle\rangle\langle\text{true} = \text{a}\rangle\langle\text{false} = \text{b}\rangle$$
$$= \text{X.false} \ [\langle\rangle\langle\text{X} = \langle\rangle\langle\text{true} = \text{a}\rangle\langle\text{false} = \text{b}\rangle\rangle]$$
$$= (\langle\rangle\langle\text{true} = \text{a}\rangle\langle\text{false} = \text{b}\rangle).\text{false}$$
$$= \text{b}$$

Similarly, it holds that

$$(\text{Not True}) \ \langle\rangle\langle\text{true} = \text{a}\rangle\langle\text{false} = \text{b}\rangle$$
$$= (\lambda(\text{V}) \ \text{B} \ \text{V}\langle\text{true} = \text{V.false}\rangle\langle\text{false} = \text{V.true}\rangle \ [\langle\rangle\langle\text{B} = \text{True}\rangle])$$
$$\langle\rangle\langle\text{true} = \text{a}\rangle\langle\text{false} = \text{b}\rangle$$
$$= (\text{True} \ \text{V}\langle\text{true} = \text{V.false}\rangle\langle\text{false} = \text{V.true}\rangle) \ [\langle\rangle\langle\text{V} = \langle\rangle\langle\text{true} = \text{a}\rangle\langle\text{false} = \text{b}\rangle\rangle]$$
$$= \text{True} \ \langle\rangle\langle\text{true} = \text{b}\rangle\langle\text{false} = \text{a}\rangle$$
$$= \text{X.true} \ [\langle\rangle\langle\text{X} = \langle\rangle\langle\text{true} = \text{b}\rangle\langle\text{false} = \text{a}\rangle\rangle]$$
$$= (\langle\rangle\langle\text{true} = \text{b}\rangle\langle\text{false} = \text{a}\rangle).\text{true}$$
$$= \text{b}$$

We use denotational semantics to formalize the interpretation of forms and $\lambda\mathcal{F}$-terms. The underlying semantic model of forms is that of interacting systems [17]. Informally, the interpretation of forms (that is, their observable behavior) is defined by an evaluation function $[\![\ ]\!]^F$, which guarantees that feature access is performed from right-to-left [15]. The reader should note, however, that in contrast to standard records, a given binding may not be observable[1] in a form and, therefore, may not be used to redefine or hide an existing one.

Form composition may yield form expressions in which many of their bindings have become inaccessible due to extension or restriction. Those bindings can be garbage collected. Garbage collecting inaccessible bindings of a form F yields a so-called *normalized form* $\overline{F}$ containing solely observable binding extensions. In other words, form normalization yields an expression that is isomorphic to a classical record. However, we still maintain position independency. That is,

---

[1] A binding is not observable if it cannot be distinguished from $\mathcal{E}$ or $\langle\rangle$. For example, the forms $\langle\rangle\langle\text{m} = \mathcal{E}\rangle$, $\langle\rangle\langle\text{m} = \langle\rangle\rangle$, and $\langle\rangle$ are all considered equivalent.

$\langle\rangle\langle 1 = a\rangle\langle m = b\rangle$ and $\langle\rangle\langle m = b\rangle\langle 1 = a\rangle$ are behaviorally equivalent. Moreover, it holds that for every form F that there exists a normalized form $\overline{F}$, such that F is behaviorally equivalent to $\overline{F}$, written $F \approx \overline{F}$. We use $\overline{F}, \overline{G}, \overline{H}$ to range over the set, $\overline{\mathcal{F}}$, of normalized forms, which is the smallest set that satisfies the specification given in Figure 2. There exists an algorithm, called **normalize**, that can generate a behaviorally equivalent normalized form $\overline{F}$ for every given form F [15].

$$\overline{F} ::= \begin{cases} \langle\rangle \\ \langle\rangle\langle l_1 = v_1\rangle\langle l_2 = v_2\rangle \ldots \langle l_n = v_n\rangle \ n > 0 \end{cases}$$

$$\forall\, i,j \in \{1\ldots n\} \wedge i \neq j: \ l_i \neq l_j \quad \text{and} \quad \forall\, i \in \{1\ldots n\}: \ v_i \neq \mathcal{E} \ \wedge \ v_i \neq \langle\rangle$$

Fig. 2. Normalized Forms

The meaning of a $\lambda\mathcal{F}$-term depends on its deployment context. A deployment context is represented by a normalized form. We write $[\![a]\!]^{LF}[\overline{H}]$ to evaluate the $\lambda\mathcal{F}$-expression a in a deployment context $\overline{H}$. For example, we can use the encoding of Booleans as shown above to build a deployment context $\overline{B}$. This context defines three bindings: True, False, and Not:

$$\overline{B} = \langle\rangle\langle\text{True} = \lambda(\text{X}) \ \text{X.true}\rangle$$
$$\langle\text{False} = \lambda(\text{X}) \ \text{X.false}\rangle$$
$$\langle\text{Not} = \lambda(\text{B}) \ \lambda(\text{V}) \ \text{B V}\langle\text{true} = \text{V.false}\rangle\langle\text{false} = \text{V.true}\rangle\rangle$$

We can use $\overline{B}$ to evaluate (Not True) $\langle\rangle\langle\text{true} = a\rangle\langle\text{false} = b\rangle$, written

$$[\![(\text{Not True}) \ \langle\rangle\langle\text{true} = a\rangle\langle\text{false} = b\rangle]\!]^{LF}[\overline{B}],$$

which yields

$$\textbf{apply} \ ([\![(\text{Not True})]\!]^{LF}[\overline{B}], \ \overline{B}) \ \langle\rangle\langle\text{true} = a\rangle\langle\text{false} = b\rangle$$
$$= b.$$

The evaluation rules for forms and $\lambda\mathcal{F}$-terms are shown in Figure 3.

The operator **apply** is the heart of the $\lambda\mathcal{F}$-evaluation process. It actually implements a *lazy evaluation* mechanism. The reason for this is that the first argument (i.e., the operator) may not yield a closure.

Form evaluation:

$$[\langle\rangle]^F[\overline{H}] \qquad = \langle\rangle \qquad\qquad\qquad\qquad\qquad\qquad\qquad\text{(F-EMPTY)}$$

$$[X]^F[\overline{H}] \qquad = \langle\langle\overline{H} \to X\rangle\rangle \qquad\qquad\qquad\qquad\qquad\text{(F-VAR)}$$

$$[F\langle l = V\rangle]^F[\overline{H}] = ([F]^F[\overline{H}])\langle l = [V]^V[\overline{H}]\rangle \qquad\qquad\text{(F-BIND)}$$

$$[F \cdot G]^F[\overline{H}] \qquad = ([F]^F[\overline{H}]) \cdot ([G]^F[\overline{H}]) \qquad\qquad\text{(F-PBIND)}$$

$$[F\backslash G]^F[\overline{H}] \qquad = ([F]^F[\overline{H}])\backslash([G]^F[\overline{H}]) \qquad\qquad\text{(F-PRES)}$$

$$[F \to l]^F[\overline{H}] \qquad = \langle\langle([F]^F[\overline{H}]) \to l\rangle\rangle \qquad\qquad\text{(F-DEREF)}$$

$$[F[G]]^F[\overline{H}] \qquad = [F]^F[\textbf{normalize }(([G]^F[\overline{H}]) \cdot \overline{H})] \qquad\text{(F-CONTEXT)}$$

Value evaluation:

$$[\mathcal{E}]^V[\overline{H}] = \mathcal{E} \qquad\qquad [a]^V[\overline{H}] = a \qquad\qquad [M]^V[\overline{H}] = [M]^{LF}[\overline{H}]$$

Form normalization:

$$[F]^{\overline{F}}[\overline{H}] = \textbf{normalize }([F]^F[\overline{H}]) \qquad\qquad\qquad\text{(F-NORM)}$$

$\lambda\mathcal{F}$-evaluation:

$$[F]^{LF}[\overline{H}] \qquad = \begin{cases} v & \text{if } F \equiv X \wedge v = [\overline{H}.X] \neq \mathcal{E} \\ [F]^{\overline{F}}[\overline{H}] & \text{otherwise} \end{cases} \qquad\text{(LF-FORM)}$$

$$[M.l]^{LF}[\overline{H}] \qquad = [([M]^{LF}[\overline{H}]).l] \qquad\qquad\qquad\text{(LF-PROJ)}$$

$$[\lambda(X)\ M]^{LF}[\overline{H}] = \lambda(X)\ (M[\overline{H}]) \qquad\qquad\qquad\text{(LF-ABS)}$$

$$[M\ N]^{LF}[\overline{H}] \qquad = \textbf{apply } M\ N\ \overline{H} \qquad\qquad\qquad\text{(LF-APP)}$$

$$[M[F]]^{LF}[\overline{H}] \qquad = [M]^{LF}[\textbf{normalize }(([F]^F[\overline{H}]) \cdot \overline{H})] \qquad\text{(LF-CONTEXT)}$$

Projection evaluation ($\hat{F} = [F]^F[\overline{H}]$ and $\hat{G} = [G]^F[\overline{H}]$ for some $\overline{H}$):

$$\left. \begin{array}{l} [(\langle\rangle).l],\ [a.l],\ [\mathcal{E}.l] \\ [(\lambda(X)\ (M[\overline{H}])).l] \end{array} \right\} = \mathcal{E}$$

$$[(\hat{F}\langle m = \hat{V}\rangle).l] \qquad = [\hat{F}.l] \qquad \text{if } m \neq l$$

$$[(\hat{F}\langle l = \hat{V}\rangle).l] \qquad = \begin{cases} \hat{V} & \text{if } \hat{V} \in \mathcal{V} \\ \mathcal{E} & \text{otherwise} \end{cases}$$

$$[(\hat{F} \cdot \hat{G}).l] \qquad = \begin{cases} [\hat{G}.l] & \text{if } [\hat{G}.l] \neq \mathcal{E} \vee \langle\langle\hat{G} \to l\rangle\rangle \neq \langle\rangle \\ [\hat{F}.l] & \text{otherwise} \end{cases}$$

$$[(\hat{F}\backslash\hat{G}).l] \qquad = \begin{cases} \mathcal{E} & \text{if } [\hat{G}.l] \neq \mathcal{E} \vee \langle\langle\hat{G} \to l\rangle\rangle \neq \langle\rangle \\ [\hat{F}.l] & \text{otherwise} \end{cases}$$

Form dereference evaluation ($\hat{F} = [F]^F[\overline{H}]$ and $\hat{G} = [G]^F[\overline{H}]$ for some $\overline{H}$):

$$\langle\langle\langle\rangle \to l\rangle\rangle \qquad = \langle\rangle$$

$$\langle\langle(\hat{F}\langle m = \hat{V}\rangle) \to l\rangle\rangle = \langle\langle\hat{F} \to l\rangle\rangle \qquad \text{if } m \neq l$$

$$\langle\langle(\hat{F}\langle l = \hat{V}\rangle) \to l\rangle\rangle \ = \begin{cases} \langle\rangle & \text{if } \hat{V} \in \mathcal{V} \\ \textbf{normalize } \hat{V} & \text{otherwise} \end{cases}$$

$$\langle\langle(\hat{F} \cdot \hat{G}) \to l\rangle\rangle \qquad = \begin{cases} \langle\langle\hat{G} \to l\rangle\rangle & \text{if } [\hat{G}.l] \neq \mathcal{E} \vee \langle\langle\hat{G} \to l\rangle\rangle \neq \langle\rangle \\ \langle\langle\hat{F} \to l\rangle\rangle & \text{otherwise} \end{cases}$$

$$\langle\langle(\hat{F}\backslash\hat{G}) \to l\rangle\rangle \qquad = \begin{cases} \langle\rangle & \text{if } [\hat{G}.l] \neq \mathcal{E} \vee \langle\langle\hat{G} \to l\rangle\rangle \neq \langle\rangle \\ \langle\langle\hat{F} \to l\rangle\rangle & \text{otherwise} \end{cases}$$

Fig. 3. Evaluation Rules

The $\lambda\mathcal{F}$-operator **apply** is defined as follows:

> **apply** M N $\overline{F}$ =
>   **cases** $[\![M]\!]^{LF}[\overline{F}]$ **of**
>
> | | | |
> |---|---|---|
> | $\overline{G}$ | : $[\![N]\!]^{LF}[\,[\overline{F}\cdot\overline{G}]^{\overline{F}}\,]$ | (c1) |
> | a | : $a\,([\![N]\!]^{LF}[\overline{F}])$ | (c2) |
> | $\mathcal{E}$ | : $\mathcal{E}$ | (c3) |
> | $\lambda(X)\,(M'\,[\overline{H}])$: | $[\![M'\,[\overline{H}]]\!]^{LF}[\,\langle\rangle\langle X=[\![N]\!]^{LF}[\overline{F}]\rangle\,]$ | (c4) |
>
>   **end**

The first rule states that if the operator, denoted by M, evaluates to a (normal) form expression $\overline{G}$, we evaluate the argument N in a new extended context $[[\overline{F}\cdot\overline{G}]^{\overline{F}}]$, where $\overline{G}$ defines a local refinement of $\overline{F}$. Consider, for example, the following evaluation

$$\begin{aligned}
&\langle\rangle\langle\texttt{True}=\lambda(\texttt{X})\ \texttt{X.true}\rangle\ (\texttt{True}\ \langle\rangle\langle\texttt{true}=\texttt{a}\rangle\langle\texttt{false}=\texttt{b}\rangle)\\
&=(\texttt{True}\ \langle\rangle\langle\texttt{true}=\texttt{a}\rangle\langle\texttt{false}=\texttt{b}\rangle)[\,\langle\rangle\langle\texttt{True}=\lambda(\texttt{X})\ \texttt{X.true}\rangle\,]\\
&=(\lambda(\texttt{X})\ \texttt{X.true})\ (\langle\rangle\langle\texttt{true}=\texttt{a}\rangle\langle\texttt{false}=\texttt{b}\rangle)\\
&=(\langle\rangle\langle\texttt{true}=\texttt{a}\rangle\langle\texttt{false}=\texttt{b}\rangle).\texttt{true}\\
&=\texttt{a}
\end{aligned}$$

Here, the form $\langle\rangle\langle\texttt{True}=\lambda(\texttt{X})\ \texttt{X.true}\rangle$ provides a proper environment that allows for the evaluation of the expression $(\texttt{True}\ \langle\rangle\langle\texttt{true}=\texttt{a}\rangle\langle\texttt{false}=\texttt{b}\rangle)$ in a meaningful way. This approach is similar to way the so-called sandbox expressions are handled in the PICCOLA-calculus [2]. When evaluating a sandbox expression $\texttt{A;B}$ the term left to the semicolon defines a *root* context or *controlled environment* for the right-hand side agent. However, $\texttt{A}$ in $\texttt{A;B}$ may not evaluate to a form. In this case the agent $\texttt{A;B}$ is *stuck* and identified with $\mathcal{E}$.

The second rule defines the evaluation of a system-depended expression, that is, when the operator M evaluates to an abstract value a. The actual meaning of a lies outside the $\lambda\mathcal{F}$-calculus. Therefore, the target system is responsible for the proper handling of the expression $a\,([\![N]\!]^{LF}[\overline{F}])$. We have chosen this approach, rather than using $\perp$ (i.e., undefined), because the meaning of $a\,([\![N]\!]^{LF}[\overline{F}])$ is not really undefined, but merely our knowledge about it is incomplete.

The third rule defines *error propagation*. If the operator (i.e., M) evaluates to "no value", the whole expression has no value. It will simply be discarded.

The fourth rule states that if operator M evaluates in context $[\overline{F}]$ to a closure $\lambda(X)\,(M'\,[\overline{H}])$, then the body of the closure (i.e., $(M'\,[\overline{H}])$) is being evaluated in a new context $[\langle\rangle\langle X=[\![N]\!]^{LF}[\overline{F}]\rangle]$. Thus, actual parameters are passed to a functions as bindings in the evaluation context.

To illustrate the $\lambda\mathcal{F}$-evaluation process, consider the following example. To simplify the presentation, we assume that both F_1 and F_2 do not contain any free variables:

$$\llbracket F_1 \ (\lambda(X) \ (\lambda(Y) \ Y) \ X) \ F_2 \rrbracket^{LF}[\langle\rangle]$$
$$= \mathbf{apply} \ F_1 \ ((\lambda(X) \ (\lambda(Y) \ Y) \ X) \ F_2) \ \langle\rangle \qquad\qquad (\text{LF-APP})$$
$$= \llbracket (\lambda(X) \ (\lambda(Y) \ Y) \ X) \ F_2 \rrbracket^{LF}[\llbracket \langle\rangle \cdot F_1 \rrbracket^{\overline{F}}] \qquad\qquad (\text{c1})$$
$$= \llbracket (\lambda(X) \ (\lambda(Y) \ Y) \ X) \ F_2 \rrbracket^{LF}[F_1] \qquad\qquad (\text{F-NORM})$$
$$= \mathbf{apply} \ (\lambda(X) \ (\lambda(Y) \ Y) \ X) \ F_2 \ F_1 \qquad\qquad (\text{LF-APP})$$
$$= \llbracket ((\lambda(Y) \ Y) \ X \ [F_1]) \rrbracket^{LF}[\langle\rangle\langle X = \llbracket F_2 \rrbracket^{LF}[F_1]\rangle] \qquad\qquad (\text{c4})$$
$$= \llbracket ((\lambda(Y) \ Y) \ X \ [F_1]) \rrbracket^{LF}[\langle\rangle\langle X = F_2\rangle] \qquad\qquad (\text{LF-FORM})$$
$$= \llbracket (\lambda(Y) \ Y) \ X \rrbracket^{LF}[\llbracket (\llbracket F_1 \rrbracket^{F}[\langle\rangle\langle X = F_2\rangle]) \cdot \langle\rangle\langle X = F_2\rangle \rrbracket^{\overline{F}}] \qquad\qquad (\text{LF-CONTEXT})$$
$$= \llbracket (\lambda(Y) \ Y) \ X \rrbracket^{LF}[\llbracket F_1 \cdot \langle\rangle\langle X = F_2\rangle \rrbracket^{\overline{F}}]$$
$$= \llbracket (\lambda(Y) \ Y) \ X \rrbracket^{LF}[F_1\langle X = F_2\rangle] \qquad\qquad (\text{F-NORM})$$
$$= \mathbf{apply} \ (\lambda(Y) \ Y) \ X \ (F_1\langle X = F_2\rangle) \qquad\qquad (\text{LF-APP})$$
$$= \llbracket Y \ [F_1\langle X = F_2\rangle] \rrbracket^{LF}[\langle\rangle\langle Y = (\llbracket X \rrbracket^{LF}[F_1\langle X = F_2\rangle])\rangle] \qquad\qquad (\text{c4})$$
$$= \llbracket Y \ [F_1\langle X = F_2\rangle] \rrbracket^{LF}[\langle\rangle\langle Y = F_2\rangle] \qquad\qquad (\text{LF-FORM})$$
$$= \llbracket Y \rrbracket^{LF}[\llbracket (\llbracket F_1\langle X = F_2\rangle \rrbracket^{F}[\langle\rangle\langle Y = F_2\rangle]) \cdot \langle\rangle\langle Y = F_2\rangle \rrbracket^{\overline{F}}] \qquad\qquad (\text{LF-CONTEXT})$$
$$= \llbracket Y \rrbracket^{LF}[\llbracket (F_1\langle X = F_2\rangle) \cdot \langle\rangle\langle Y = F_2\rangle \rrbracket^{\overline{F}}]$$
$$= \llbracket Y \rrbracket^{LF}[(F_1\langle X = F_2\rangle)\langle Y = F_2\rangle] \qquad\qquad (\text{F-NORM})$$
$$= \llbracket Y \rrbracket^{\overline{F}}[(F_1\langle X = F_2\rangle)\langle Y = F_2\rangle] \qquad\qquad (\text{LF-FORM})$$
$$= F_2 \qquad\qquad (\text{F-NORM})$$

The above example illustrates that keyword-based parameter-passing can effectively be modeled with form-based explicit contexts (e.g., $[\langle\rangle\langle X = F_2\rangle]$). Actual function arguments are encoded as bindings in the form that represents the current context.

In $\lambda\mathcal{F}$, forms take the role of λ-calculus variables. But is it possible to embed the λ-calculus in $\lambda\mathcal{F}$ itself? Assume, for example, a closed λ-calculus term M. Then the embedding of M into $\lambda\mathcal{F}$ is given by the translation $\llbracket M \rrbracket$ as specified below:

$$\llbracket x \rrbracket \quad = x.arg$$
$$\llbracket \lambda x. \ M \rrbracket = \lambda(x) \ \llbracket M \rrbracket$$
$$\llbracket M \ N \rrbracket \ = (\llbracket M \rrbracket \ \langle\rangle\langle arg = \llbracket N \rrbracket\rangle)$$

Here, λ-calculus variables are encoded as projections, which extract the actual value. The encoding of abstractions maps a position-dependent function to a position-independent functions, whereas the encoding of application builds a form expression for the λ-term in argument position.

Unfortunately, a simple translation of a λ-calculus term does not necessarily yield a position-independent $\lambda\mathcal{F}$-term. Suppose we want to specify a recursive function definition (e.g., the length function for lists) of the form $\mathtt{f} = \lambda\mathtt{x}.\{body\ containing\ f\}$. That is, we want to write a function where the term on the right-hand side of the $=$ uses the very function that we are defining. To solve this problem, we define a function $\mathtt{g} = \lambda\mathtt{f}.\lambda\mathtt{x}.\{body\ containing\ f\}$ and a function $\mathtt{h} = (\mathtt{fix}\ \mathtt{g})$, where $\mathtt{fix}$ is the applicative-order fixed-point combinator

$$\mathtt{fix} = \lambda\mathtt{f}.((\lambda\mathtt{x}.\mathtt{f}\ (\lambda\mathtt{y}.(\mathtt{x}\ \mathtt{x})\ \mathtt{y}))\ (\lambda\mathtt{x}.\mathtt{f}\ (\lambda\mathtt{y}.(\mathtt{x}\ \mathtt{x})\ \mathtt{y})))$$

Now, we can translate $(\mathtt{fix}\ \mathtt{g})$ into $\lambda\mathcal{F}$, but the result would still be position-dependent, since the sub-term $(\lambda\mathtt{x}.\mathtt{f}\ (\lambda\mathtt{y}.(\mathtt{x}\ \mathtt{x})\ \mathtt{y}))$ forces a position-dependent order on g's arguments. In particular, $[\![g]\!]$ is a $\lambda\mathcal{F}$-function that has to be applied to a "self-replicator" (i.e., the fixed-point) before it can consume any additional arguments. Further analysis reveals that in order to achieve a position-independent encoding of (fix g), we need to be able to convert g into an equivalent "uncurried" function, which can consume the self-replicator and any additional arguments at the same time. But the application of g in term $(\lambda x.f\ (\lambda y.(x\ x)\ y))\{f/g\}$ does not allow this. We solve this problem by applying f later. That is, we move the application of f underneath the innermost abstraction: $\lambda x.\lambda y.(f\ (x\ x)\ y)$. We observe now that f has become a function that takes two arguments. Replacing the sequence of arguments with a structured argument (i.e., uncurrying f) yields the desired effect that the self-replicator and any additional arguments are consumed at the same time. We call a fixed-point operator with this property *late applicative-order fixed-point combinator*, which is defined as

$$\text{fix}_L = \lambda f.((\lambda x.\lambda y.(f\ (x\ x)\ y))\ (\lambda x.\lambda y.(f\ (x\ x)\ y)))$$

The encoding[2] of fix_L into $\lambda\mathcal{F}$ is as follows:

$$[\![\text{fix}_L]\!] = \lambda(f)\ [\![(\lambda x.\lambda y.(f\ (x\ x)\ y))\ (\lambda x.\lambda y(f\ (x\ x)\ y))]\!]$$
$$= \lambda(f)\ [\![(\lambda x.\lambda y.(f\ (x\ x)\ y))]\!]\ \langle\rangle\langle\text{arg} = [\![(\lambda x.\lambda y(f\ (x\ x)\ y))]\!]\rangle$$
$$= \lambda(f)\ (H\ \langle\rangle\langle\text{arg} = H\rangle)$$
$$\text{where } H\ = \lambda(x)\ \lambda(y)\ (f.\text{arg}\ \langle\rangle\langle\text{arg} = (x.\text{arg}\ \langle\rangle\langle\text{arg} = x.\text{arg}\rangle)\rangle$$
$$\langle\rangle\langle\text{arg} = y.\text{arg}\rangle)$$

By further analyzing the expression H, we notice that a form expression of the kind $\langle\rangle\langle\text{arg} = X.\text{arg}\rangle$ is the same as X. Thus, we can rewrite H as follows:

$$H\ = \lambda(x)\ \lambda(y)\ (f.\text{arg}\ \langle\rangle\langle\text{arg} = (x.\text{arg}\ x)\rangle\ y)$$

In the next step, we use the fact that f.arg actually has to denote a position-independent function, which can consume all arguments in any order at once:

$$H\ = \lambda(x)\ \lambda(y)\ (f.\text{arg}\ y\langle\text{arg} = (x.\text{arg}\ x)\rangle)$$

Thus, a position-independent applicative-order fixed-point combinator in $\lambda\mathcal{F}$, written FIX, can be defined as follows:

$$\text{FIX} = \lambda(\text{Fun})\ (H\ \langle\rangle\langle\text{self} = H\rangle)$$
$$[\langle\rangle\langle H = \lambda(\text{Fix})\ \lambda(\text{Args})\ (\text{Fun}.f\ \text{Args}\langle\text{self} = (\text{Fix}.\text{self}\ \text{Fix})\rangle)\rangle)]$$

The ability to define the fixed-point operator FIX in $\lambda\mathcal{F}$ suggests that it should be possible to embed arbitrary λ-terms in the $\lambda\mathcal{F}$-calculus. However, a simple translation of a λ-term into a $\lambda\mathcal{F}$-term does not guarantee a position-independent result. A more detailed study of embedding λ-calculus into $\lambda\mathcal{F}$ is part of future work.

---

[2] In the encoding of fix_L, the term H is still position-dependent, but the application of the recursive function, denoted by Fun.f, is not.

3 Contractual Specifications

The contractual specification of component interfaces has to guarantee that a component can be safely combined with other components or deployed in a new context. Ideally, all conditions of a contract should be stated explicitly and formally as part of an interface specification. The information contained in a contract should tell us *what* a component offers without entering into the details of *how* it is provided. Beugnard et al [5] have identified four levels of component contracts:

- Syntactic contracts to specify data type compatibility,
- Behavioral contracts to specify pre- and postconditions invariants,
- Synchronization contracts to specify constraints in concurrent contexts, and
- Quality-of-service contracts to specify quantitative properties like maximum response time.

Each of these four levels is important, but in this paper we focus only on syntactic contracts.

Consider, for example, the following code written in C#-like language:

```
using System;
public class OneMinute : MarshalByRefObject {
    public override ILease InitializeLifetimeService() {
        ILease lease = base.InitializeLifetimeService();
        lease.InitialLeaseTime = TimeSpan.FromMinutes(1);
        return lease;
    }
}
```

This code defines a class *OneMinute*, which can be used to instantiate .NET Remoting [21] objects with a lease time of one minute. *OneMinute* is derived from *MarshalByRefObject*, a .NET class that enables access to objects across application domain boundaries. The .NET Remoting infrastructure is an abstract approach to support interprocess communication. The .NET lifetime service associates a lease with each remotely activated object and after the lease expires, the object is removed from the system. The system assigns a default lifetime to each Remoting object, but the user can redefine the default by overriding the method `InitializeLifetimeService`. In the case of *OneMinute*, the lease will expire after one minute.

Now, we can represent the class *OneMinute* as a $\lambda\mathcal{F}$-term using the approach of Lumpe and Schneider [16]. The behavior of the class *OneMinute* can be captured by $\Delta_{OneMinute}$ denoting the incremental modification defined by this class:

$$
\begin{aligned}
\Delta_{OneMinute} = \\
\lambda(\texttt{I})\langle\rangle\langle\ \texttt{InitializeLifetimeService} = \\
\lambda()\ ((\texttt{I} \rightarrow \texttt{super}).\texttt{InitializeLifetimeService}\ \langle\rangle) \\
\langle\texttt{InitialLeaseTime} = (\textit{TimeSpan}.\texttt{FromMinutes}\ (\langle\rangle\langle\texttt{value} = 1\rangle)))\rangle
\end{aligned}
$$

The term $(\texttt{I} \rightarrow \texttt{super}).\texttt{InitializeLifetimeService}\ \langle\rangle$ implements the call to the inherited method `InitializeLifetimeService`, which returns a lease form. The binding `InitialLeaseTime` is then overridden to set the lease time to one minute. To create the class *OneMinute*, we use the abstraction `Class` that when applied to an appropriate model generator for C# yields a class builder for C#-classes. We use `CSharpClass` to denote this class builder and apply it the both the super class *MarshalByRefObject* and the incremental modification $\Delta_{OneMinute}$ to construct *OneMinute*:

$$OneMinute = \texttt{CSharpClass} \; (MarshalByRefObject \langle \Delta = \Delta_{OneMinute} \rangle)$$

Suppose now that we would like to verify the correctness of this definition without excessive dependencies on the features imported from the `System` namespace. Based on a static analysis of this code, we might express what it *provides* as the following form, where values are type expressions:

$$P = \langle \rangle \langle \texttt{OneMinute} = () \rightarrow \langle \rangle \langle \texttt{InitializeLifetimeService} = () \rightarrow ILease \rangle \rangle$$

that is, a default constructor called `OneMinute`, which yields an instance of *OneMinute* that understands at least the `InitializeLifetimeService` method, which returns a lease object that implements the interface *ILease*. We can, however, say even more about the assumptions this definition places on its environment. In particular, instances of *OneMinute* will safely provide their services if and only if the environment (i.e., the namespace `System`) satisfies the following requirement:

$$\overline{R} =$$
$$\langle \rangle \langle MarshalByRefObject = () \rightarrow \langle \rangle \langle \texttt{InitializeLifetimeService} = () \rightarrow ILease \rangle$$
$$\langle ILease = \langle \rangle \langle \texttt{InitialLeaseTime} = TimeSpan \rangle \rangle$$
$$\langle TimeSpan = \langle \rangle \langle \texttt{FromMinutes} = ((\langle \rangle \langle \texttt{value} = Integer \rangle) \rightarrow TimeSpan \rangle \rangle$$

that is, the environment `System`, denoted by $\overline{R}$, has to provide suitable definitions for the types *MarshalByRefObject*, *ILease*, and *TimeSpan*. In particular, the class *MarshalByRefObject* must define a default constructor and has to provide a method `InitializeLifetimeService`, which returns a value that implements the *ILease* interface. Furthermore, it is required that the *ILease* interface must define a virtual field `InitialLeaseTime` that can be assigned a *TimeSpan* structure, which has at least a suitable `FromMinutes` method.

Thus, we can say that `System` denotes the required type, which expresses the requirements posed by the free variables of class *OneMinute*. If we close *OneMinute* by composing it with an environment or component like `System`, written $P[\overline{R}]$, we must then check whether the services provided by `System` satisfy the required type of *OneMinute*.

4   Conclusion and Future Work

In this paper, we have presented the $\lambda\mathcal{F}$-calculus, a substitution-free variant of the λ-calculus in which names are replaced with forms and parameter passing is modeled using explicit contexts. The $\lambda\mathcal{F}$-calculus, like Dami's λN, is a calculus in which parameters are identified by names rather than positions. Position-independent parameter specification allows for the development of extensible, flexible, and reliable component-based application. The resulting flexibility of a form-based programming model can also be seen, for example, in XML/HTML forms [30], where fields are encoded as named (rather than positional) parameters, in Python [29] and Common Lisp [27], where functions can be defined to take arguments by keywords, and in Perl [31] where it is a common technique to pass a map of name/value pairs as arguments to a function or method.

The definition of explicit contexts is inspired by the work of Achermann's PICCOLA-calculus [2] and the work on *explicit substitutions* by Abadi et al [1]. Substitution, as used in the classical λ-calculus, is actually a meta-level concept and not part of the language. By making it part of the language, Abadi et al argue that we can achieve a better correspondence between the language theory and its implementation.

However, Abadi et al do not address the problem of position dependency. In fact, explicit substitutions use de Bruijn indices [11] to correctly map parameters to their actual values. The resulting operational semantics of substitutions is not trivial and makes it cumbersome to trace the actual effects of them. On the other hand, forms provide a convenient way to record parameter bindings in a small and expressive framework.

We can use the $\lambda\mathcal{F}$-calculus to define (syntactic) contractual specifications. Contractual specifications raise explicitly the confidence level in the development of applications involving third-party components. The fundamental purpose of a contractual specifications is to prevent the occurrence of *run-time errors* while executing a component-based program, that is, contractual specifications should impose a well-balanced set of constraints to enforce the correctness of a component-based application. However, the verification process of contractual specifications must be defined in a way such that the programmer can easily predict whether a contract is satisfiable or not [6]. That is, a contract should be defined in a manner that the reasons why the verification of it has failed are self-evident.

The key challenge of the design of contractual specifications will be the proper characterization of incomplete system knowledge and the definition of the verification rules for both form extension and form restriction. The form extension operator is similar to *asymmetric record concatenation* [7,22,32] and takes two forms and returns a new form in which the bindings of the argument forms are merged. The specific nature of this operation makes it hard to find a suitable type assignment. Some type systems [7,32] cannot assign a type to this operator at all. In type systems that incorporate a *subsumption rule* the form extension operator requires an additional set of constraints that limits the number of applicable subtypes. Early results from recent work in this area [13,18] indicate that the definition of a suitable component type system will go beyond "traditional" type theories.

Acknowledgement. The author thanks Jean-Guy Schneider, Oscar Nierstrasz, and the anonymous reviewers for their valuable comments and discussions.

References

1. Martín Abadi, Luca Cardelli, Pierre-Louis Curien, and Jean-Jacques Lèvy. Explicit Substitutions. In *Conference Record of the Seventeenth Annual ACM Symposium on Principles of Programming Languages, San Francisco, California*, pages 31–46. ACM, 1990.

2. Franz Achermann. *Forms, Agents and Channels: Defining Composition Abstraction with Style*. PhD thesis, University of Bern, Institute of Computer Science and Applied Mathematics, January 2002.

3. Franz Achermann and Oscar Nierstrasz. Explicit Namespaces. In Jürg Gutknecht and Wolfgang Weck, editors, *Modular Programming Languages*, LNCS 1897, pages 77–89. Springer, September 2000.

4. Uwe Assmann. *Invasive Software Composition*. Springer, 2003.

5. Antoine Beugnard, Jean-Marc Jézéquel, Noël Plouzeau, and Damien Watkins. Making Components Contract Aware. *IEEE Computer*, 32(7):38–45, July 1999.

6. Luca Cardelli. Type Systems. In *Handbook of Computer Science and Engineering*, chapter 103, pages 2208–2236. CRC Press, 1997.

7. Luca Cardelli and John C. Mitchell. Operations on Records. In Carl Gunter and John C. Mitchell, editors, *Theoretical Aspects of Object-Oriented Programming*. MIT Press, 1994. Also appeared as SRC Research Report 48, and in *Mathematical Structures in Computer Science*, 1(1):3–48, March 1991.

8. Francisco Curbera, Sanjiva Weerawarana, and Matthew J. Duftler. On Component Composition Languages. Proceedings of ECOOP 2000 Workshop on Component-Oriented Programming, June 2000.

9. Laurent Dami. *Software Composition: Towards an Integration of Functional and Object-Oriented Approaches*. PhD thesis, Centre Universitaire d'Informatique, University of Geneva, CH, 1994.

10. Laurent Dami. A Lambda-Calculus for Dynamic Binding. *Theoretical Computer Science*, 192:201–231, February 1998.

11. Nikolas G. de Bruijn. Lambda Calculus Notation with Nameless Dummies. *Indagationes Mathematicae*, 34:381–392, 1972.

12. Frank DeRemer and Hans H. Kron. Programming in the Large versus Programming in the Small. *IEEE Transactions on Software Engineering*, SE–2(2):80–86, June 1976.

13. Markus Lumpe. *A π-Calculus Based Approach to Software Composition*. PhD thesis, University of Bern, Institute of Computer Science and Applied Mathematics, January 1999.

14. Markus Lumpe, Franz Achermann, and Oscar Nierstrasz. A Formal Language for Composition. In Gary Leavens and Murali Sitaraman, editors, *Foundations of Component-Based Systems*, chapter 4, pages 69–90. Cambridge University Press, March 2000.

15. Markus Lumpe and Jean-Guy Schneider. Form-based Software Composition. In Mike Barnett, Steve Edwards, Dimitra Giannakopoulou, and Gary T. Leavens, editors, *Proceedings of ESEC '03 Workshop on Specification and Verification of Component-Based Systems (SAVCBS '03)*, pages 58–65, Helsinki, Finland, September 2003.

16. Markus Lumpe and Jean-Guy Schneider. A Form-based Metamodel for Software Composition. *Science of Computer Programming*, 56:59–78, April 2005.

17. Robin Milner. *Communicating and Mobile Systems: the π-Calculus*. Cambridge University Press, 1999.

18. Oscar Nierstrasz and Franz Achermann. A Calculus for Modeling Software Components. In Frank S. de Boer, Marcello M. Bonsangue, Susanne Graf, and Willem P. de Roever, editors, *Proceedings of First International Symposium on Formal Methods for Components and Objects (FMCO 2002)*, LNCS 2852, pages 339–360, Leiden, The Netherlands, 2003. Springer.
19. Oscar Nierstrasz and Laurent Dami. Component-Oriented Software Technology. In Oscar Nierstrasz and Dennis Tsichritzis, editors, *Object-Oriented Software Composition*, pages 3–28. Prentice Hall, 1995.
20. Oscar Nierstrasz and Theo Dirk Meijler. Requirements for a Composition Language. In Paolo Ciancarini, Oscar Nierstrasz, and Akinori Yonezawa, editors, *Object-Based Models and Languages for Concurrent Systems*, LNCS 924, pages 147–161. Springer, 1995.
21. Ingo Rammer. *Advanced .NET Remoting*. APress, 2002.
22. Didier Rémy. Typing Record Concatenation for Free. Technical Report RR-1739, INRIA Rocquencourt, August 1992.
23. Johannes Sametinger. *Software Engineering with Reusable Components*. Springer, 1997.
24. Jean-Guy Schneider. *Components, Scripts, and Glue: A conceptual framework for software composition*. PhD thesis, University of Bern, Institute of Computer Science and Applied Mathematics, October 1999.
25. Jean-Guy Schneider and Markus Lumpe. Synchronizing Concurrent Objects in the Pi-Calculus. In Roland Ducournau and Serge Garlatti, editors, *Proceedings of Langages et Modèles à Objets '97*, pages 61–76, Roscoff, October 1997. Hermes.
26. João Costa Seco and Luís Caires. A Basic Model of Typed Components. In Elisa Bertino, editor, *Proceedings of ECOOP 2000*, LNCS 1850, pages 108–128. Springer, 2000.
27. Guy L. Steele. *Common Lisp the Language*. Digital Press, Thinking Machines, Inc., 2nd edition, 1990.
28. Clemens Szyperski. *Component Software: Beyond Object-Oriented Programming*. Addison-Wesley / ACM Press, second edition, 2002.
29. Guido van Rossum. Python Reference Manual. Technical report, Corporation for National Research Initiatives (CNRI), October 1996.
30. W3C. *Extensible Markup Language (XML) 1.0 (Third Edition)*. W3C Recommendation, February 2004. http://www.w3.org/TR/REC-xml.
31. Larry Wall, Tom Christiansen, and Randal L. Schwartz. *Programming Perl*. O'Reilly & Associates, 2nd edition, September 1996.
32. Mitchell Wand. Type Inference for Record Concatenation and Multiple Inheritance. *Information and Computation*, 93:1–15, 1991. Preliminary version appeared in *Proc. 4th IEEE Symposium on Logic in Computer Science* (1989), pp. 92–97.

A Model of Components
with Non-regular Protocols

Mario Südholt

INRIA/EMN, LINA,
OBASCO project, Département Informatique,
École des Mines de Nantes,
4 rue Alfred Kastler, 44307 Nantes cedex 3, France
www.emn.fr/sudholt

Abstract. Behavioral specifications that are integrated into component interfaces are an important means for the correct construction of component-based systems. Currently, such specifications are typically limited to finite-state protocols because more expressive notions of protocol do not support reasonable basic composition properties, such as compatibility and substitutability.

In this paper, we present first results of the integration into component interfaces of a notion of non-regular protocols based on "non-regular process types" introduced by Puntigam [17]. More concretely, we present three contributions: (i) a motivation of the usefulness of non-regular protocols in the context of peer-to-peer applications, (ii) a language for non-regular protocols and an outline of a suitable formal definition, (iii) a discussion of basic composition properties and an analysis of how to adequately integrate protocol-modifying operators in the model.

1 Introduction

Component-based programming promises to facilitate the construction of large-scale applications by supporting the composition of simple building blocks into complex applications. Explicit interfaces are commonly seen as being a fundamental means of components for this endeavor. Interfaces are intended to impose strong restrictions on components: they should make explicit all the means for communication and coordination of components. This requires a much stronger notion of interface than is common in object-oriented programming languages, where interactions may occur in a hidden fashion, *e.g.*, through a state global to two collaborating objects.

Interfaces of most component models, many academic ones (see, *e.g.*, [22,2]) but in particular the major industrial ones, such as Sun's Enterprise JavaBeans (EJB) [4], define component interfaces as sets of method signatures representing the services a component provides or requires. Such interfaces do not provide much information about component implementations and the correctness of their implementation is therefore very difficult to establish. Consequently, a large number of specification methods, such as Rational Rose [11] and State

T. Gschwind, U. Aßmann, and O. Nierstrasz (Eds.): SC 2005, LNCS 3628, pp. 99–113, 2005.

Charts [9] enable specifications for component interfaces to be separated from component implementations.

The integration of behavioral specifications into component interfaces has been recognized early as a means to solve certain deficiencies of approaches relying on such specifications, in particular, the maintainability problem of separated evolution of component specifications and implementations. By far the largest class of approaches featuring integrated behavioral specifications are component models which include regular, *i.e.*, finite-state, protocols into interfaces (see, *e.g.*, [25,24,3,15,7]). Regular protocols enable the definition of several properties, such as compatibility and substitutability, useful for correctness proofs of components and can be implemented quite simply.

While more expressive notions of protocol in interfaces are highly interesting from a programming point of view, well-understood classes of protocols, such as protocols based on context-free languages, do not offer reasonable definitions of the above-mentioned basic composition properties. Consequently, more expressive protocols are rarely used in interfaces in order to construct components (two notable exceptions being counter-constrained finite state machines [19] and protocols based on symbolic transitions systems [14]).

In this paper, we present first results in the integration of a notion of non-regular protocols into component interfaces based on the "non-regular process types" introduced by Puntigam [17]. More concretely, we present three contributions. First, we motivate the usefulness of non-regular protocols in the context of peer-to-peer (P2P) applications, which, due to their distributed and large-scale nature, benefit from a component-based structure. Second, we present a protocol language in which such protocols can be defined and show how this language can be formally grounded in Puntigam's calculus. Third, we discuss how basic composition properties are addressed in such a component model and present an analysis how protocol operators defined for regular protocols can be integrated into components with non-regular protocols.

The paper is structured as follows. In Sect. 2, we introduce trust management in P2P applications as a motivating problem for the use of non-regular protocols. Sect. 3 presents our component model, the corresponding protocol language, and sketch its formal definition. In Sect. 4, we investigate basic composition properties and the integration of protocol-modifying operators in our model. Sect. 5 discusses related work. Finally, we conclude and discuss future work in Sect. 6.

2   Motivation: Trust Management in P2P Applications

In order to motivate that expressive protocols are useful and later illustrate our approach, we first consider peer-to-peer (P2P) architectures. P2P applications are distributed applications which are characterized by the importance of scalability and self-organization properties because of their typically very large user base, and the use of unstable and often low-bandwidth connections on the client but also server side [20].

The need for scalability and support for reorganization has led to the development of a large number of algorithms using P2P-specific protocols, among others, for routing, data replication, and trust management in such networks. Protocols are generally very useful for system-level applications (for recent work on protocols and protocol manipulations in system-level C applications and relevant references, see [5]). However, there is reason to believe that declarative protocol descriptions are particularly interesting in the context of P2P applications. In fact, these applications do not only require relations to be managed within a protocol but also among different instances of a protocol which are executing at the same time, *e.g.*, all instances of a protocol fetching different pieces of the same video. Furthermore, P2P applications are usefully implemented using components due to their size (note that components here may mean sets of strongly encapsulated C functions).

A specific algorithm for trust management in P2P networks to which protocols can usefully be applied has been proposed by Aberer and Despotovic [1]. Their approach can be summarized as follows. Trust is computed by a statistical analysis of past transactions of agents in a network. After each transaction, agents may register complaints which are stored in a distributed, partially-replicated, data structure which is organized into a virtual binary search tree. The evaluation of trustworthiness of an agent in the network is essentially done by searching for complaints about her. Moreover, the algorithm recursively searches for complaints about complaining agents in order to judge whether the latter could have attributed complaints maliciously. Without any further control, this recursive process would obviously traverse all of the network. The crucial property of this algorithm is that the search is "localized" by a cut-off heuristic consisting in judging an agent trustworthy when a certain number of agents yields a small enough number of complaints.

In order to illustrate our approach, we consider three specific (classes of) protocols which are part of this algorithm.

- *Optimizing Data Transfer.* A P2P application typically stores data (complaint data in the trust algorithm) in a partially-replicated manner. In such cases, data transfer may be sped up by first choosing faster connection links to duplicated data. (This is similar to the selection of the closest/fastest mirror before downloading a popular software distribution such as Debian Linux.) To this end, a protocol can be used which, optionally, first accesses a list of links suggested by the system to locations where data replicas are stored, and then repeatedly performs three operations: opening a connection, send/receive data to evaluate the available bandwidth to/from the current connection, and a close operation. Such a protocol can obviously be concisely described using a regular, *i.e.*, finite-state, protocol.
- *Trust Computation.* The algorithm for trust computation above essentially relies on a sequence of send operations of queries for trust information about an agent a_1 and the corresponding responses containing the requested data. This computation must be performed recursively because a response involving information returned from another agent a_2 results in a query about the

trustworthiness of a_2. A correct evaluation of trust needs the reception of all information in the right order (because the cut-off heuristic may rely on that order). Such a protocol can be concisely defined in terms of a context-free language mechanism for the specification of well-balanced nested structures.

– *Cut-off Heuristic.* It is frequently the case that heuristics which iteratively gather information from an (even small) number of neighboring nodes can be described (concisely) only using protocols of context-sensitive structure, *i.e.*, whose interaction structure is not even context-free. This is, *e.g.*, the case if an interaction structure involving four neighbors is equivalent to two interleaved nested structures involving different pairs of neighbors (because, in language-theoretic terms, the word $a^n b^m c^n d^m$ cannot be generated by a context-free grammar).

In the following we investigate support for the definition of protocols of such structure and their property-based manipulation.

3   Components with Non-regular Protocols

There are by now a number of proposals of component models with explicit protocols, *e.g.*, CwEP [7,6] and SOFA [15]. These models augment traditional component interfaces consisting of sets of method signatures by one or several protocols. Furthermore, some additional protocol state may be present, *e.g.*, component identities in the case of CwEP.

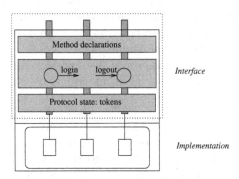

Fig. 1. Structure of components with non-regular protocols

In this paper, we consider an integration of non-regular protocols introduced by Puntigam [17]. Our components have the structure shown in Fig. 1. Components consist of an interface and a set of method implementations. The interface consists of three parts: a set of method signatures, a protocol declaration, and an additional protocol state consisting of a set of tokens used as guards governing method application. Besides being able to define more expressive protocols than regular ones, we are also interested in providing declarative means for the description of such protocols.

3.1   Syntax and Informal Semantics

Concretely, we propose to define component interfaces in terms of the language generated by the grammar shown in Fig. 2. Such interfaces consist of a signature, a protocol, and token declarations. We will now discuss the form and informal semantics of these parts in turn.

The *signature* defines a set of method signatures each of which consists of five constituents: the first three are the standard return types, method identifier, and formal parameter declarations, respectively. The last two constituents define the method's dependencies on the token state: the fourth constituent specifies the tokens which must be present in the token state for the method to be applicable, in this case the specified tokens are removed from the state; the fifth constituent specifies the tokens to be added to the token state when the method is executed. Dependencies on method applicability expressed in terms of tokens enable non-regular relationships within a protocol: it is, in particular possible to make the application of a method call depend on a specific but arbitrary number of tokens, which includes '∞' representing an infinite number.

A *protocol* is a (parenthesized) sequence or choice of primitive constituents, which are method call expressions or nested expressions. A method call is of the standard form *id(params)*. Method calls are executed asynchronously, synchronization is to be performed by coordination between different components. A nested protocol consists of a protocol delimited by an entering call and an exit call. Note that nested expressions are the only protocol expressions which can be named. This enables balanced nesting to be expressed on the protocol level without forgoing automatic verification of composition properties. We will come back to this issue in the discussion of a formalization of the protocol language below.

Finally, the *token state* defines an initial set of tokens, *i.e.*, a multiset consisting of different token ids of different multiplicity. Furthermore, the declaration of the token state may define symbolic ids for tokens.

Interface	::=	Signature Protocol Token
Signature	::=	(MethodSig)*
MethodSig	::=	Type Id(Formals) [Toks] [Toks]
Toks	::=	(Id[×nat])*
Protocol, P	::=	Prim*	P⋆	P+	[P]	(P ∨ P)	(P)
Prim	::=	Call	NestedExp
Call	::=	Id(Actuals)
NestedExp	::=	[Id =] nestedExp(Call,P,Call)	Id
Token	::=	(Id[×nat] (Id = Id×nat)*)*

Fig. 2. Syntax of non-regular protocols

Note that while the increased expressiveness of the protocols generated by this language is due to the dependence of method acceptance on tokens, the language includes declarative support for regular and context-free structures.

3.2   P2P Trust Management Revisited

We are now ready to formulate the protocols for P2P trust management introduced in Sect. 2 using our language:

- *Optimizing Data Transfer.* A protocol to evaluate the bandwidth of connections can be defined by the following protocol (to improve readability, we take the liberty in the following to separate primitive protocol expressions by semicolons.):

  [init;] (open; send ; receive ; close ; calculateBandwith)+

  This protocol defines sequences of an optional initialization, followed by repeated sequences of bidirectional communications followed by a bandwidth computation using the finite-state constructions of our protocol language.
- *Trust Computation.* Gathering of trust data up to a point when sufficient data has been collected (as determined by a suitable heuristic) can be defined as follows:

  (G = nestedExp(sendQuery,G,getData); isSufficient)+

  Through the use of the construct nestedExp, this protocol makes explicit that acquisition of trust-related data can be recursive (in which case it must be done in a well-balanced manner).
- *Cut-off Heuristic.* Certain protocols which are not of context-free structure or which are difficult to describe using context-free structures can be defined (easily) using token-based protocols. As a simple example of the latter case consider a heuristic which prunes the trust data acquisition process by limiting the nesting depth to a fixed but arbitrary depth n. This heuristic can be defined by the following protocol:

  t×n
  void sendQuery(query) [t] []
  (G = nestedExp(sendQuery,G,getData) ; isSufficient)+

  This protocol first declares an appropriate number of tokens. The signature declaration of method sendQuery states that it can only be applied in presence of a token. Furthermore the token is removed since it is not re-injected in the token state (the last signature argument is empty). Therefore, the nested expression in the last line will be applicable exactly n times after which the token state will be empty.

3.3   Outline of a Formal Semantics

The protocol language shown in Fig. 1 has been designed such that its semantics can be defined by a translation into the notion of non-regular process types introduced by Puntigam [17]. This gives us a precise formal framework without reinventing the wheel. Furthermore, we can reuse notions of type correctness and subtyping on process types to investigate basic properties of component-based systems, in particular, compatibility and substitutability of components.

Since the contributions of this paper are the protocol language, motivation of its usefulness (rather than its formal definition), and mechanisms for the manipulation of such protocols, we limit the presentation of the formal underpinnings to the following two issues: a brief overview of non-regular process types as introduced by Puntigam, and an analysis of how the protocol language defined by Fig. 1 can be translated into non-regular process types.

Non-Regular Process Types. The basic notions of non-regular process types (henceforth also referred to simply as types) can be summarized as follows. Types, denoted by $\{\overline{m}\}[\overline{s}]$, consist of a set of (static) message signatures m and a (dynamic) token state s. The token state is composed of descriptors of the form $x^{p|q}$ indicating that p copies of token x exist and that the set of tokens x has been divided q times. Using divisions, tokens can be passed to collaborators, which at the same time updates the types of the sending and receiving component accordingly. The dividend p can mainly be a natural number, '∞', which represents an infinite number of tokens, or an addition of two dividends. The latter case permits to gather new tokens from a collaborator; analogously to a division operation, this operation results in an update of the types of the sending and receiving component. A divisor $q = 0$ indicates that all tokens are present in the current token state.

Message signatures, denoted by $m(\overline{t})(\overline{p})[\overline{i}][\overline{o}]$, consist of an identifier m, type parameters t associated to the message, types p for formal parameters, and incoming and outgoing tokens $\overline{i}, \overline{o}$. Message acceptance is defined similarly as introduced previously: for a method to be acceptable, each state descriptor $x^{p|q} \in \overline{i}$ must be present in the dynamic token state of the enclosing object and if $q = 0$ that descriptor must be the only one relating to x in the token state. The token state is then updated by removing the tokens from $\overline{i}$ and adding the tokens in $\overline{o}$. In this way types keep track of exact numbers of tokens and allow them to be passed around between objects.

The type-checking algorithm from [16] can also be used for the static checking of non-regular process types. Hence, conditions involving exact token numbers (including ∞) are statically checkable. Note, however, that the type system of [17] allows such conditions to be applied only to components which contain all token expressions of the types occurring in such conditions. In cases where the underlying language does not explicitly support such types, they can be passed along and checked during runtime.

Translation of the protocol language of Fig. 1. The protocol language shown in Fig. 1 has been designed in order to be based on the formalism of non-regular process types.

Our notions of token state and token manipulation through methods whose signatures make token manipulations explicit are essentially defined as in Puntigam's approach.

Our language has two features which have no direct counterpart in non-regular types: regular expressions and nested expressions. Both of these can, however, be expressed using types. Two essential constituents of the corresponding translation are the following:

- Repetition of a method call can simply be defined using a token which is consumed from and immediately re-injected in the token state to enable the following call in the repetition.

$$m\star := \{m()(p)[x^{1|0}][x^{1|0}]\}[x^{1|0}]$$

  Hence, m's token state initially contains one x. A call to m (with arguments conforming to p) requires one occurrence of x, which is removed from the token state as part of method acceptance but immediately re-injected.
- Nesting can be defined by a type using tokens to count method invocations. The main part of the corresponding translation is the following:

  nestedExp(m,ϵ,n) :=
$$\{m()(\_)[x^{1|0}][x^{1|0}, y], n()(\_)[x^{1|0}, y][x^{2|0}], n()(\_)[x^{2|0}, y][x^{2|0}]\}[x^{1|0}]$$

  Here, m generates tokens y which are consumed by n. Furthermore, once the first n has been accepted, m cannot be accepted anymore because no state $x^{1|0}$ is present in the token state anymore. Technically, this is achieved by using the dividends 1 and 2, which, intuitively speaking, separate execution of such a nested expression in two exclusive phases.

4   Protocol-Based Component Composition

One of the main advantages of the introduction of explicit protocols in components is that composition of components can be defined in terms of protocol composition. This enables, in particular, reasoning about black-box component compositions which is almost impossible in the case of interfaces consisting of method signatures only (since almost no knowledge about component implementations is available).

In this section we present first results relating to (properties of) the composition of components based on non-regular protocols. Since there is very little directly related work, it is reasonable to start from results developed in the context of components with regular protocols. To this end we have studied the non-regular case by leveraging our previous work on the property-based composition of components based on finite-state protocols [8,6]. Concretely, we present how two different issues related to properties of component composition carry over (or not) from the regular to the non-regular case:

- *Basic composition properties*: compatibility and substitutability, which are fundamental composition properties in component-based systems, have to be defined differently in the non-regular case compared to finite-state protocols.
- *Composition operators*: we consider the definition of operators modifying the structure of a protocol as well as operators modifying the protocol state.

4.1   Basic Composition Properties

In component-based programming two fundamental composition properties are traditionally considered: *compatibility* (the technical notion ensuring that components flawlessly work with each other) and *substitutability* (which addresses the question if a component can be substituted for another one without causing faulty service provision). Approaches which use finite-state protocols to make explicit part of the semantics of objects or components typically employ equivalence and containment relationships over sets of traces and failures to define such composition properties [13].

In contrast to finite-state languages, no decision procedures are known (or can even exist) for these correctness notions in the case of context-free or even more expressive languages. Non-regular process types enjoy, however, two decidable relations, *type equivalence* and *subtyping*, which can be used to similar effect. In fact, if t_1 is equivalent to (a subtype of) t_2 the set of traces generated by t_1 is equal to (larger than) the trace set of t_2. Compatibility between collaborators can therefore be expressed in terms of compatibility of the manipulation of token states and type equivalence. Substitutability can be proven by using the subtype relation and type equivalence.

To give an example of the usefulness of these type-based relationships for substitutability of components, reconsider the cut-off heuristic introduced in the context of trust computation in P2P networks. Different cut-off heuristics which explore the complaint data base to different depths can be proved to obey subtype relationships, thus ensuring that deeper-reaching heuristics are substitutable for shallower ones (reflecting the fact that the former will yield better trust evaluations than the latter).

An important property of the type-based relationships is that they are defined for *deterministic types* only. Informally speaking, deterministic types are characterized by having a unique follow state for any application of a method declared within the type. The protocol language defined by Fig. 2 has been designed to yield only deterministic types. In particular, all types corresponding to protocols discussed in Sect. 3 are deterministic.

4.2   Composition Operators for Non-regular Protocols

In a model of components with protocol-based interfaces, composition of components is naturally expressed through composition of protocols. Furthermore, component composition can then be supported by a set of protocol-composition operators which preserve (to a reasonable degree) fundamental composition properties, such as component substitutability.

In previous work [7,6], we substantiated these claims for components with regular protocols. In particular, we have defined a set of operators for the modification of the static structure of finite-state automata and operators for the modification of a dynamic state associated to regular protocols. In the following we present an analysis of how such operators can be integrated into a model of components with non-regular protocols.

Before considering concrete operators, let us note that there is a fundamental difference between the regular case and the non-regular one: protocol structure is much more explicit in finite-state automata than in the non-regular process types. The former directly represent execution traces through the automata structure, while a non-regular type $\{\overline{m}\}[\overline{t}]$ represents traces only indirectly through an inductive construction. Furthermore, it would be very unwieldy to define the operators directly in terms of non-regular traces because the notions of equivalence and subtyping are constructively defined only on types not sets of traces. This issue is alleviated by using a protocol language such as that defined in Fig. 2 because its constructs directly correspond to trace sets; an example giving evidence for this claim can be found in the discussion of the definition of start states for the union composition operator below. (We strongly believe that declarative protocols even provide a reasonable solution to the issue. This is the subject of on-going work, though, and not further discussed here.)

Structural Operators. We first consider the definition of three basic and fundamental structural operators, namely "union" (which, informally speaking, allows to add at a certain state new branches to protocols), "concatenation" of protocols, and general "insertion" of a protocol into another one.

Since process types do not represent the trace sets of protocols directly as explained above, the definition of structural operators based on non-regular process types therefore either has to be limited to structural properties directly expressible on the type level or includes rather complex proofs involving the trace sets generated by types.

It turns out that the three basic operators can be defined quite adequately in terms of non-regular process types:

- A union operation, denoted $\{\overline{m_1}\}[\overline{t_1}] \cup_s \{\overline{m_2}\}[\overline{t_2}]$, which adds a new protocol (*e.g.*, a new branch) to an existing protocol at a state s, can be directly defined on the type level. Informally, the method signatures and token states have to be merged, *i.e.*, the result can be defined as $\{\overline{m_1} \oplus_m \overline{m_2}\}[\overline{t_1} \oplus_t \overline{t_2}]$. However, the functions $\oplus_m, \oplus_t$ cannot simply be defined to be multiset union because two technical problems have to be resolved regarding the merge:
  - Interference of the new parts and old parts of the resulting protocol has to be avoided: when the new part is executed the state related to the old part should not be affected. This can be achieved by an appropriate renaming of the methods and tokens of the newly added protocol *and* introduction of an adapter definition translating new names in case of communication with collaborators expecting old ones.
  - The definition of the starting state s is not obvious. In the case of regular protocols the state typically is one explicitly enumerated in the definition of the corresponding finite-state automata and related to other states by the automata's transition relation. For non-regular process types, the state would have to be defined in terms of elements of the trace set generated by the original protocol, however, only the token state is directly accessible given the type definition and tokens do not represent states meaningful *w.r.t.* to positions in method sequences.

One approach to (partially) solve this problem is to introduce new tokens and modify methods of the type such that they emit these new tokens in order to mark specific positions as part of the type's token state. Note that this technique is strongly supported by our declarative protocol language. The translation, *e.g.*, of a regular repetition such as ⋆m into a non-regular type, can automatically yield position markers useful to define protocol states for composition operators.

– Concatenation can be treated similarly to the union operation in that it can be defined as a union operation on final states. Its definition thus reduces to the identification of final states which can frequently be done by using specific tokens as end markers.

– Insertion can also be treated using the means above, requiring mainly identification of start and end states within protocols.

In order to conclude the discussion of these operators, let us note that the properties of these operators carry over from the regular case (cf. [7,6]) to the non-regular one. For instance, a protocol resulting from an application of the union operator above can be substituted for any of the two original protocols from the state s on.

State-manipulating Operators. A second group of protocol-related operators allows the modification of the dynamic state of protocols. These include protocol-modifying operators directly working on the protocol state but also operators modifying the program execution and the protocol state at the same time. In the following, we briefly discuss the integration into our model of two (classes) of such operators which are analogous to operators put forward in the context of components with regular protocols [7,8].

A first class of operators directly modifies the token state $\bar{t}$ of a type $\{\overline{m}\}[\bar{t}]$. Some of these operators introduce new tokens, *e.g.*, to support the implementation of the structural operators discussed above. In this case, compatibility and substitutability properties of the protocol are preserved. Other such operators modify existing tokens, thus modifying the compatibility and substitutability properties of the corresponding protocols. The extent to which such properties still hold then have to be investigated on a case by case basis.

Another class of state-manipulating operators provide for the "spontaneous" emission of messages without directly modifying the underlying protocol. Such operators are useful, *e.g.*, in order to adapt a component temporarily. In the case of the trust management algorithm for P2P applications, such an operator could be used, *e.g.*, to temporarily augment the depth to which the underlying distributed complaint data base is explored. Composition properties of such operators also have to be proved on a case by case basis.

5   Related Work

There is little directly related work, *i.e.*, work on protocols more expressive than regular ones and which, in particular, consider their constructive use as part of a component model. One notable exception is recent work by Puntigam [18] who proposes an integration of non-regular process types into a Java-like language and discusses issues of such types related to hot-swapping of components. However, he does not consider a more declarative language for protocol definition nor composition operators as discussed in this paper. Another interesting approach is Reussner's work on counter-constraint finite state machines [19]. This approach is close to our approach in terms of expressiveness: such automata allow the definition of certain non-regular (even some context-sensitive) protocols, similar to the approach presented here. The exact relationship w.r.t. expressiveness between our approach and his approach is an interesting open research question. However, Reussner does not consider a user-level language like that presented here, does not provide an underlying typing discipline, and does not consider composition operators. Finally, another approach which goes beyond regular protocols is that by Pavel et al [14], who endow components with protocols based on symbolic transition systems (STS). However, that work does not include static property support as provided by non-regular process types and does not consider composition operators.

The work presented in this paper has been motivated by a lack of expressiveness of the (many) approaches using finite-state protocols. However, as exploited in this paper, work on regular protocols is still relevant for the non-regular case w.r.t. the kinds of properties useful for component-based programming, be it properties of protocol composition operators (e.g., those presented in [7,6]) or adaptation properties (see, e.g., [25,21,24]).

There are several approaches using aspect-oriented techniques (in the sense introduced by Kiczales [10]) to manipulate protocols, which share many of the problems the present paper raises related to the definition of protocol-modifying operators. Walter and Viggers [23] propose an aspect language using context-free grammars to define patterns to be matched against Java source code. Their protocol language therefore is more restricted than ours. Furthermore, they do not consider any issues related to component encapsulation. Recently, we have worked [8,6] on an aspect language for the manipulation of regular protocols. This work defines, in particular, an aspect language for protocol manipulations. Furthermore, it provides a discussion of several properties over regular protocols which are subject to aspect weaving: in particular, preservation of finitude of protocols in the presence of operators modifying the structure of protocols and techniques for the analysis of interaction properties of aspects over components with regular protocols.

There is a large body of work using specification means for non-regular protocols in the context of component-based programming. As two examples among many more let us cite the work by Braccialia et al., who use protocol specifications based on the π-calculus in order to semi-automatically synthesize component adapters, and work using symbolic transition systems (STS) for component analysis [12]. Such approaches feature notions of protocols which are even more expressive than that considered in this paper but cannot be used constructively and, for a large part, do not support automatic checking of composition properties.

6   Conclusion and Further Work

In this paper we have presented the integration of a notion of non-regular protocols in component interfaces. Concretely, we have presented three contributions. We have motivated that such protocols naturally arise in P2P applications and that our approach allows the concise formulation of the required protocols. We have defined a protocol language for non-regular protocols including declarative constructs for regular and context-free protocols. Furthermore, we have outlined a translation of the protocol language into Puntigam's calculus of non-regular process types. Finally, we have discussed composition properties in our setting as well as the integration of several protocol composition operators.

This paper presents a first step towards the definition of a component model with non-regular protocols and much interesting work remains to do. As to the protocol language, the current proposal provides a limited set of declarative constructs (nested and regular expressions). This set of constructs should be extended, thus reducing the use of token manipulations in protocol definitions. As to the composition properties, operators should be more deeply explored and more specific operators defined, *e.g.*, for component adaptation. Finally, there are open question concerning the underlying formal framework, in particular its support for composition properties relevant for components and its efficient realization.

Aknowledgements. The author would like to thank the anonymous reviewers and his colleagues Jacques Noyé and Sebastien Pavel for their many helpful remarks.

References

1. K. Aberer and Z. Despotovic. Managing trust in a Peer-2-Peer information system. In Henrique Paques, Ling Liu, and David Grossman, editors, *Proceedings of the Tenth International Conference on Information and Knowledge Management (CIKM-01)*, pages 310–317, New York, November 5–10 2001. ACM Press.
2. E. Bruneton, T. Coupaye, M. Leclercq, V. Quéma, and J.-B. Stefani. An open component model and its support in Java. In I. Crnkovic et al., editors, *Proc. of the 7th Int. Symposium on Component-Based Software Engineering (CBSE 2004)*, volume 3054 of *LNCS*, pages 7–22. Springer-Verlag, 2004.
3. L. de Alfaro and T. A. Henzinger. Interface automata. In V. Gruhn, editor, *Proc. of the Joint 8th European Software Engineering Conference and 9th ACM SIGSOFT Symposium on the Foundation of Software Engeneering (ESEC/FSE-01)*, volume 26, 5 of *SOFTWARE ENGINEERING NOTES*, pages 109–120, New York, September 10–14 2001. ACM Press.
4. L.G. DeMichiel et al. *Enterprise JavaBeans^{TM} Specification*. SUN Microsystems, November 2003. Version 2.1, Final Release.
5. R. Douence, T. Fritz, N. Loriant, J.-M. Menaud, M. Ségura, and M. Südholt. An expressive aspect language for system applications with Arachne. In *Proc. of 4th International Conference on Aspect-Oriented Software Development (AOSD'05)*. ACM Press, March 2005.

6. A. Farías. *Un modèle de composants avec des protocoles explicites.* PhD thesis, École des Mines de Nantes/Université de Nantes, December 2003.

7. A. Farías and M. Südholt. On components with explicit protocols satisfying a notion of correctness by construction. In *International Symposium on Distributed Objects and Applications (DOA)*, volume 2519 of *LNCS*, pages 995–1006, 2002.

8. A. Farías and M. Südholt. Integrating protocol aspects with software components to address dependability concerns. Technical Report 04/6/INFO, École des Mines de Nantes, November 2004.

9. D. Harel. Statecharts: A visual formalism for complex system. *Science of Computer Programming*, 8(3):231–274, March 1987.

10. G. Kiczales et al. Aspect-Oriented Programming. In M. Aksit and S. Matsuoka, editors, *Proc. of the 11th European Conference on Object-Oriented Programming (ECOOP)*, volume 1241 of *LNCS*, pages 220–242. Springer-Verlag, 1997.

11. P. Kruchten. *Rational Unified Process: an Introduction.* Addison-Wesley, Reading, Massachusetts, USA, 1998.

12. O. Maréchal, P. Poizat, and J.-C. Royer. Checking Asynchronously Communicating Components Using Symbolic Transition Systems. In Z. Tari R. Meersman and al., editors, *Proc. of Distributed Objects and Applications (DOA'04)*, volume 3291 of *LNCS*, pages 1502–1519. Springer-Verlag, 2004.

13. O. Nierstrasz. Regular types for active objects. In *Proceedings of the Conference on Object-Oriented Programming Systems, Languages, and Applications (OOPSLA)*, volume 28(10) of *ACM SigPlan Notices*, pages 1–15. ACM Press, October 1993.

14. S. Pavel, J. Noyé, P. Poizat, and J.-C. Royer. Java implementation of a component model with explicit symbolic protocols. In *Proceedings of the 4th International Workshop on Software Composition (SC'05)*, LNCS. Springer-Verlag, April 2005. To appear.

15. F. Plasil and S. Visnovsky. Behavior protocols for software components. In *Transactions on Software Engineering*. IEEE, January 2002.

16. F. Puntigam. Coordination requirements expressed in types for active objects. In Mehmet Akşit and Satoshi Matsuoka, editors, *ECOOP'97—Object-Oriented Programming*, volume 1241 of *Lecture Notes in Computer Science*, pages 367–388. Springer-Verlag, 1997.

17. F. Puntigam. Non-regular process types. In P. Amestoy et al., editors, *Proceedings of the 5th European Conference on Parallel Processing (Euro-Par'99)*, number 1685 in LNCS, Toulouse, France, September 1999. Springer-Verlag.

18. F. Puntigam. State information in statically checked interfaces. 8th Int. WS on Component-Oriented Programming at ECOOP, July 2003.

19. R. H. Reussner. Counter-constraint finite state machines: A new model for resource-bounded component protocols. In B. Grosky, F. Plasil, and A. Krenek, editors, *Proc. of the 29th Annual Conference in Current Trends in Theory and Practice of Informatics (SOFSEM 2002)*, Milovy, Tschechische Republik, volume 2540 of *LNCS*. Springer-Verlag, November 2002.

20. M. Ripeanu, I. Foster, and A. Iamnitchi. Mapping the Gnutella network: Properties of large-scale peer-to-peer systems and implications for system design. *IEEE Internet Computing Journal*, 6(1), September 25 2002. Special issue on peer-to-peer networking.

21. H. W. Schmidt and R. Reussner. Generating adapters for concurrent component protocol synchronisation. In *Proc. of the 5th IFIP International conference on Formal Methods for Open Object-based Distributed Systems*, pages 213–229. Kluwer, March 2002.

22. J. C. Seco and L. Caires. A basic model of typed components. In *Proc. of ECOOP*, volume 1850 of *LNCS*, pages 108–128. Springer-Verlag, 2000.
23. R. J. Walker and K. Viggers. Implementing protocols via declarative event patterns. In *Proceedings of the ACM SIGSOFT International Symposium on Foundations of Software Engineering (FSE-12)*, 2004.
24. B. Wydaeghe. *PACOSUITE — Component Composition Based on Composition Patterns and Usage Scenarios*. PhD thesis, Vrije Universiteit Brussel (VUB), November 2001.
25. D. M. Yellin and R. E. Strom. Protocol specifications and component adaptors. *ACM Transactions of Programming Languages and Systems*, 19(2):292–333, March 1997.

A Java Implementation of a Component Model with Explicit Symbolic Protocols

Sebastian Pavel[1], Jacques Noyé[1], Pascal Poizat[2], and Jean-Claude Royer[1]

[1] OBASCO project, École des Mines de Nantes-INRIA,LINA,
4 rue Alfred Kastler, 44307 Nantes cedex 3, France
{Sebastian.Pavel, Jacques.Noye, Jean-Claude.Royer}@emn.fr
[2] LaMI, UMR 8042 CNRS-Université d'Évry Val d'Essonne, Genopole,
Tour Évry 2, 523 place des terrasses de l'Agora, 91000 Évry, France
poizat@lami.univ-evry.fr

Abstract. Component-Based Software Engineering (CBSE) has now emerged as a discipline for system development. An important issue is to fill the gap between high-level models (needed for analysis) and implementation. This paper describes a component model with explicit symbolic protocols based on Symbolic Transition Systems (STSs), and its implementation in Java. This implementation relies on controllers that encapsulate protocols and channels devoted to (possibly remote) communications between components.

Keywords: CBSE, Behavioural IDL, Explicit Protocols, Symbolic Transition Systems, Java, Controllers, Channels.

1 Introduction

With the increase in complexity of software systems, Component-Based Software Engineering (CBSE) has emerged as a discipline that yields promising results such as trusted and Off-The-Shelf components (COTS), improved component reusability, semi- or automatic composition and adaptation of components into architectures, better middleware, and so on.

The first important issue when designing a component model is related to the definition of the component *interfaces* using Interface Description Languages (IDLs). This has been initially addressed by industrial component infrastructures to statically (*i.e.*, at compile time) generate skeletons and stubs for distributed components. More recently, this issue has turned to be at the core of the most challenging issues in CBSE: component validation and trusted components, (dynamic) adaptation, negotiation and choreography. The limit of IDLs based on signature types has now been demonstrated [27]. For instance, type correct communicating components may deadlock because they do not have compatible protocols. Hence, it is now widely accepted that IDLs have to take into account *behavioural protocols*, yielding Behavioural IDLs (BIDLs). These protocols may be used either as a piece of documentation for the components, in a design-by-contract process, to compose and check connections between components or even

T. Gschwind, U. Aßmann, and O. Nierstrasz (Eds.): SC 2005, LNCS 3628, pp. 115–124, 2005.
© Springer-Verlag Berlin Heidelberg 2005

build adapters [8,27] when component interfaces do not match. Several formal models dealing with such IDLs and protocols have been proposed. However, as components exchange data using their provided and required services, formal models have to take data into account while managing potential state-explosion problems.

In this paper, we suggest using Symbolic Transition Systems [7,10,15] (STSs) as the basis of a BIDL. This expressive formalism makes it possible to control state explosion thanks to the use of guards and typed parameters associated to the transitions. We show how STSs can be used as explicit protocols in a hierarchical component model supporting multiple interfaces with heterogeneous services (synchronous and asynchronous communications). We present the implementation principles of the model in Java whereby the code of a primitive component is synthesized from an STS protocol and Java code. A controller intercepts the communications and calls the related service of the inner Java code according to the protocol. The subcomponents of a compound component communicate via channels dealing with the guarded synchronous and asynchronous communications.

The paper is organized as follows. Section 2 describes our component model. Then Sect. 3 explains how our model can be implemented in Java to deal with explicit protocols and explicit component binding mechanisms. Section 4 presents related approaches and Sect. 5 concludes.

2   STS-Oriented Component Model

Like any component model, our model builds on the ADL ontology [19]: architectures or configurations made of components (with ports) and connectors (with roles), and bindings between component ports and connector roles.

The specificities of our model are: heterogeneous interfaces incorporating typed services of different kinds, explicit behavioural protocols, and the use of Symbolic Transition Systems. We rely on a simple binding mechanism rather than on complex connectors. For the time being, we only consider one-to-one, one-way messages. We are also dealing only with static architectures. Our syntax for interfaces was inspired by various component graphical notations, mainly from the Olan ADL [5] (for the port symbols) and from process algebras such as LOTOS [25] (for the input/output event schemes).

Symbolic Transition Systems (STS) [7,15] have initially been developed as a solution to the state and transition explosion problem in value-passing process algebras using substitutions associated to states and symbolic values in transition labels. Our STSs (see example in Fig. 2) are a generalisation of these, associating a symbolic state and transition system with a data type description. This description may be given using algebraic specifications [10,23], model-oriented specifications [4] or even Java classes. STSs can be related to statecharts (see [22] for details) but are simpler as far as semantics is concerned. They also improve readability and abstraction of behavioural descriptions and makes it possible to control the state and transition explosion problems.

2.1   Architecture Example

In order to illustrate our proposal, we present a simplified flight ticket reservation system. The reservation system (see Fig. 1) contains a Company component, a Bank component, and a Counter component. The Company is responsible for proposing the available flights corresponding to a particular request. The Bank manages the bank accounts of the clients. The Counter is the most important component as it receives the requests from clients and then coordinates the search, confirmation (by interacting with the Company), and payment (by calling the Bank services) of the flight. As a coordinator, the Counter exposes three interfaces: bookingIntf, paymentIntf and orderingIntf. While the first two interfaces are used to connect the Counter to the Company and the Bank, respectively, orderingIntf is used to interact with the clients. Here we omit service types for conciseness. Boxes correspond to synchronous services and circles to asynchronous ones. Black symbols denote required services (emissions) and white ones denote provided services (receipts).

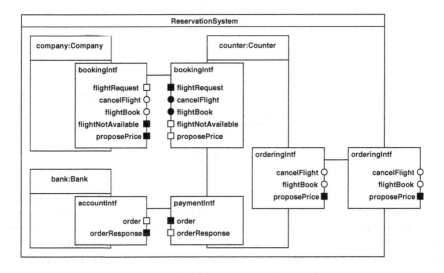

Fig. 1. A Simplified Ticket Reservation System

Once connected, the Company, the Bank, and the Counter form a compound component called ReservationSystem. A client component does not have to know the internals of this component. It will only communicate through the interface exposed by ReservationSystem. The interaction between a client and the system is actually implemented within the Counter component, the exposed interface is orderingIntf. Once the architecture has been built, all requests coming from a client are transferred to the orderingIntf in the Counter.

2.2   Primitive Component Protocol

In order to facilitate the understanding of STS protocols associated to components we use a graphical description of STSs. The protocol described in Fig. 2
represents the allowed behaviour associated to the **Company** component. The
protocol consists of three states and several transitions between these states
corresponding to the messages that are received and emitted to and from the
component. In addition, the protocol specifies the message ordering. For example, a booking (**flightBook**) or cancellation (**cancelFlight**) message cannot
be exchanged before a **proposePrice** message is received. The **flightBook** and
cancelFlight messages are guarded. They will be processed only if the corresponding guard, a bracketed boolean expression depending on message parameters, evaluates to true.

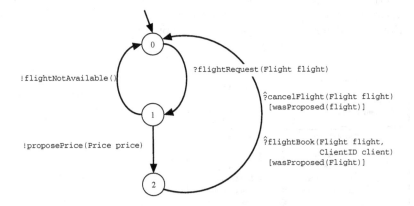

Fig. 2. The Company STS Protocol

A ? character denotes the reception of a message and a ! character the sending of a message. A ^ character further distinguishes asynchronous messages from
synchronous messages. Graphical descriptions of protocols are useful for human
understanding of dynamic systems. However, automated computation requires
a textual representation. We have defined a minimal component language [20]
based on Java to describe the interfaces and the protocol of a basic component.

A primitive component results from the combination of an STS protocol and
existing Java code (henceforth referred to as a *bare component*). One important
issue is the compatibility or coherence between the bare component intrinsic
protocol (*i.e.*, the execution protocol) and the externally-defined STS protocol.
There are different ways to address this issue. It is possible to provide a method
that extracts a compatible data type from the STS description [23]. But the bare
component and the protocol can also be developed separately. However they
have to be both syntactically and behaviourally compatible. Behavioural compatibility has been addressed in process algebra [6] and in state machines [3,27]
approaches.

3 Implementation of the Model

The general idea of the implementation is depicted in Fig. 3. The purpose is to attach an STS protocol to an already defined bare component. After attaching the protocol, the result is another component (henceforth referred to as a *controlled component*) with the same functionality as the initial one and in addition a mechanism to check and impose the specified protocol. A bare component would connect into an architecture using simple binding mechanisms (if the correspondent is local) or RMI connections (if the correspondent is remote). A controlled component would connect using a special connection based on communication channels as we will see later in this section.

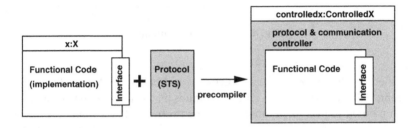

Fig. 3. General Idea

The guidelines to follow in order to implement a component in Java are discussed in Sect. 3.1. Our approach to attach a given protocol to a given component is described in Sect. 3.2. Finally, Sect. 3.3 describes how channels are used to connect components in an architecture.

3.1 Bare Components

In order to strictly encapsulate a bare component, we use an approach similar to the one presented in [2]. A package is declared for each component. It includes a class representing the interface of the component. This class is the only public class in the package and only methods of this class can be public. As a result, the internal classes and methods are invisible from outside the component boundaries. The clear advantage of such an approach is that the access to a component is possible only through its explicitly specified interface, without imposing any strong condition on the details of the implementation. At runtime, a bare component instance may be composed of one or more objects, one or more active entities, etc.

3.2 Protocol Implementation

To integrate protocols expressed as STSs, we have identified two major approaches. First, we could modify the code of a bare component so that it behaves

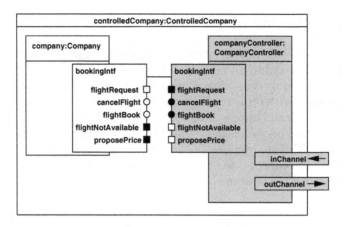

Fig. 4. Controlled Company

as specified by the protocol. One solution would be to use Aspect-Oriented Programming [16], or bytecode altering techniques [9] to create a new Java class hierarchy implementing the component with the protocol. The second approach does not modify the initial code but rather creates a framework of classes around the initial code. Once instantiated, this framework will become a component (with the same functionality as the initial one) integrating the specified protocol.

We choose to implement our proposal by following the second approach (see Fig. 4). In order to associate a protocol to a component at runtime, we use a single, complementary active entity that plays the role of a controller for the component (hence the name *controlled component* for the association of a bare component and a protocol). The role of a controller is to: (i) intercept the messages sent or received by the actual component and (ii) decide whether these messages are either allowed or forbidden. This can be achieved by implementing the LogicalState pattern [14].

This pattern is implemented in two steps. First, all the possible states of the protocol are declared as private variables in the controller (a Java thread). Second, the actions to be taken when the component can receive a request (according to the protocol state) are defined in the run method. The actions to be taken when the component can send a message are defined in the methods implementing the required operation of the component.

Before actually forwarding a message, the controller entity has to implement two checks. The first check is related to the current state of the component (*i.e.*, the component has to be in a state that allows the emission or reception of that particular message). The second is the guard check. The guard is a conditional expression implemented as a boolean operation in the bare component. While the two conditions are not true, the message is not forwarded, and the execution is possibly blocked. If the two checks succeed, the message is forwarded to the bare component (for an incoming message) or to the correspondent controlled component (for an outgoing message) and the current state of the protocol is

updated. Outgoing messages are transmitted by employing a special entity called
`channel`.

3.3 Channel Connections

In order to connect components into an architecture, we follow [2] and employ
channels. A channel represents a one-to-one anonymous connection mechanism.
It is also directed: messages flow from its *source* (where messages are sent) to
its *sink* (where messages are received). Channels can be synchronous or asynchronous, mobile, with conditions, etc. In addition to its coordination role, a
channel can be used in more sophisticated connection schemes. In this paper,
we consider that all the components are local and that the architecture is static.
However, a channel can also be employed to connect remote component instances, possibly dynamically created at runtime.

To connect two interfaces we need two different channels. One channel is
oriented from interface I1 to interface I2. The second channel is oriented from I2
to I1. Created within the scope of the compound component, the channel ends are
transmitted as parameters to the communicating components (subcomponents)
at instantiation time. The fact that the channels are not exported outside the
scope of the compound component ensures that they are exclusively used by the
connected components.

In our implementation, we have created a class called `Channel`. This class
implements two interfaces `WriteChannel` and `ReadChannel`. The `WriteChannel`
interface defines the operation `write` related to the channel source. The
`ReadChannel` interface defines the operations `read`, `commit`, and `cancel` related
to the channel sink. The execution behaves differently depending on the communication type. If the communication is synchronous, the sender blocks on the
`write` method until the receiver reads (and commits or cancels, depending on
the evaluation of the associated guard) the message. If the communication is
asynchronous, the `write` method blocks until the message is saved into a buffer,
built inside the channel entity. Our scenario considers only local applications. In
case of a distributed environment, a solution like the one given in [2] could be
easily reused.

While the `Channel` class can be reused as is in many different connections,
the controller classes have to be created for each bare component in the architecture. This can be done manually of course, but an automated solution is
under development. In fact, the language used to define the interfaces and the
protocol of a component contains enough information to allow a tool to automatically create the required classes for an application. A pre-compiler based
on the SableCC [13] framework has been developed. The pre-compiler takes as
input the description of (either primitive or compound) component classes and
generates the necessary controller classes.

In terms of performance we expect that our implementation imposes some
overhead computation when the full power of the STSs (for instance guards) is
not required due (i) to employing the communication channels that reify messages, (ii) to the message interception and forwarding, and (iii) to guard evalua-

tion. Moreover, on reception, all asynchronous messages are initially saved into incoming buffers inside the controller entity. Optimizations are possible in some cases. For example, when components are located on the same machine, channels could be replaced by direct connections. If components employ only synchronous communication, the controller implementation can be simplified and some overhead computation and memory space could be saved.

4 Related Work

In the last decade, formal models with behavioural descriptions have been proposed either on their own [27,11,24] or in the context of software architectures [1,17]. However, if they propose different analysis mechanisms for component architectures, they do not address the issue of taking protocols into account within the implementation, which is a mandatory issue for seamless CBSE development.

In the concurrent object-oriented community, PROCOL [26] is one of the oldest proposals that deals with explicit protocols. PROCOL is a parallel C-based object-oriented language with communication based on one-way synchronous messages. As far as the protocols are concerned, PROCOL relies on rational expressions extended with variables and guards. Each object is implemented as a process within the Unix environment and communicates under the control of a unique arbiter. Action sequencing is implemented by a nondeterministic finite automaton that is equivalent (in the accepting language sense) to the regular expression protocol of the object. Apart from the graphical presentation, PROCOL protocols have the same expressive power as STSs.

In [18], the authors present techniques to relate concurrent Java programs with a behavioural description given in the FSP (Finite State Processus) process algebra. Rather than really taking into account FSP protocols within a programming language, their goal is to be able to use FSP in a development process and to analyse models of threaded concurrent Java programs before coding them.

In [12], the authors propose to integrate protocols within EJBs, at different levels. These protocols are given as labelled FSMs (Finite State Models) enriched by very specific data types (for instance, to handle lists of allowed receivers) and related guards. Our context of work is different: we consider a hierarchical component model, and our protocols are not limited to using a few specific data types.

SOFA [21] introduces the notion of interface, compound and primitive architectures as well as usual means to connect services between the subcomponents of an architecture. The description language introduces behavioural protocols and employs first-class connectors. The behaviour protocols are regular expressions denoting traces, i.e., sequences of events (required, provided, and internal calls). These protocols may be associated with an interface, a frame, and an architecture. [21] presents a model for the protocol-based description of hierarchical components. Regular expressions are concise but less readable than STSs. Another limitation is that they do not consider data types and conditions.

5 Conclusions

We have presented in this paper a hierarchical component model supporting multiple interfaces with asynchronous and synchronous services. The main feature of this model is the introduction of explicit protocols based on symbolic transition systems. Then, we have presented the principles of the implementation in Java of our model. A component corresponds to a controller encapsulating the STS part and a Java application provided with a well-defined component interface. The controller has the responsibility of intercepting communications and of triggering the right service on the inner Java code, depending on the state of the protocol. The communications are implemented thanks to channels, a construct providing benefits such as mobility, remote connections, and reusability. Channels are used in our implementation to ensure that a message arrives to its destination and also to notify the sender when the guard does not hold on the destination side.

Acknowledgment. This work was partly supported by the ACI Sécurité Informatique, DISPO project. We would also like to thank Mario Südholt and the anonymous reviewers for their comments.

References

1. R. J. Allen. *A formal approach to software architecture.* PhD thesis, Carnegie Mellon University, 1997.
2. F. Arbab, J. V. Guillen Scholten, F.S. de Boer, and M. M. Bonsangue. A channel-based coordination model for components. Technical report, Centruum voor Wiskunde en Informatica, 2002.
3. A. Arnold. *Finite transition systems.* Prentice-Hall, 1994.
4. C. Attiogbé, P. Poizat, and G. Salaün. Integration of formal datatypes within state diagrams. In *FASE 2003*, volume 2621 of *Lecture Notes in Computer Science*, pages 344–355. Springer-Verlag, 2003.
5. L. Bellissard, S. B. Atallah, A. Kerbrat, and M. Riveill. Component-based programming and application management with Olan. In J. Briot, J. Geib, and A. Yonezawa, editors, *Object-Based Parallel And Distributed Computation*, volume 1107 of *Lecture Notes in Computer Science*, pages 290–309. Springer-Verlag, Berlin, 1995.
6. J. A. Bergstra, A. Ponse, and S. A. Smolka, editors. *Handbook of Process Algebra.* Elsevier, 2001.
7. M. Calder, S. Maharaj, and C. Shankland. A modal logic for full LOTOS based on symbolic transition systems. *The Computer Journal*, 45(1):55–61, 2002.
8. C. Canal, J. M. Murillo, and P. Poizat, editors. *WCAT'2004 - Int. Workshop on Coordination and Adaptation Techniques for Software Entities*, 2004. Available at http://wcat04.unex.es.
9. S. Chiba. Load-time structural reflection in Java. In E. Bertino, editor, *Proceedings of the European Conference on Object-oriented Programming (ECOOP 2000)*, volume 1850 of *Lecture Notes in Computer Science*, pages 313–336, France, June 2000. Springer-Verlag.
10. C. Choppy, P. Poizat, and J.-C. Royer. A global semantics for views. In T. Rus, editor, *International Conference, AMAST 2000*, volume 1816 of *Lecture Notes in Computer Science*, pages 165–180. Springer-Verlag, 2000.

11. L. de Alfaro and T.A. Henzinger. Interface automata. In *Proceedings of the Joint 8th European Software Engineering Conference (ESEC) and 9th ACM SIGSOFT Symposium on the Foundations of Software Engineering (FSE-9)*, pages 109–120, Vienna, Austria, September 2001.

12. A. Farías, Y.-G. Guéhéneuc, and M. Südholt. Integrating behavioral protocols in Enterprise Java Beans. In K. Baclawski and H. Kilov, editors, *Eleventh OOPSLA Workshop on Behavioral Semantics: Serving the Customer*, pages 80–89, 2002.

13. E. Gagnon. *SableCC, An Object-Oriented Compiler Framework*. PhD thesis, School of Computer Science McGill University, Montreal, November 1998.

14. E. Gamma, R. Helm, R. Johnson, and J. Vlissides. *Design Patterns*. Addison Wesley Professional Computing Series. Addison Wesley, 1995.

15. A. Ingólfsdóttir and H. Lin. *A Symbolic Approach to Value-passing Processes*, chapter 7 in [6], pages 427–478. Elsevier, 2001.

16. I. Kiselev. *Aspect-Oriented Programming with AspectJ*. Sams Publishing, Indianapolis, 2003.

17. J. Magee, N. Dulay, S. Eisenbach, and J. Kramer. Specifying distributed software architectures. In *Proceedings of ESEC'95*, pages 137–53. IEEE, 1995.

18. J. Magee and J. Kramer. *Concurrency: State Models & Java Programs*. Wiley, 1999.

19. N. Medvidovic and R. N. Taylor. A classification and comparison framework for software architecture description languages. *IEEE - Transactions on Software Engineering*, 26(1):70–93, 2000.

20. S. Pavel, J. Noyé, P. Poizat, and J.-C. Royer. A formal component model with explicit symbolic protocols and its Java implementation. Technical report, École des Mines de Nantes, 2005.

21. F. Plasil and S. Visnovsky. Behavior protocols for software components. *IEEE - Transactions on Software Engineering*, 28(11):1056–1076, November 2002.

22. P. Poizat and J.-C. Royer. Korrigan: a formal ADL with full data types and a temporal glue. Technical Report 83–2002, Laboratoire de Méthodes Informatiques, 2002. Available at http://www.lami.univ-evry.fr/~poizat/publications-fr.php.

23. J.-C. Royer. The GAT approach to specify mixed systems. *Informatica*, 27(1):89–103, 2003.

24. Mario Südholt. A model of components with non-regular protocols. In *Proceedings of the 4th International Workshop on Software Composition (SC'05)*, Lecture Notes in Computer Science. Springer-Verlag, April 2005.

25. K. J. Turner, editor. *Using Formal Description Techniques, An introduction to Estelle, LOTOS and SDL*. Wiley, 1993.

26. J. van den Bos and C. Laffra. PROCOL: A parallel object language with protocols. In Norman Meyrowitz, editor, *OOPSLA'89 Conference Proceedings*, pages 95–102. ACM Press, 1989.

27. D. M. Yellin and R. E. Strom. Protocol specifications and component adaptors. *ACM Transactions on Programming Languages and Systems*, 19(2):292–333, 1997.

Towards Distributed Contract Negotiation in Component-Based Systems

Mesfin Mulugeta and Steffen Göbel

Institute for System Architecture,
Dresden University of Technology, Germany
{mulugeta, goebel}@rn.inf.tu-dresden.de

Abstract. The consideration of non-functional properties like QoS or security is crucial for many software applications, but it is also a challenging task. The combination of non-functional aspects and component-based software engineering aims at simplifying the development of those applications.

The COMQUAD project has employed this approach and has allowed the specification of required and provided non-functional properties as well as resource demand at the component level. The runtime environment, in particular the component container, negotiates contracts between components of an application.

In this paper we report on work in progress about a distributed contract negotiation mechanism between components running in different component containers on multiple nodes. We introduce a layered negotiation approach consisting of a coarse-grained negotiation between component containers and a fine-grained negotiation between components within a single container and across containers. We demonstrate our ideas with a distributed video on-demand application.

1 Introduction

Component-based software engineering allows the composition of complex systems and applications out of well-defined parts. Nowadays several mature and commercial component models (e.g. EJB, JavaBeans, .NET, COM+, etc.) exist on the market. However, they provide only limited support for the development of components and applications with Non-Functional Properties (NFPs). The consideration of NFPs like Quality of Service (QoS) or security is crucial for many software applications, e. g. video on-demand or banking scenarios. In the COMQUAD project [7,9,16] we have developed a component model together with a runtime environment that allows specifying NFPs of components. The component model follows a classification by Cheesman and Daniels [4]: A component specification defining the functional interfaces can have multiple implementations and each implementation can support multiple QoS profiles. A QoS profile of a COMQUAD component represents an operating range describing provided and required NFPs and the resource demand (cf. Fig. 1).

T. Gschwind, U. Aßmann, and O. Nierstrasz (Eds.): SC 2005, LNCS 3628, pp. 125–134, 2005.

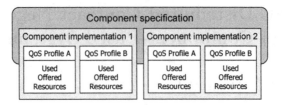

Fig. 1. Relationship between component specification, implementations, and QoS profiles

The component container, which is the runtime environment for COMQUAD components, selects appropriate implementations and QoS profiles based on requirements of a client at runtime. This process is called contract negotiation and results in a network of interconnected components that collaborate to fulfill the non-functional requirements of clients. The contract negotiation phase also involves the reservation of necessary resources for all components of a net. The underlying real-time operating system DROPS [10] together with resource managers provides the necessary reservation capabilities for the component container. So far the COMQUAD runtime environment only supports a single component container, which means that all components must run on a single computer. Obviously, this restriction is inappropriate for many applications.

In this paper, we introduce an approach for the distributed contract negotiation between components running in different component containers on multiple nodes. This two phased process consists of a coarse-grained negotiation between the multiple containers, followed by a fine-grained negotiation of NFPs between components.

The paper is structured as follows: In the next section we explain some additional details of COMQUAD by means of a sample video on-demand application. In the third section we first discuss the requirements and challenges inherent in a distributed contract negotiation and then present our two phase negotiation approach. The paper closes with an examination of related work, a conclusion, and an outlook to future work.

2   Example Scenario

In this section we introduce a Video-on-Demand (VoD) application to motivate our distributed contract negotiation approach in the next section. The scenario consists of one or more clients that access a video on a remote server and control the playback, for example by issuing commands like play, rewind, pause, etc. A component diagram of the sample application is shown in Fig. 2. For the sake of clarity, we have omitted some components and interfaces that are not necessary to illustrate the scenario.

The `VideoServer` component reads media files from the hard disk and streams them to its remote clients via the `ICompVideo` interface. The media

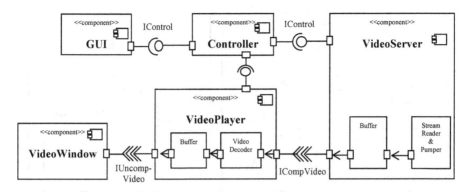

Fig. 2. Component diagram of the VoD application

files stored on the hard disk have been encoded in several versions with different formats and data rates. COMQUAD supports streams as special interface type [9] and allows to specify NFPs for them. A `Controller` component acts as intermediator between the `GUI` component implementing the user interface and the `VideoServer`. The `IControl` interface controls the transmission of the video flow through the `ICompVideo` interface by means of operations like play, stop, rewind, and fast-forward. The `VideoPlayer` receives a remote video stream by the `ICompVideo` interface, decompresses the video, and outputs the uncompressed stream via the `IUncompVideo` interface to the `VideoWindow` component where it is finally displayed.

Several different implementations of the `VideoServer` and `VideoPlayer` components are available to handle the streaming of different qualities of encoded media files, for example, depending on the available network bandwidth and the client's requirements. The implementations adhere to the same functional specification but differ in NFPs associated to the stream interfaces. The `VideoPlayer` component also provides different QoS profiles for each implementation to offer different levels of video preprocessing depending on the available CPU resources. These QoS profiles are mapped to different internal configurations of the `VideoPlayer` component. See [6] for more details.

Important NFPs used for stream and operational interfaces in the VoD application are, for example, data rate, frame rate, and response time. For the specification of NFPs—offers, requirements, and resource demand—we use CQML+ [14], which is an extension of CQML [1].

A possible deployment scenario of the VoD application is depicted in Fig. 3. To simplify our discussion, we considered only two nodes—`ClientNode` and `ServerNode`—and a network between them as the target environment. `ClientNode` is the client computer and `ServerNode` is a server at the service provider. The `Controller` component is deployed on the same node as the `VideoPlayer` and the `VideoWindow` component.

The `GUI` component is the client triggering the instantiation of all other components. The component containers of `ClientNode` and `ServerNode` work

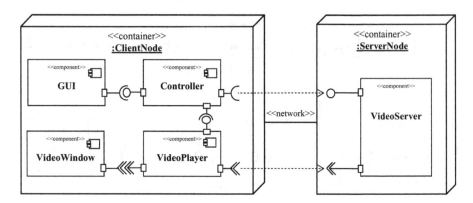

Fig. 3. Deployment of the VoD application

together to select implementations and QoS profiles based on the client's non-functional requirements.

3   Contract Negotiation

In [3] four classes of contracts have been identified for a software component: syntactic, behavioral, synchronization, and QoS. In this paper, we deal with the fourth class of component contract: QoS. Our usage of the term contract involves the collaborating components, containers, and platforms [19]. A QoS contract between components is negotiated at runtime and defines the provided and required QoS properties of each component. This component–component contract depends on the contract that exists between the components and their respective containers and the container–platform contract.

A QoS contract between two components can only be established if the level of QoS offered by one component satisfies the expectations of the other one. Otherwise, if no available implementation and QoS profile fulfills this condition, a collaboration of the components is impossible. However, the client's requirements might be relaxed and the negotiation is restarted.

In our approach the container negotiates contracts between collaborating components by selecting appropriate implementations and QoS profiles. In this section we first discuss contract negotiation within a single container. We then extend the approach to the contract negotiation between multiple containers hosted on different computers.

3.1   Negotiation in a Single Container

Our current COMQUAD implementation supports contract negotiation in a single container. This means that all the collaborating components are hosted in one node. All required resources of these components are also provided by this node. The client's QoS requirements, specifying minimum and maximum values, drive the whole negotiation process. They have to be captured before the negotiation begins. The contract negotiation is initiated when a client wants to create a specified component instance via the home interface of this component. The client transmits QoS requirements together with the create request to the container. Before the actual contract negotiation is started, the client's QoS requirements are translated into a QoS requirements of one or more components. The contract negotiation is then performed in the container as outlined below [8].

1. Select a valid component net configuration. A component net represents components that collaborate to handle the particular client's request. A valid component net configuration is one where the required and provided quality statements for each connection in the component net conform to one another. Some heuristics need to be done in the selection in order to decrease the complexity of the search.
2. Compute the resource demand of the selected configuration.
3. Make resource reservations.
4. If reservation was successful, create component instances of the selected implementation. Otherwise, if reservation failed and there are still more valid configurations, go to step 1.

3.2   Negotiation in Multiple Containers

The multiple container case differs from the single container case in the following aspects:

- The collaborating components are spread across different computers and their resource demand is provided by the multiple nodes and a shared network resource. The negotiation process needs to consider configurations and available resources of multiple nodes (containers) and the network both in isolation and collectively.
- QoS properties of component implementations across containers cannot be simply matched based on their QoS expectation and QoS offer. The influence of the network like latency and packet loss needs to be considered for NFPs like response time, frame rate, etc.
- The network between the containers increases the complexity of the negotiation process. Different communication service models are supported by the network: guaranteed, priority-based, or best-effort. Moreover, component implementations could require a specific network protocol.
- Multiple containers exchange messages during the negotiation process to come to an agreement. For performance reasons the number of message exchanges between the containers must be minimized.

We propose a distributed contract negotiation approach to address the identified requirements. Each container integrates a contract manager acting as a negotiating agent in the interaction between containers, in addition to its role in local contract negotiation. We have identified two phases in our approach:

(i) *coarse-grained negotiation* between the multiple containers and (ii) *fine-grained negotiation* of the NFPs of components. The second phase is further divided into negotiations between containers and negotiations locally in a single container.

Coarse-grained negotiation: The agents of multiple containers need to negotiate general terms before the actual NFP negotiations take place. For instance, the containers need to agree on the type of communication service model provided by the network, or on a specific transport protocol (TCP, RTP/UDP, etc) that must be used to transfer data between components across containers.

In the VoD application example, a client may not support RSVP (Resource Reservation Protocol) [18] while the server supports it. Hence, RSVP based guaranteed connections cannot be used and the parties need to agree on a different connection type. In another case, the video service provider may offer its service in two modes – interactive VoD and near VoD. Interactive VoD allows clients to view a video using VCR-style functions such as pause, rewind and fast-forward. In near-VoD some interactivity and part of the on-demand nature are sacrificed to achieve cost-effectiveness or other objectives [2]. Each of these modes may have their own requirements on the total number of clients supported and time when the service is available. Before the negotiation of the NFPs, the client and server need to agree either on interactive-VoD or near-VoD.

Fine-grained negotiation of the NFPs: Once the negotiating agents have agreed on higher level terms, the fine-grained negotiation on the NFPs continues, with the objective of selecting implementations and QoS profiles of components. This selection can be done either (i.) centrally by one container, or (ii.) in a step by step manner; i.e., first by selecting implementations of components that are connected across containers followed by selections in each local container, or first making selections in the client (server) container, then for components connected across containers, and finally for components in the server (client) containers. In a VoD or similar applications, the number of involved components can be many and/or some components provide many implementations and QoS profiles. An application that has four components, where two implementations are available for each component and two QoS-profiles exist for each implementation, already results in $4^4 = 256$ configurations. Heuristic approaches are thus important to decrease the negotiation time. Negotiation is made first between the containers, followed by the local container negotiations. We believe this choice of ordering helps in narrowing the search space of available configurations and reducing the amount of message exchanges between containers. Moreover, it gives local containers the freedom in the selection of local component implementations and QoS profiles once agreement is reached between containers. As remote access is a costly operation and as network failure is the most common cause of system failure in the context of distributed environment, components are mostly co-located in a node as far as possible. Component connections across containers should be minimized.

The fine-grained distributed contract negotiation is performed as outlined below:

1. Do container–container negotiation. This is done by the container on the server node assuming it has information about the QoS specification of all components.
   (a) Select a valid component net configuration as done for the single container case but only consider components that are connected across containers. The computation of a valid configuration should take into account the network by appropriately modifying the NFPs of the components.
   (b) Compute network resource demand of the selected configuration.
   (c) If available resources are sufficient, go to step 2.
   (d) If available resources are insufficient and other valid configurations are still available, go to step (a). If there are no more valid configurations, relax the user's requirements and go to step (a). If the user's requirements cannot be further relaxed, then notify the user and exit.
2. Repeat this step for all containers: Do local container negotiation with additional constraints of the valid configuration obtained in step 1.
3. If all negotiations in step 2 are successful, make local container and container–container resource reservations.
4. If any negotiation in step 2 fails or requires a change of the configuration selected in the step 1, go to step 1.
5. If all negotiations are successful, create component instances of the selected implementation. This establishes QoS contracts between the collaborating components and the multiple containers.

We take the VoD application to demonstrate our ideas. The user's QoS requirements might be "high quality media and fast interactive functions". This is translated into requirements on collaborating components as follows: (i) The VideoPlayer's ICompVideo interface expects to receive a QoS offer of $dataRate = 96kbit/s$ and $frameRate > 25s^{-1}$; (ii) the Controller's IControl interface expects $responseTime < 200ms$. How this translation can be achieved is out of scope of this paper. Component's offered QoS depend on available resources and the level of its used QoS. This dependency is captured in the QoS profiles of components. A measurement framework [12] is used to estimate QoS offer of components. The contract negotiation then proceeds as follows:

- The components that are connected across containers are VideoPlayer, Controller, and VideoServer. To get a valid component configuration, a matching is made between the available implementations and QoS profiles of the VideoServer and the VideoPlayer, and also between the VideoServer and the Controller. Table 1 shows different implementations of these components and the NFPs of the specified interfaces.
- Based on the translated user's requirements, the third implementation of VideoServer is selected and this should be matched with the QoS expectations of the other two components. The $responseTime$ property of VideoServer.IControl must be modified before matching it with Controller.IControl. This could be done by analyzing the network load and estimating the latency introduced by the network. If the overall time is less than 200 ms, the selected VideoServer implementation is valid for the

Table 1. Component Implementations

Controller		VideoPlayer		VideoServer		
Imp no.	IControl *(responseTime)*	Imp no.	ICompVideo *(dateRate, frameRate)*	Imp no.	ICompVideo *(dateRate, frameRate)*	IControl *(responseTime)*
1	< 200 ms	1	(56 kbit/s, 25 s^{-1})	1	(56 kbit/s, 25 s^{-1})	< 50 ms
		2	(96 kbit/s, 25 s^{-1})	2	(56 kbit/s, 15 s^{-1})	< 100 ms
				3	(96 kbit/s, 25 s^{-1})	< 50 ms
				4	(96 kbit/s, 15 s^{-1})	< 100 ms

Controller component. Matching between the VideoServer and Video-Player components results in selecting the 2nd implementation of the VideoPlayer.

- For the selected configuration, network resource demand is computed. If resources are available, local contract negotiation proceeds in the two containers under the constraint that the 3rd, 2nd, and 1st implementations have been selected for the VideoServer, VideoPlayer, and Controller components, respectively.
- If the available bandwidth is not enough, other configurations that fulfill client's minimum requirements are searched from Table 1. For instance, the 1st implementations of both VideoServer and VideoPlayer component can be selected. Then the local negotiation process is repeated.

The distributed contract negotiation protocol proposed is not an optimal algorithm in the sense that the selected configurations are not the ones with the minimal resource requirements. Moreover, we have simplified our considerations of the matching process of implementations and QoS profiles across the network. Under a simplified scenario, for a network that provides QoS guarantees, latency can be estimated on condition that the allocated bandwidth and the size of the transported data are known. The effect of the different service models of the network—guaranteed, priority-based, and best-effort—on the NFPs of components needs an in-depth investigation.

In our example, user's requirements are fulfilled by the selected implementations and QoS profiles on all the NFPs. This does not always work. In more complex situations the requirements for some NFPs (e.g. data rate and frame rate) can be fulfilled while for the rest (e.g. response time) it is not possible. In this case, other matching strategies should be applied. Capturing the user's relative preference for each NFP is useful for the selection. There are still more complex situations of contract negotiation like the case when non-functional requirements are conflicting. We would like to address these issues in the future.

4   Related Work

The work in [5] proposes a QoS-aware component framework that extends the EJB container by integrating QoS services like resource reservation and negotiation. The EJB container implements basic negotiation algorithms and isolates the business components from reservation services. The approach allows clients to negotiate a single QoS dimension of method calls per second. But it does not explain how component contracts can be negotiated in the multiple nodes.

Menascé et al [11] describe a model where a component provides a set of interrelated services to other components. These components are QoS-aware and are capable of engaging in QoS negotiations with other components of a distributed application. The paper attempts to create a framework for software components that are capable of negotiating QoS goals in a dynamic fashion using analytic performance models. The QoS negotiation between two components occurs by taking performance as a QoS requirement and concurrency level as a means of negotiation element. Our treatment of QoS negotiation is generic, which may be applied for a larger set of problems. Moreover, the negotiation between components is handled in the container.

Some other projects that currently work on QoS support in software components are CIAO and QuA. CIAO [17] builds a QoS-enabled CCM implementation on top of TAO [15]. CIAO's philosophy is a strong adherence to existing OMG specifications such as RT/CORBA and CCM, and the extension of those. QuA [13] aims at precisely defining an abstract component architecture, including the semantics for general QoS specifications. The proof of concept is provided by implementing an open framework for platform managed QoS.

5   Conclusions and Outlook

In this paper, we have discussed that contract negotiation of collaborating components and their runtime environment is important for the support of non-functional requirements in component-based applications. In our approach, the container mediates the negotiation of the collaborating components. Contract negotiation has been discussed for a single container and multiple containers case. Important challenges for supporting multiple container contract negotiations are the consideration of resource constraints and possible conflicts at different nodes and the network as well as the required negotiation time in large-scaled scenarios. We proposed a two-phased negotiation approach to tackle these challenges.

However, the presented algorithm is not optimal in the sense that it does not find configurations with minimal resource demand in all cases. In the future, we want to come up with a more efficient algorithm or apply some heuristics. Moreover, we would like also to address the effect of the different service models of the network—guaranteed, priority-based, and best-effort—on the NFPs of components.

References

1. J. Ø. Aagedal. *Quality of Service Support in Development of Distributed Systems.* PhD thesis, University of Oslo, 2001.
2. K. C. Almeroth and M. H. Ammar. The use of multicast delivery to provide a scalable and interactive video-on-demand service. *IEEE Journal of Selected Areas in Communications*, 14(6):1110–1122, 1996.

3. A. Beugnard, J.-M. Jézéquel, N. Plouzeau, and D. Watkins. Making components contract aware. *IEEE Computer*, 32(7):38–45, July 1999.
4. J. Cheesman and J. Daniels. *UML Components: A Simple Process for Specifying Component-Based Software*. Addison Wesley Longman, Inc., 2001.
5. M. de Miguel, J. F. Ruiz, and M. Garca-Valls. Qos-aware component frameworks. In *10th International Workshop on Quality of Service (IWQoS 2002)*, Miami Beach, USA, May 2002.
6. S. Göbel. Encapsulation of structural adaptation by composite components. In *Workshop on Self-Managed Systems (WOSS '02)*, Newport Beach, CA, USA, October 2004.
7. S. Göbel, C. Pohl, R. Aigner, M. Pohlack, S. Röttger, and S. Zschaler. The COMQUAD component container architecture. In J. Magee, C. Szyperski, and J. Bosch, editors, *4th Working IEEE/IFIP Conf. on Software Architecture (WICSA)*, pages 315–318, Oslo, Norway, June 2004. IEEE.
8. S. Göbel, C. Pohl, R. Aigner, M. Pohlack, S. Röttger, and S. Zschaler. The comquad component container architecture and contract negotiation. Technical Report TUD-FI04-04, Technische Universität Dresden, April 2004.
9. S. Göbel, C. Pohl, S. Röttger, and S. Zschaler. The COMQUAD Component Model—Enabling Dynamic Selection of Implementations by Weaving Nonfunctional Aspects. In *3rd International Conference on Aspect-Oriented Software Development (AOSD'04)*, Lancaster, UK, 22–26 Mar. 2004.
10. H. Härtig, R. Baumgartl, M. Borriss, C.-J. Hamann, M. Hohmuth, F. Mehnert, L. Reuther, S. Schönberg, and J. Wolter. DROPS: OS support for distributed multimedia applications. In *Proc. 8th ACM SIGOPS European Workshop: Support for Composing Distributed Applications*, Sintra, Portugal, Sept. 1998.
11. D. A. Menascé, H. Ruan, and H. Gomaa. A framework for qos-aware software components. In *The fourth international workshop on Software and performance*, pages 186–196, Redwood Shores, CA, USA, 2004.
12. M. Meyerhfer and C. Neumann. Testejb - a measurement framework for ebjs. In I. C. (Hrsg.), editor, *International Symposium on Component-based Software Engineering (CBSE7)*, volume 3054 of *Lecture Notes in Computer Science*, Edinburgh, Scotland, 24–25May 2004. Springer.
13. Qua project. http://www.simula.no:8888/QuA.
14. S. Röttger and S. Zschaler. CQML$^+$: Enhancements to CQML. In J.-M. Bruel, editor, *Proc. 1st Int'l Workshop on Quality of Service in Component-Based Software Engineering, Toulouse, France*, pages 43–56. Cépaduès-Éditions, June 2003.
15. D. C. Schmidt, D. L. Levine, and S. Mungee. The design of the tao real-time object request broker. *Computer Communications*, 21(4), 1998.
16. COMQUAD Project – Components with Quantitative Properties and Adaptivity. http://comquad.org/.
17. N. Wang, C. D. Gill, D. C. Schmidt, A. Gokhale, B. Natarajan, C. Rodrigues, J. P. Loyall, and R. E. Schantz. Total quality of service provisioning in middleware and applications. *Microprocessors and Microsystems*, 27(2):45–54, March 2003.
18. L. Zhang, S. Berson, S. Herzog, and S. Jamin. RFC 2205: Resource reservation protocol (rsvp) – version 1, functional specification, September 1997. URL http://www.ietf.org /rfc /rfc2205.txt.
19. S. Zschaler and S. Röttger. Types of quality of service contracts for component-based systems. In *The IASTED International Conference on Software Engineering (IASTED SE 2004)*, Innsbruck, Austria, 2004.

On Typesafe Aspect Implementations in C++

Daniel Lohmann and Olaf Spinczyk

Friedrich-Alexander-University Erlangen-Nuremberg, Germany
{dl, os}@cs.fau.de

Abstract. Compared to other languages, the C++ language offers a less powerful runtime type system, but a very powerful static type system. In AspectC++, this is addressed by an extended join-point API that provides static type information at compile-time and type-safe access to join-point-specific context information. In this paper we show, how the use of static type information leads to the development highly generic, but type-safe aspects that fit well into the C++ language model. This is demonstrated by an example.

1 Introduction

Compared to languages like Java and C#, the C++ language has a less powerful runtime type system, but a more powerful compile-time (static) type system. C#, while still beeing a statically typed language, implements a unified type system where even primitive value types offer the interface of the one and only root class System.object. In Java all class types derive from Java.lang.Object. Due to autoboxing it is possible in both languages (Java beginning with Java 5) to pass value type instances as object references. Basically, Java and C# allow to treat "everything as an object" at runtime[1]. This facilitates the development of "type generic code", in the sense that such code can deal with objects of any type *at runtime*.

In C++ there is no such common root class and the C++ runtime type information (RTTI) system offers only a very limited set of runtime services. On the other hand, C++ implements a static type system that offers a very high level of expressive power, based on operator and function overloading, argument dependend name lookup and C++ templates. This facilitates the development of highly generic code that can be instantiated *at compile-time* with any type. In general, the C++ philosphy is to use *genericity at compile time*, while Java and C# advise *genericity at runtime*[2]. The C++ model of compile-time genericity has some clear advantages, as it allows a good separation of concerns, typically results in very efficient code, and implicitly ensures type-safety.

Type genericity is particularly important for the development of aspects, as aspects are typically intended to be broadly reusable and applicable. For example, the implementation of a tracing aspect that logs all actual parameter and result values of function invocations, should be independent of the affected function's signature, i.e. on its argument and result types. In AspectJ this is realized by providing a *runtime join-point*

---

[1] Actually, it is the Smalltalk language that carried the "everything is an object" idea to the extremes. However, Smalltalk offers no static type system.

[2] This is even true with Java generics introduced in the Java 5, which are basically a syntatic wrapper around the "treat everyting as an object" philosophy.

T. Gschwind, U. Aßmann, and O. Nierstrasz (Eds.): SC 2005, LNCS 3628, pp. 135–149, 2005.

API to advice implementations, which offers a unified interface to access the join-point's context information. This information includes the number of parameters, the argument and return values (as `Object`), and (via the interface of `Object` and Java's reflection capabilities) their runtime types. Our AspectC++ language offers very similar runtime mechanisms. Additionally, the AspectC++ join-point API supports an alternative *type-safe* access to all parameter and result values. For this purpose, we extended the AspectC++ runtime join-point API by a *compile-time join-point API*, which provides static type information about the current join-point at compilation time. We call advice, which depends on static type information from the compile-time join-point API *generic advice* [10].

1.1   Outline

The aim of this paper is to show, how the AspectC++ notion of generic advice can be used to develop reusable, but type-safe aspect implementations that fit well into the C++ philosphy of "doing as much as possible statically". This is demonstrated by an example. The example is an aspect that facilitates exception-based error propagation for legacy third-party C-libraries like the Win32 API.

The rest of this paper is structured as follows. The next section provides a brief introduction into the AspectC++ language and terminology and describes the AspectC++ join-point API. Section 3.1 explains the example project. Afterwards, some details about the weaving process of AspectC++ are given in section 4. This is followed by a discussion of the advantages and limitations of our approach in section 5. Finally, we give an overview of related work and briefly summarize the paper.

2   AspectC++ Concepts and Terminology

AspectC++ [13] is a general purpose aspect-oriented language extension to C++ designed by the authors and others. It is aimed to support the well-known AspectJ programming style in areas with stronger demands on runtime efficiency and code density. While beeing strongly influenced by the AspectJ language model [7,8], AspectC++ has to support many additional concepts that are unique to the C++ domain. This ranges from operator overloading, const correctness and multiple inheritance up to weaving in template code.

The AspectC++ compiler, plugin for Eclipse, and documentation are available under open source license from the AspectC++ homepage [1].

2.1   Basic Concepts [10]

The AspectC++ terminology is inspired by the terminology introduced by AspectJ. The most relevant terms are *join-point* and *advice*. A *join-point* denotes a specific weaving position in the target code (often called component code, too). Join-points are usually given in a declarative way by a join-point description language. Each set of join-points, which is described in this language, is called a *pointcut*. In AspectC++ the sentences of the join-point description language are called *pointcut expressions*. For example the pointcut expression

```
call("% Service::%(...)")
```

describes all calls to member functions of the class Service. The pointcut expression

```
call("% Service::%(...)")
    && cflow( execution( "void error_%(...)" ) )
```

describes again all calls to member functions of the class Service. By combining (&& operation) these join-points with the cflow pointcut function these join-points become conditional. They are only affected by advice if the flow of control already passed a function with a name beginning with error_. Users may define pointcut expressions of arbitrary complexity to describe the crosscutting nature of their aspects. A list of all built-in pointcut functions of AspectC++ is available in the *AspectC++ Language Quick Reference Sheet* [1].

The core of the join-point language are match-expressions. In AspectC++ these expressions are quoted strings where % and ... can be used as wildcards[3]. They can be understood as regular expressions matched against the names of known program entities like functions or classes.The aspect code that is actually woven into the target code at the join-points is called *advice*. Advice is bound to a set of join-points (given by a pointcut expression). For example by defining the advice

```
advice call( "% Service::%(...)" ) : before() {
    cout << "Service function invocation" << endl;
}
```

the program will print a message *before* any *call* to a member function of Service. The advice code itself has access to its context, i.e. the join-point which it affects, at runtime by a *join-point API*. Very similar to the predefined this-pointer in C++, AspectC++ provides a pointer called tjp, which provides the context information. For example the advice

```
advice call( "% Service::%(...)" ) : before() {
    cout << tjp->signature() << " invocation";
    cout << endl;
}
```

prints a message that contains the name of the function that is going to be called.

2.2   The AspectC++ Join-point API

Table 1 shows an excerpt from the join-point API, describing those parts that are relevant in the context of this paper. The elements that are based on join-point-specific static type information are emphasized. The upper part (types and enumerators) provides compile-time type information, which can be used to instantiate generic code or template metaprograms by advice. The lower part (non-static methods) provides a

---

[3] In AspectJ * is used as a wildcard, but this would result in ambiguities in C++. However, the match mechanism exists in AspectJ, too.

type-safe interface to the join-point context. These methods are bound at compile-time, but called at runtime. For example, the function `Arg<i>::ReferredType *arg()` offers a type-safe way to access argument values if the argument index is known at compile time. Inside the advice body, the static part of the join-point API is provided as a class `JoinPoint`. At runtime, the non-static members are accessed using the `JoinPoint *tjp` pointer.

Table 1. An Excerpt from the AspectC++ Join-point API

compile-time types and enumerators:	
`That`	type of the affected class
`Target`	type of the destination class (for call join-points)
`Arg<i>::Type`	type of the i'th argument
`Arg<i>::ReferredType`	with $0 \leq i <$ ARGS
`Result`	result type
`ARGS`	number of arguments
`JPID`	unique numeric identifier for this join-point
`JPTYPE`	type of this join-point (call / execution / construction / destruction)

runtime static methods:	
`const char *signature()`	signature of the affected function
•••	

runtime non-static methods:	
`void proceed()`	execute original code (around advice)
`That *that()`	object instance referred to by this
`Target *target()`	target object instance of a call (for call join-points)
`Arg<i>::ReferredType *arg()`	argument value instance of the i'th argument
`Result *result()`	result value instance
•••	

3   Using Static Typing in Aspects - An Example

3.1   Motivation

Every program has to deal with the fact that operations may fail at runtime. Programming language concepts for propagation and handling of runtime errors have evolved over time. Today most developers favor *exceptions* for this purpose. However, especially in the C/C++ world, there are still hundreds of legacy libraries that do not support exception handling and follow a more traditional approach of error handling by reporting an error situation via the function's *return value*. An error is returned either as an error code, a boolean flag or as a special "magic value". In the latter cases, a more descriptive error code can typically be retrieved by calling a special library function or reading a global variable. The C runtime library (CRT), for instance, provides the global variable errno for this purpose.

Many libraries overload the indication of a runtime error with the functions regular result. In such libraries, the result value has to be checked against a "magic value" to

```
1  #include <windows.h>
2  HANDLE g_hConfigFile = NULL;
3
4  LRESULT WINAPI WndProc( HWND hWnd, UINT nMsg, WPARAM wParam, LPARAM lParam ) {
5    HDC     dc = NULL;
6    PAINTSTRUCT ps = {0};
7
8    switch( nMsg ) {
9      case WM_PAINT:
10       dc = BeginPaint( hWnd, &ps );
11       ...
12       EndPaint(hWnd, &ps);
13       break;
14
15     case ...
16
17     default:
18       return DefWindowProc(hWnd, nMsg, wParam, lParam);
19     }
20     return 0;
21 }
22
23 int WINAPI WinMain( ... ) {
24   g_hConfigFile = CreateFile( "example.config", GENERIC_READ, 0,
25                               NULL, OPEN_EXISTING, 0, NULL );
26
27   WNDCLASS wc = {0, WndProc, 0, 0, ... , "Example_Class"};
28   RegisterClass( &wc );
29
30   HWND hwndMain = CreateWindowEx( 0, "Example Class", "Example", ... );
31   UpdateWindow( hwndMain );
32
33   MSG msg;
34   while( GetMessage( &msg, NULL, 0, 0 ) ) {
35     TranslateMessage( &msg );
36     DispatchMessage( &msg );
37   }
38   return 0;
39 }
```

Fig. 1. A Typical Win32 Application

determine if there was an error. The "magic value" itself often depends on the result type. For instance, functions that perform floating point calculations return a double which is either the result of the calculation or the special not-a-number (NaN) value in case of an error. The CRT function fopen() returns a FILE* that is the handle to the opened file or NULL in case of an error.

Error checking and handling by validation of function results is cumbersome. Typically, in the client code each function call needs to be surrounded by an if statement with at least two or three additional lines to do the error handling. This results in heavily tangled and almost unreadable code. As a consequence, this kind of error handling is often "forgotten" as C-style languages allow programmers to simply ignore the results of a function call. At runtime this may lead to undefined behavior when the program continues execution with invalid internal state. With error propagation by exceptions this could not happen, as an exception "can't be ignored" and reported faults are thereby detected as early as possible. Hence, it is a good idea to integrate calls to legacy libraries into the error-handling-by-exception model. As this is a crosscutting concern, we strive for a generic aspect-oriented solution. In the following we describe such a generic aspect for one of most popular (and disliked) legacy libraries: the Win32 API.

3.2 The Example Application

Figure 1 shows the listing of a typical Win32 application. WinMain() is the entry point, which performs the usual sequence of Win32 API calls to initialize the application and start the main message loop: First a configuration file is opened (CreateFile()) and the window class for the application's main window is registered (RegisterClass()). Afterwards the main window is created (CreateWindowEx()) and an initial WM_PAINT message is sent to it (UpdateWindow()). The WM_PAINT message is handled by the WndProc() window procedure, which acquires a device context (BeginPaint()), draws the window's content (not shown here) and then releases the device context (EndPaint()). After the main window was created, the application finally enters the message loop to perform all further processing.

Even if the application does not contain any error checking code, any of the above mentioned API functions may fail at runtime. They all follow the Win32 convention by indicating a failure by a "magic" return value and, in case of failure, providing more information about the reason via GetLastError().

3.3 An Aspect to Throw on Win32 Errors

Our goal is now to develop an aspect that implements an exception-based error handling for calls to the Win32 API. The general idea is to give after call advice to all Win32 API functions. In the advice body, the return value of the API function is checked and, in case of an error, an exception is thrown:

```
#include "Win32Error.h"
aspect ThrowWin32Errors {
  advice call( win32::Win32API() ) : after() {
    if( win32::IsError( *tjp->result() ) {
      throw win32::Exception(...);
    }
  }
};
```

The advice affects all calls to API functions that are described by the (externally defined) pointcut win32::Win32API(). Its implementation uses a helper function win32::IsError() that returns true if the passed result value, retrieved via tjp->result(), indicates a failure. This is done by checking the result against the "magic value". The actual implementation of the helper function depends on the API function called, or, more precisely, on its return type. In the example the following Win32 API functions are used:

– EndPaint() and UpdateWindow() are of type BOOL.
  BOOL functions indicate an error by returning FALSE.

- BeginPaint() is of type HDC.
  HDC functions indicate an error by returning NULL.
- CreateWindowEx() is of type HWND.
  HWND functions indicate an error by returning NULL.
- RegisterClass() is of type ATOM.
  ATOM functions indicate an error by returning 0.
- CreateFile() is of type HANDLE.
  HANDLE functions indicate an error by either returning NULL or INVALID_HANDLE_VALUE.

These few API functions already cover a significant part of the different return types and "magic values" used by the Win32 API. The win32::IsError() helper function is overloaded for each of these types to perform the check against the type-dependent "magic values" (Figure 3, lines 12–26). The compiler's overload resolution deduces (at compile-time) for each join-point the correct helper function to call (Figure 2). In the case the advice affects calls to a function of a type no compatible helper function is defined for, the overload resolution process fails and results in a compile-time error. Note that this generic implementation of the advice code is only possible, because tjp->result() is type-safe, as it returns a pointer of the real static type of the affected function.

3.4   Providing Context Information

Our aspect performs a type-safe validation of the results of Win32 API calls and throws a win32::Exception in case of an error. The exception object should include all context information that can be helpful to figure out the reason for the actual failure. Besides the Win32 error code, this should include a human readable string describing the error, the signature of the called function (retrieved with tjp->signature()) and the actual parameter values that were passed to the function.

The tricky part is to build a string from the actual parameter values. In AspectJ one would iterate at *runtime* over all arguments and call Object.toString()on each argument. However, in C++ it is not possible to perform this at runtime, as C++ types

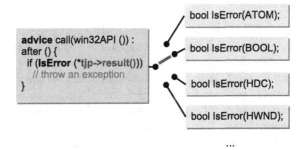

Fig. 2. A Join-Point specific Compile-Time Switch

```
1  namespace win32 {
2
3    struct Exception {
4      Exception( const std::string& w, DWORD c )
5        : where( w ), code( c )
6      {}
7
8      std::string where;
9      DWORD    code;
10   };
11
12   inline bool IsError( HANDLE res ) {
13     return res == NULL || res == INVALID_HANDLE_VALUE;
14   }
15   inline bool IsError( ATOM res ) {
16     return res == 0;
17   }
18   inline bool IsError( HWND res ) {
19     return res == NULL;
20   }
21   inline bool IsError( HDC res ) {
22     return res == NULL;
23   }
24   inline bool IsError( BOOL res ) {
25     return res == FALSE;
26   }
27
28   // Translates a Win32 error code into a
29   // readable text message using the Win32
30   // FormatMessage() function
31   std::string GetErrorText( DWORD code ) {
32     char res[ 256 ];
33     FormatMessage(... , code, 0, res, ...);
34     return res;
35   }
36
37
38   pointcut  Win32API() = "% CreateWindow%(...)"
39                       || "% RegisterClass%(...)"
40                       || "% BeginPaint(...)"
41                       || "% UpdateWindow(...)"
42                       || "% CreateFile%(...)"
43                       || ...;
44   } // namespace Win32
```

Fig. 3. Win32 Errorhandling Helper

do not share a common root class that offers services like toString(). The C++ concept to get a string representation of any type is based, once again, on static typing. It is realized by overloading the stream operator ostream& operator <<(ostream&, T) for each type T. Therefore, we have to iterate at *compile-time* over the join-point-specific list of argument types to generate a sequence of stream operator calls, each processing (later at runtime) an argument value of the correct type. This is implemented by a small template metaprogram (Figure 4, lines 4–19), which is instantiated at compile-time with the JoinPoint type (line 35) and iterates, by recursive instantiation of the template, over the join-point-specific argument type list JoinPoint::Arg<I>. For each argument type, a stream_params class with a process() method is generated, which later at runtime will stream the typed argument value (retrieved via tjp->arg<I>()) and recursively

```
1  #include "Win32Error.h"
2
3  aspect ThrowWin32Errors {
4    // template metaprogram to stream a commaseparated sequence of
5    // arguments available at a joinpoint
6    template< class TJP, int N >
7    struct stream_params {
8      static void process( ostream& os, TJP* tjp ) {
9        os << *tjp->arg<TJP::ARGS-N>() << ", ";
10       stream_params< TJP, N - 1 >::process( os, tjp );
11     }
12   };
13   // specialization to terminate the recursion
14   template< class TJP >
15   struct stream_params< TJP, 1 > {
16     static void process( ostream& os, TJP* tjp ) {
17       os << *tjp->arg< TJP::ARGS - 1 >();
18     }
19   };
20
21   advice call( win32::Win32API() ) : after() {
22     if( win32::IsError( *tjp->result() ) ) {
23       ostringstream os;
24       DWORD c = GetLastError();
25
26       os << "WIN32 ERROR " << c << ": "
27          << win32::GetErrorText(c) << endl;
28       os << "WHILE CALLING: "
29          << tjp->signature() << endl;
30       os << "WITH: " << "(";
31
32       // Generate joinpoint-specific sequence
33       // of operations to stream all argument
34       // values
35       stream_params< JoinPoint, JoinPoint::ARGS >::process( os, tjp );
36       os << ")";
37
38       throw win32::Exception( os.str(), c );
39     }
40  } };
```

Fig. 4. An Aspect to Throw Win32 Errors as Exceptions

```
1  #include "Win32Error.h"
2
3  aspect CatchWin32Errors {
4    advice execution("% WinMain(...)"
5          || "% WndProc(...)" ) : around() {
6      try {
7        tjp->proceed();
8      }
9      catch( win32::Exception& e ) {
10       MessageBox( NULL, e.where.c_str(), NULL, MB_ICONERROR );
11     }
12  } };
```

Fig. 5. A Simple Aspect to Catch Win32 Errors

call `stream_params::process()` for the next argument (line 10). This implementation is, again, type-safe. The compiler automatically deduces the stream operator to call for a specific type. If no compatible operator is available, a compile-time error is thrown.

3.5 Handling Error Conditions

The exception handling itself is implemented, for demonstration purposes, as another simple aspect (Figure 5). It just displays the context information in a message box. If, for instance, the `CreateFile()` call (Figure 1, line 24) fails, because the configuration file `example.config` does not exist, the following error message pops up:

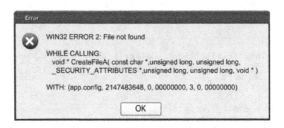

For real-world applications, the `CatchWin32Errors` aspect can be easily extended to implement advanced error handling concepts. For instance, a detailed error log can be created and the Win32 debugger API might be used to dump the call stack before the application is terminated.

4   Implementation Details

AspectC++ is a source-to-source weaver that transforms AspectC++ programs into C++ programs. The woven code can then be built with any standard-conforming C++ compiler, like g++ or VisualC++. In this section we show some details about this transformation process, focussing on generic advice code and the compile-time join-point API.

4.1   Aspect Transformation

AspectC++ generates a C++ class with a unique name for each join-point that is affected by advice code. Advice code is transformed into a template member function of the aspect, which in turn is transformed to a class. The unique join-point class is passed as a template argument to the advice code. Thus, the advice code is generic and can access all type definitions (C++ typedefs) inside the join-point class with `JoinPoint::Typename`. Indirectly these types can also be used by using the type-safe argument and result access function. The following code fragment shows advice code after its transformation into a template function.

```
// ...
template< class JoinPoint >
void __a0_after( JoinPoint *tjp ) {
  if( win32::IsError( *tjp->result() ) ) {
    // ...
  }
};
```

4.2 Argument Type Sequences

In AspectC++ template-metaprograms can be used to iterate over the argument type sequence of a join-point at compile time, as shown in the example. However, these sequences have to be provided in a "metaprogram-friendly" way. Just generating ArgType0, ArgType1, ..., ArgTypeN would not allow metaprograms to iterate over these types. For this purpose, the generated join-point-specific classes contain a template class Arg<I> which provides all the type information for the I'th argument as typedefs.

Sequences of types can be implemented by recursive template definitions as in the Loki[2] Typelist. For the AspectC++ we decided for an implementation with less demands on the back-end compiler, based on explicit template specialization. The following code shows a part of the generated type for the call join-point to RegisterClass() in the WinMain() function (Figure 1, line 28).

```
struct TJP_main_1 {
  typedef ::ATOM Result;
  typedef void That;
  typedef void Target;
  enum { ARGS = 1 };
  template <int I> struct Arg {};
  template <> struct Arg<0> {
    typedef ::WNDCLASSA *Type;
    typedef ::WNDCLASSA *ReferredType;
  };
  void **_args;
  Result *_result;
  inline Result *result() {return _result;}
  inline static const char *signature () {return ...;}
  inline void *arg (int n) {return _args[n];}
  template<int I> typename Arg<I>::ReferredType *arg (){
    return (typename Arg<I>::ReferredType *) arg(I);
  }
};
```

Note that only the _result and _args attributes consume memory at runtime, as everything else is resolved at compile-time.

5   Discussion

As demonstrated by the `ThrowWin32Errors` aspect, the technique of using static typing for generic advice implementations has some clear advantages regarding genericity and type-safety. On the other hand, the strong focus on static typing and the template-based implementation also implies some potential drawbacks. In this section we discuss the major advantages and limitations of our approach.

5.1   Advantages of Generic Advice

Genericity is achieved, as generic advice can be applied to functions with any signature, even if they use primitive or POD data types. This seamless support of non-class types is particulary important in the C/C++ domain. It is not possible to implement a unified access to instances of such types by extending their interface, e.g. using (baseclass-) introductions or other typical AOP idioms.

Separation of concerns is improved, as type-specific parts of the implementation (like the comparison with a "magic value") are separated out from the advice implementation in own external program entities. Thereby most of the advice code can be reused. Moreover, this makes the aspect code more stable with respect to changes in the component code. If, for instance, the result type of a function is changed to some unknown new type, the missing helper function is detected at compile-time. A non-generic aspect implementation that gives one advice per return type would silently miss to match the function's new signature.

Type-safety is guaranteed, as type errors are detected early at compile-time. Costly and potentially dangerous runtime casts are avoided. In languages that do not offer a type-safe access to the join-point's context information, problems (like a missing helper function) may not be detected before runtime.

5.2   Potential Limitations and Disadvantages

Code bloating is a potential problem, as generic advice is intantiated per join-point which might result in a high number of (similar) template instantiations, each being compiled seperately into the machine code. This is a general and well known issue in the C++ domain. It is difficult to judge its effects on real applications, as they depend on many other properties, especially the optimization capabilities of the compiler. For small template functions, which are inlined anyway, it has no effect at all.

In the example application, around 200 (`BeginPaint()`, 2 arguments) to 1000 (`CreateWindowEx()`, 11 arguments) additional bytes of code are generated for each of the Win32 function matched by the `ErrorException` aspect. Most of this overhead is induced by the generated streaming code. We estimate that a hand-written tangled implementation of the same crosscutting concern would result in similar costs, as it has to contain the same amount of streaming code. However, *additional* calls of the same Win32 function result in (almost) *no* additional overhead. In these cases the build system seems to be able to detect and optimize away the semantically identical template instantiations[4].

---

[4] All measurements were done using Microsoft Visual C++ 2003 using /O1 optimizations.

Compile-time fixation limits the approach to those types that are known at build-type. Generic advice can not be instantiated for additional types loaded dynamically at runtime. This is an implicit property of static typing. It is no real limitation for languages like C++ or Ada, as these languages do not support runtime type loading anyway. However, for Java or C#, which provide runtime class loading, this might be an issue. A possible solution for such languages is to rely on static type information as much as possible, but fall back to runtime type checking for types that are not known at build time.

Strong type semantics is a prerequisite of taking advantage of the approach. If, for instance, there is no general policy which "magic values" of a return type indicate a failure, it is not possible to bind the required test function solely on the base of the return type. However, if there are only a few exceptions from an otherwise general rule, they can be handled by seperate advice.

The example `ThrowWin32Errors` aspect, for instance, can already be applied to most functions of the Win32 base API in any program. It is easy to achieve complete coverage by implementing the helper functions for the remaining return types. Very few API functions, however, do not follow the general Win32 error handling conventions[5]. Luckily, these few exceptions can easily be handled by giving specific advice for them.

5.3 Conclusions

Overall, the approach fits well into languages like Ada and C++ that have a static typing philosophy. Languages like Java or C#, which support static, but emphazise dynamic typing, would even benefit from generic advice, although it might be necessary to extend the approach for these languages by some runtime mechanism that deals with dynamically loaded classes. Such combination would make the most of both worlds.

6   Related Work

So far, no publications focus on the development of generic, but type-safe aspects in languages with a sophisticated static type system as C++. C#, being currently a language with focus on dynamic typing, will be extended by additional static concepts (templates) in the next version [6]. However, the proposed extensions for integrating AOP into C# (e.g. [12,11]) do not cover static typing in aspects, yet.

Several extensions have been suggested to increase the static genericity of AspectJ. Instead of an extended join-point API, they are based on an extension of the join-point description language by context-dependend logic variables that are bound at weaving-time. *Sally* [5] focusses on genericity for structural aspects and proposes *parametric introductions* as an extension of the inter-type declaration mechanism in AspectJ and Hyper/J. *LogicAJ* [9] supports a similar mechanism called *generic introductions* and facilitates the development of generic advice code as well as reasoning over non-type

---

[5] The `TlsGetValue()` function, which is used to retrieve a thread-local storage value, is an example. It does not use a "magic value", but indicates success by clearing the `GetLastError()` value.

program entities like method names. While the use of of a logical language for this purposes has some clear advantages, it also leads to a high level of complexity. As C++ is already a "rich" multi-paradigm language with respect to complexity and expressive power, such an approach implies the risk of introducing redundant language concepts. For instance, a compile-time type deduction engine is already available through templates. For AspectC++, our goal is therefore to *carefully integrate* AOP concepts with the *existing* idioms and the philosophy of the C++ language.

The few existing work in the AOP/C++ domain focusses on using the preprocessor or static type concepts like overloading and advanced template techniques to "simulate" AOP in pure C++ [3,15,4].

7   Summary

The aim of this paper was to demonstrate, how static type information and a type-safe join-point API can be used in generic advice for the development of broadly applicable and type-safe aspects. By seperating out the type-specific parts (like the detection of an error result) into own external functions, both a good separation of concerns and a high level of type-safety is achieved.

Generic advice integrates well with the idioms of a language with a strong static type system as C++, where it is common and desirable to "decide things at compile time". As shown in the example, this involves even the utilization of template-metaprogramming techniques in advice code, e.g. to iterate over the function's arguments. Template-metaprogramming is known to be tricky and cumbersome, however, there are promising attempts to reduce its complexity by carefully extending the C++ language [14]. Currently, templates permit to reach a level of genericity and type-safety that is otherwise not feasable. Both, genericity and type-safety are very important properties for any aspect that is intended for reuse, like aspects from an aspect library. Such aspects are potentially applied to functions with any signature, which includes functions that use primitive and POD types. Thus, they should be able to deal with all those types and, even more important, raise potential type errors at compile-time.

References

1. AspectC++ homepage. http://www.aspectc.org/.
2. Andrei Alexandrescu. *Modern C++ Design: Generic Programming and Design Patterns Applied*. Addison-Wesley, 2001.
3. Krysztof Czarnecki, Lutz Dominick, and Ulrich W. Eisenecker. Aspektorientierte Programmierung in C++, Teil 1–3. *iX, Magazin für professionelle Informationstechnik*, 8–10, 2001.
4. Christopher Diggins. Aspect-Oriented Programming & C++. *Dr. Dobb's Journal of Software Tools*, 408(8), August 2004.
5. Stefan Hanenberg and Rainer Unland. Parametric introductions. In Mehmet Akşit, editor, *Proceedings of the 2nd International Conference on Aspect-Oriented Software Development (AOSD '03)*, pages 80–89, Boston, MA, USA, March 2003. ACM Press.
6. Andrew Kennedy and Don Syme. The design and implementation of generics for the .NET Common Language Runtime. In *Proceedings of the ACM SIGPLAN Conference on Programming Language Design and Implementation (PLDI '00)*, June 2001.

7. Gregor Kiczales, Erik Hilsdale, Jim Hugunin, Mik Kersten, Jeffrey Palm, and William G. Griswold. Getting started with AspectJ. *Communications of the ACM*, pages 59–65, October 2001.
8. Gregor Kiczales, Erik Hilsdale, Jim Hugunin, Mik Kersten, Jeffrey Palm, and William G. Griswold. An overview of AspectJ. In J. Lindskov Knudsen, editor, *Proceedings of the 15th European Conference on Object-Oriented Programming (ECOOP '01)*, volume 2072 of *Lecture Notes in Computer Science*, pages 327–353. Springer-Verlag, June 2001.
9. Günter Kniesel, Tobias Rho, and Stefan Hanenberg. Evolvable pattern implementations need generic aspects. In *Proceedings of the ECOOP'04 Workshop on Reflection, AOP and Meta-Data for Software Evolution (RAM-SE'04)*, Oslo, Norway, June 2004.
10. Daniel Lohmann, Georg Blaschke, and Olaf Spinczyk. Generic advice: On the combination of AOP with generative programming in AspectC++. In G. Karsai and E. Visser, editors, *Proceedings of the 3rd International Conference on Generative Programming and Component Engineering (GPCE '04)*, volume 3286 of *Lecture Notes in Computer Science*, pages 55–74. Springer-Verlag, October 2004.
11. Hridesh Rajan and Kevin Sullivan. Eos: Instance-level aspects for integrated system design. In *Proceedings of the 4th Joint European Software Engineering Conference and ACM Symposium on the Foundations of Software Engineering (ESEC/FSE '03)*, September 2003.
12. Mario Schüpany, Christa Schwanninger, and Egon Wuchner. Aspect-oriented programming for .NET. In *Proceedings of the 1st AOSDWorkshop on Aspects, Components and Patterns for Infrastructure Software (AOSD-ACP4IS '02)*, March 2002.
13. Olaf Spinczyk, Andreas Gal, and Wolfgang Schröder-Preikschat. AspectC++: An aspect-oriented extension to C++. In *Proceedings of the 40th International Conference on Technology of Object-Oriented Languages and Systems (TOOLS Pacific '02)*, pages 53–60, Sydney, Australia, February 2002.
14. Daveed Vandevoorde. Reflective metagrogramming. In *Presentation held on the ACCU 2003 Spring Conference*, Oxford, UK, April 2003. http://www.open-std.org/jtc1/sc22/wg21/docs/papers/2003/n1471.pdf.
15. Detlef Vollmann. Visibility of join-points in AOP and implementation languages. In *Second GI Workshop on Aspect-Oriented Software Development*, Bonn, Germany, February 2002.

Flexible Binding for Reusable Composition of Web Services*

Cesare Pautasso and Gustavo Alonso

Department of Computer Science,
Swiss Federal Institute of Technology (ETHZ),
ETH Zentrum, 8092 Zürich, Switzerland
{pautasso, alonso}@inf.ethz.ch

Abstract. In addition to publishing composite services as reusable services, compositions can also be reused by applying them to orchestrate different component services. To do so, it is important to describe compositions using flexible bindings, which define only the minimal constraints on the syntax and semantics of the services to be composed. This way, the choice of which service to invoke can be delayed to later stages in the life cycle of the composition. In the context of Web service composition, we refine the concept of binding beyond the basic distinction of static and dynamic binding. Bindings can be evaluated during the design, the compilation, the deployment, the beginning of the execution of a composition, or just before the actual service invocation takes place. Considering the current limited support of dynamic binding in the BPEL service composition language, we show how we addressed the problem in JOpera, where modeling bindings does not require a specific language construct as it can be considered a special application of reflection.

1 Introduction

Software components are – by definition – reusable [28]. In this paper we look at reusability from the opposite perspective and ask the following question: are compositions also reusable? Clearly, thanks to the recursive nature of most composition languages, compositions as a whole can be immediately reused as components. Web services, a particular kind of component used to build service oriented architectures [26], are also intended to be reused in many different combinations (e.g., [34]). Likewise, composite services are typically published themselves as Web services [24].

In addition to reuse based on packaging entire compositions as components, compositions – as opposed to basic components – can also be reused along a qualitatively different dimension. As it was informally exemplified by W. Tracz in [28]:

---

* Part of this work is supported by grants from the *Hasler Foundation* (DISC Project No. 1820) and the *SODIUM* EU Project (IST-FP6-004559)

T. Gschwind, U. Aßmann, and O. Nierstrasz (Eds.): SC 2005, LNCS 3628, pp. 151–166, 2005.

If you have components to reuse then you need to glue them together. If you have patterns to reuse, then you have the glue into which you have to stick pieces. After you glue pieces together long enough and you start seeing a pattern, then you can reuse the glue too.

Along these lines, the main contribution of this paper consists of applying such idea to Web service composition. In particular, we discuss what are the requirements for service composition languages, techniques and tools to support reusable composition. To this end, the notion of *binding* is very important, as it captures the relationship between the composition and its component services and defines what are the corresponding reusability constraints.

In practice, reusability is not the only issue related to the flexible binding of services into compositions. Other interesting ones concern the testability and the reliability of the compositions. These are also two very important aspects to be taken into account when building distributed applications out of the composition of Web services.

From a different perspective, current Web service technologies can be seen as an evolutionary step of existing RPC [4] based middleware to cover distribution at a World-wide-web scale [1]. In this sense, SOAP [29] is used as a wire-protocol, WSDL [30] as the interface description language (IDL), while UDDI [19] was meant to provide the foundation for a global registry infrastructure. Based on this, the focus of this paper is to discuss how to apply the notion of binding to address the Web service composition problem and to determine how well the existing Web services composition languages and tools support it.

Given the current limited level of support for static and dynamic binding in BPEL4WS [16], in this paper we present how reusable service compositions can be built using JOpera. JOpera is an open research platform for service composition developed at the Swiss Federal Institute of Technology. It features a visual composition language [22], a set of rapid composition tools based on Eclipse [20] and supports an extensible set of composition techniques [23].

This paper is organized as follows. We introduce the problem of binding in service oriented architectures by showing some of the limitations of BPEL in Section 2. Then, we refine the notion of flexible binding according to different orthogonal aspects: its scope and its evaluation time. In Section 4 we present how the JOpera system uses reflection to support flexible binding. In Section 5 we discuss related work in the context of Web service composition. In Section 6 we draw some conclusions.

2 Motivation

In service oriented architectures, binding is an abstraction mechanism to separate implementation specific details from a high-level description of the functionality of the services to be accessed. As an example, consider the approach followed by WSDL, which separates the abstract description of a service interface (the *port type*) from the transport protocols and the addressing information used to access

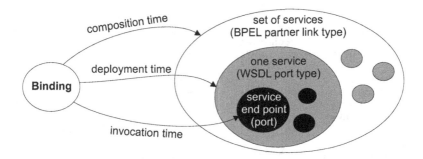

Fig. 1. Progressive refinement of a binding using BPEL

the corresponding service provider (the *port*). This separation of interface from implementation fulfills the important requirement of adaptability that make a composition reusable in an ever-changing distributed environment.

Building on this, BPEL[1] uses the notion of *abstract process* and *partner* to reflect the idea that the business processes modeling how different Web services should be composed can be applied to different service providers. By extending the WSDL standard service interface description with the declaration of a *partner link type*, the process which defines how to compose different services does not depend on specific services but can be customized to use different ones as long as they fit with the expected link type.

As represented in Figure 1, during the life time of a process, a binding is progressively refined going from a set of services to one specific service end point. When a process is designed, it does not contain any reference to a specific service, but it only lists partner port types. An abstract process is reused by constructing a mapping between concrete service port type definitions and the *roles* played by the various partners in the process. This mapping between WSDL definitions and partners is set once the composition is deployed and it is fixed for all executions of the composition.

As shown in the example (Figure 2), the only form of dynamic binding supported by BPEL consists of re-assigning end points which identify specific ports within a service interface at runtime. End points are identified with the WS-Addressing proposed standard [32]. Although this feature can be used to establish call-back relationships and allows to tap the flexibility offered by the separation between port types (interfaces) and ports (communication end-points), the values for the port type and the operation themselves are fixed for each **invoke** activity and cannot be changed as the process runs.

---

[1] The Business Process Execution Language for Web Services (BPEL4WS or BPEL) language specification represents the current state of the art in process-oriented Web service composition languages. It is currently undergoing a standardization process at OASIS, which may change some of its capabilities. In this example we refer to version 1.1 [14].

```
<process
  xmlns="http://schemas.xmlsoap.org/ws/2003/03/business-process/"
  name="AsyncEchoService" targetNamespace="urn:asyncEcho:Service"
  xmlns:this="urn:asyncEcho:Service" suppressJoinFailure="no"
  enableInstanceCompensation="no" abstractProcess="no">

  <partnerLinks>
    <partnerLink name="caller" partnerLinkType="this:EchoPLT"
      myRole="service" partnerRole="client"/>
  </partnerLinks>

  <variables>
    <variable name="echoMessage" messageType="this:EchoMessage"/>
  </variables>

  <sequence>
    <receive name="echoReceive" partnerLink="caller"
      portType="this:EchoService" operation="echo"
      variable="echoMessage" createInstance="yes"/>

    <assign>
      <copy>
        <from variable="echoMessage" part="replyTo"/>
        <to partnerLink="caller"/>
      </copy>
    </assign>

    <invoke name="echoReply" partnerLink="caller"
            portType="this:EchoClient" operation="echoCallback"
            inputVariable="echoMessage"/>
  </sequence>
```

Fig. 2. Example of dynamic redirection of service end points with BPEL. The **assign** activity copies a service end point reference from the incoming message to the partner link which is going to be invoked afterwards.

Thus, BPEL limits the scope of a binding depending on the time it is evaluated. Although a static binding can refer to different services identified by their port types, a dynamic binding is restricted to switch between the various ports of the service. This limits the reusability of composite services modeled with BPEL. Furthermore, by using WSDL port types to define constraints in the roles that can be assumed by each partner, such constraints are expressed only at the level of the syntactical description of the service interface and no explicit provision for semantics is made [16]. Thus, services which do not match the interface description contained in the binding will not be considered as potential replacements. Conversely, it is not possible to discard services that use the same syntactical signature, but provide incompatible functionality.

Before we present in detail how we address these limitations with JOpera, we introduce the notion of flexible binding abstracting from the details of a specific service composition language.

3   Flexible Binding

In general, a *binding* of a service into a composition can be defined as the reference used to choose the service to be invoked as part of the compostion. As we will discuss in the rest of this section, there are different ways of identifying the services to invoke. Furthermore, a binding can be evaluated at different times during the life cycle of a composition.

3.1   Modeling Bindings

Different composition languages may take different approaches to describing how components are bound into the composition. In this paper we make very little assumptions about how a composition language is used to model a composition. In particular, we assume that a composition contains two different kinds of information. 1) A set of bindings $\{b\}$, used to identify which services should be composed. 2) A model of the structural relationship between the bindings.

Although it is outside the scope of this paper to detail such model, it is worth noting that based on the structure of the composition it is possible to define constraints on the services that can be bound into it. For example, if the composition includes information about the data flow dependencies between the services, this information can be used to constrain the services that can be used. On the one hand, the data flow of the composition defines what data each service should be able to produce and consume. On the other hand, if two services are connected, they must fit with one another, i.e., be able to exchange messages with compatible content. As another example, if the composition includes control flow dependencies between the operations to be invoked, only services which support compatible interaction protocols can be used within such composition.

Binding by inclusion In the simplest case, services are statically bound into a composition by inclusion ($b = s$). Thus, the description of a service s is mixed with the description of the structure of the composition. Although this solution already captures the relationship between the composition and its component services, it is too simple in order to effectively model the reuse of either. With it, services can only be reused by duplicating their description in different parts of the compositions. Likewise, it is not straightforward to apply the same composition to invoke different services.

Binding by reference involves using references linking the composition to external descriptions of the services to be invoked. Thus, a binding becomes $b = t \rightarrow s$, where t represents the name referencing a service and s describes the service to be invoked. By using a reference, the service description can be stored separately from the composition. This is an important step which enables to model reuse at the level of the services, as it is now possible to have the same service referenced by more than one binding within more than one composition. However, since each binding uniquely identifies the service to be invoked, the model is not yet powerful enough to reuse compositions, where a composition can be applied to different services without modifying it.

Binding by Constraint To support reusable compositions, we extend the previous definition of binding to: $b = t \rightarrow S = \{s : C(s)\}$, where now t represents the reference to a set of services S. Thanks to this approach, a composition may be reused since its bindings only contain the constraint C modeling the requirements that a service should satisfy in order to be included in the composition.

Although this enables to reuse a composition, it remains to be defined how to model such constraints as part of each binding and when to evaluate the binding so that the actual service to be invoked can be determined based on the available known services. Depending on the available services and the actual set of constraints, it may occur that no service can be found as a result of the binding's evaluation. This condition will result in a failure of the execution of the composition. More precisely, issues such as service substitutability [7] and what is the information that should be provided to identify a service and to determine its equivalence with others remain open [11]. This is an important problem, as the services to be bound into a composition must fit within its structure. In other words, not all possible services may comply with the syntax and semantics assumed by the composition as well as by the other services which are part of it.

The problem of modeling these constraints can be addressed at different levels of abstraction. As we have shown in the example of the previous section, depending on the compostion language, it may be possible to define alternative communication end points associated with a given service interface. This way the composition does not contain hard-coded information about specific access paths to the service's functionality, but only defines how one should be chosen. Abstracting from the communication details, a larger number of services could be bound into a reusable composition as long as they have a compatible semantics [6]. Thus, as part of the binding, it should be possible to constrain the interface of the referenced service accordingly (e.g., by using ontologies [2], interface templates [8], service offerings and constraint groups [27], abstract functionalities [17], or formal functional specifications [33]).

3.2   Evaluating Bindings

Once a composition includes flexible bindings that do not uniquely identify the services to be composed, the composition system must evaluate such binding $(e(b) : b \rightarrow s \in S)$ so that the evaluation e selects the service s to be invoked among all possible ones (S) that satisfy the binding's constraints. For a composition, the result of the evaluation of all of its bindings forms a *binding configuration*, which describes which services are going to be used for each of its bindings. This evaluation can be influenced by different factors (Figure 3).

First of all, it may be useful to restrict the set of the services targeted by a binding. For example, *blacklisting* is used to guarantee that a set of services will not be used when dereferencing the binding. This mechanism allows to ensure that when an existing composition is reused, for example, untrusted providers, whose services have been added to the blacklist, are excluded from the set of services that can be bound into it.

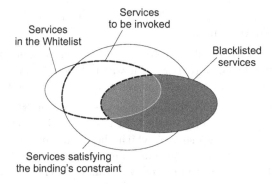

Fig. 3. Evaluating a binding using additional constraints

Conversely, *whitelisting* is used in a complementary way. Whereas a black-listed service will not be considered, a binding constrained by a whitelist will reference only services that are explicitly enumerated in such list. This way, during the evaluation of the binding it is possible to control that the services invoked by the composition, e.g., belong to a set of services that should be used only for testing purposes.

Formally, the set of services that can be invoked I is related to the original set S defined by the composition's binding as follows:

$$I = (S \cap W) \setminus B$$

where W represents the set of whitelisted services and B the blacklist. Although it is unlikely that a service belongs to both lists at the same time, with this definition the blacklist has the higher priority.

In addition to these two policies that control by exclusion or inclusion what are the services that can be chosen, the choice of the service resulting from the binding's evaluation can also be driven by Quality of Service considerations [18]. In this case a trade off is involved, e.g., each service is selected by minimizing the price (or invocation cost) associated with it, while maximizing the expected performance (e.g., in terms of the guaranteed response time of the service). This kind of metadata is typically maintained by service registries (e.g., UDDI [19]) which use a combination of automatic tools and manual validation to ensure its correctness. However, there is still a lot of work that remains to be done before issues such as *trust establishment* can be dealt with in a fully automatic manner.

3.3   Beyond Static and Dynamic Binding

In the previous section we have presented what are some of the options that can affect the evaluation of a binding, influencing the way a service is chosen to be included in a composition. However, we have not discussed when this evaluation may occur. During the life cycle of a composition, there are many opportunities for taking such decision. Thus, the traditional distinction between static vs.

dynamic (or early vs. late [10]) binding can be refined by differentiating between the following evaluation times.

Registration Time. First of all, even before a composition is defined, pre-existing services are classified using a registry. The way individual services are catalogued affects how they can be discovered and referenced from a composition [9].

Composition Time. During the definition of a composition, the developer makes a selection of the services to be invoked. At this stage, it is possible to establish a fixed binding to the exact service which should be invoked (a form of early binding). However, this limits the reusability of the composition, which would have to be modified in order to be used with different services. As an alternative it is also possible to associate some more limited constraints with each binding. These constraints will influence the choice of the service, which is delayed to a later stage.

Compilation Time. Before a composition can be executed, it is usually compiled from the representation used to model it to a representation optimized for execution. Assuming that the compiler has access to quality of service metadata about services, it can use this information to select which services should be bound into the composition based on different policies [25]. Existing approaching advocating the automatic selection of services based on whether they fit with the composition's structural constraints can also be considered as a form of compile-time binding [3]. Compilation time is also a good opportunity for checking the consistency of the binding's constraints with respect to the available services. Although it is possible that services which satisfy a binding will become available after a composition has been compiled, it may be useful to warn the developer about potential problems due to missing services and unsatisfied bindings.

Deployment Time. At this point, the compiled service composition is deployed in the execution environment. During deployment the composition changes of hands, going from the control of the developer to the end user which will manage its execution. In fact, it is the latest opportunity for the developer of the composition to customize it by selecting the specific services that should be bound into it. Thus, as part of the deployment, a developer playing the role of system integrator may select what are the actual service providers to use for the particular installation. This way, a reusable composition can be tailored to use different services each time it is deployed to be executed at a different site taking into account the characteristics of the local environment.

Startup Time. After deployment, a composition is ready to be executed. Bindings can also be evaluated at the very beginning of its execution. This way, as part of the initialization phase of a specific execution it can be decided what are the services that should be used. More precisely, binding on startup refers to the possibility of further constraining the services to be invoked in a different way each time the composition is run.

One interesting application example of this case concerns the testing of the composition. In this scenario, while a composition is developed, it may not be possible to invoke production quality services. The services to be composed may not yet be available or it may not be possible to use them for testing the composition, as they belong to a pre-existing system which is already in production. Thus, developers may find it useful to start a testing run of their composition by binding some of its services to stubs which will be invoked for testing purposes only.

Invocation Time. This case is what is mostly referred to as dynamic binding whereby the decision about which services should be used is delayed until the latest possible time, i.e., when the service is about to be invoked.

Although all of the previously described evaluation times involved a certain degree of manual intervention, in this case, we argue that is too late to do so. In practice, the choice of the service during the binding's evaluation should be fully automated for two reasons. Asking a user operator to manually bind a service invocation to a provider each time a service should be invoked would dramatically affect the execution's performance. Furthermore, it should not be assumed that users monitoring the execution of the composition have complete knowledge about details concerning bindings, which are typically under the purview of the original developers of the composition.

Failed Invocation Time. A special case of dynamic binding, which we would like to distinguish, concerns the re-evaluation of a binding in case of a failed service invocation. The main purpose of this binding on retry mechanism is to enhance the reliability of the composition by offering the capability of selecting a different service if the one resulting from the first evaluation of the binding turns out – at run-time – to be unavailable. More precisely, the default service referenced by the binding is called as if the binding would have been a static one. If the invocation succeeds, the execution of the composition continues normally. In case of failures due, for example, to the temporary unavailability of the default remote service provider, this mechanism allows to invoke a backup service which – in general – is selected by re-evaluating the binding like in the case described previously.

4   Flexible Binding with JOpera

After giving a general description about flexible binding and how it can be used, we proceed to show how these ideas have influenced the design of JOpera's visual composition language and the corresponding run-time infrastructure. In this section we are argue that a composition language may support flexible bindings without necessarily embodying this notion into a specific language construct. Instead, we will show that different kinds of bindings can be all specified by using reflection.

4.1   Modeling Bindings with Reflection

As opposed to introducing a specific language feature to support flexible bindings, in JOpera we have taken a more general approach based on *reflection*. Reflection is the ability of a computational system to represent and modify information about itself [15]. In JOpera, reflection is used to access and modify metadata about the static structure of a composition, its current state of execution, as well as to interact with the services provided by the runtime system [21].

In the first case, the composition language extends the basic service invocation construct with *system parameters* (In the visual syntax, they are shaded in gray and their name is prefixed with SYS). Thus, in addition to input and output parameters describing the data which is sent and received from a service, the system parameters allow to control the invocation mechanism and access related metadata. Furthermore, *system services* model the interaction between a composition and the underlying runtime infrastructure.

In the context of this paper, reflection is a mechanism used to expose in the composition language the binding and registry services provided by the runtime environment so that they can be controlled from within a composition. More precisely, we are interested in accessing a registry listing available services and in controlling the way a binding is evaluated.

One of the advantages of reflection is that it leaves ample freedom to model the constraints associated with a binding in many different ways. As we are going to show, with reflection it is possible to distinguish which part of the composition should be dynamically bound from the policy controlling how such binding should be evaluated. In the most advanced case, through reflection, a composition may – for instance – dynamically modify itself to bind to a service whose interface requires some form of adaptation to fit with the rest of the composition.

4.2 Bindings in the JOpera Visual Composition Language

In the rest of this section we illustrate with an example how to use reflection to model different kinds of bindings constraints: fixed bindings, where the constraint determines exactly which service should be invoked; communication level constraints, applied to the communication end points to be used by the services; structural constraints, defining minimal requirements on the syntax of a service interface; but also even how to remove all constraints, where a binding is left completely free so that a composition may call any Web service.

The examples shown in Figures 4 and 5 involves a typical (and reusable) interaction pattern between a client and a service playing the role of broker. More precisely, depending on the client's request, the broker will lookup what are the available supplier services, forward them the original client request and gather their corresponding bids, which are finally sent back to the client. Although this is a simple example, it can be implemented in different ways depending on the required level of reusability of the composition.

Fixed Binding. This is the simplest form of binding, where a service is statically bound into a composition. In case of the example shown in Figure 4, this form of binding is applied to the lookup service. With it, a default RegistryProvider is assigned to the lookup service invocation. However, with the tools provided with JOpera it is still possible to replace the registry service, both when the composition is deployed as well as each time it is started.

Communication Level Constraints. In the case of services, whose interface is bound to a given provider, it is still possible to dynamically choose the com-

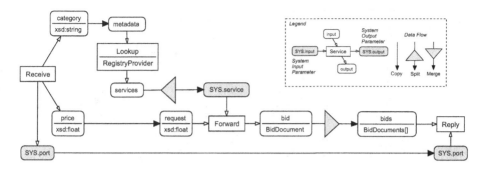

Fig. 4. The first version of the broker composite service using dynamic binding with structural constraints

munication port (or end-point, in WSDL terminology) which should be used to communicate with it. In both versions of the example, the Reply is constrained to be invoked on the same port that was used to perform the Receive. In other words, this binding constraint ensures that the answer of the broker composite service goes back to the client which submitted the original request. In general, a similar approach can be used to model constraints related to asynchronous message exchanges so that a composition can be reused to handle the interaction between different services that follow the same conversation [5].

Structural Constraints. As a general note, this example follows the principle of separating the binding of the service invocation from the strategy used to evaluate the binding. More concretely, the evaluation of a binding can be modeled as the invocation of a lookup operation of a registry service. In this case, reflection is used to expose the registry to which the appropriate query is sent. In addition to JOpera's internal registry, such lookup funcionality can also be provided by an external registry (e.g., UDDI [19]) or search engine (e.g., Woogle [8]). Thus, a binding constraint corresponds to a query to a service registry. Depending on the capabilities of such registry, a query may be based on metadata identifying the context that should be used to filter the resulting list of services, as shown in Figure 4. Not shown explicitly in the example, the query sent to the Lookup service also includes a structural constraint on the interface of the services to be returned. In particular, the composition specifies that candidate services to be bound in place of the Forward invocation must comply with its interface, i.e., they must accept at most one parameter (request) or a certain data type (a floating point number as prescribed by XML schema [31]). Furthermore, the result of the services must contain at least a parameter named bid of type BidDocument. Depending on the matching algorithm employed by the particular lookup service, these structural constraints would allow the composition to be applied to services returning additional parameters (which are simply discarded by the composition) and accepting a subset of the required input data parameters, assuming that the service interface defines default values to be used for the missing input parameters.

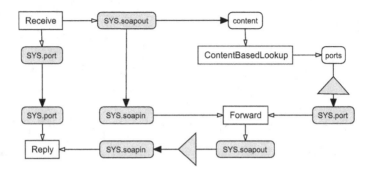

Fig. 5. The second version of the broker composite service using dynamic binding without any constraints

Unconstrained Bindings. In the second version of the example shown in Figure 5, the broker composite service can be reused with minimal constraints on the content of the messages that are exchanged between client and suppliers. By using reflection to expose details such as the content of the raw SOAP messages (the SYS.soapin and SYS.soapout parameters), it is possible to reuse this composition which only describes the interaction patterns between the services involved, abstracting from the specific syntax of their interfaces.

More precisely, this broker composite service uses a ContentBasedLookup service, which takes the content of a SOAP message to query a registry for compatible services that may be able to consume it. As opposed to the previous example, in order to identify such services, the registry only returns the port (or end-point) of the service that should be dynamically used by the Forward service invocation. Furthermore, it is the registry's responsibility to correlate the incoming message with the available services which may be able to process it. In the previous example, the extraction of the metadata to be used to find matching services was done as part of the receipt of the message.

This example shows that it is possible to use reflection to access the internal representation of a Web service invocation in order to express a binding which is left completely free to be evaluated at the latest possible time. Clearly, the example is a bit extreme, as all assumptions about the syntax of the data received and produced by the services have been removed from the composition. Thus, its expressiveness suffers as it is impossible to verify (neither statically or dynamically) that a service complies with the constraints that are associated with its interface simply because such information is not included in the composition.

However, there may be cases for which this level of flexibility is clearly the intended behavior. For these cases, the example of Figure 5 shows how to use a ContentBasedLookup service to dynamically find a service matching with a message that is going to be forwarded to it. In a similar way (Figure 6), it is possible to extend the registry service with mediation functionality so that the message used to lookup matching services can be transformed to be consumed by the selected service, in case it cannot be forwarded directly.

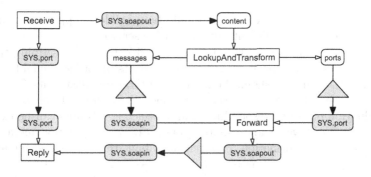

Fig. 6. The third version of the broker composite service can adapt messages before forwarding them to the chosen service end points

5 Related Work

The need for flexibile bindings was recently brought forward in [13], with the argument that the requirements of pervasive computing would challenge current component-based software engineering methodologies. In the context of Web service composition, this challenge has been addressed in different ways, mostly by including specific constructs in the corresponding composition languages. In BPEL [14], as we have exemplified in Section 2, communication end-points can be reassigned at runtime. Although this gives some limited flexibility, it does not enhance the reusability of a composition, as all information about the *port types* and *operations* that identify the Web service to be invoked are bound to constant values. This is not the case in other languages, e.g., XL [12], where flexible binding is supported by letting the argument of an invoke command represent an arbitrary XQuery expression, which is evaluated at runtime to choose the actual service to be invoked.

Reusability of Web service compositions is also the focus of [17], where composition "patterns" are modeled in terms of abstract "functionalities". Following this approach, the actual Web services come into play at "pattern-specialization time", when developers manually select the services which match the functionalities required by the composition. In the same paper the important trade-off between the abstraction (i.e., potential reusability) of a pattern and its expressiveness is identified. The example of Figure 5 can be interpreted along the same lines. Given the lack of assumptions made by the composition about its components, it is true that the composition can be reused with many services. However, the expressiveness of the composition suffers, as no constraints are given in order to choose such services.

6 Conclusion

In this paper we have presented a different perspective on how to reuse Web service compositions. Not only can compositions of Web services be published themselves as a Web service, but it should be possible to apply the same composition to coordinate different but compatible services.

To do so, we introduced the notion of flexible binding describing the relationship between a composition and its components. In order to enable reusable compositions, a binding should be modeled in terms of constraints. These identify a set of candidate services from which one will be chosen to be invoked after the evaluation of the corresponding binding. Such constraints can be expressed in many different ways: for example, queries over classification meta-data or quality of service information, requirements about the syntax and semantics of service interfaces, as well as blacklisting and whitelisting of service providers. Furthermore a binding can be evaluated at different times during the lifecycle of a composition, going beyond the classic distinction between early and late binding, we have exemplified several different points in time (registration, composition, compilation, deployment, startup, invocation and retry on failure) in which a binding may be fully evaluated or more constraints can be added to it. Thanks to the flexible binding linking the description of the composition to the description of the components, which are kept separate, not only compositions become reusable but their reliability and testability may be improved.

Given the wide range of different approaches to modeling bindings that have been introduced in existing composition languages and tools, but also considering the partial support for flexible binding of the state-of-the-art BPEL4WS language and related tools, in this paper we suggest a different approach based on reflection. With it, it is not necessary to include explicit constructs in a composition language to model flexible binding. Instead, flexible binding can be considered as a particular application of reflection, whereby – as we have shown with several examples – parts of the underlying composition infrastructure are exposed from within the composition language. One advantage of this approach is that it is possible to distinguish how a service is bound into a composition from the strategy used to evaluate such binding.

Acknowledgements. The authors would like to thank the anonymous reviewers for their insightful comments, Tone Hansen (LOCUS) for pointing out blacklisting as a good strategy from the system integrator's perspective, and Biörn Biörnstad for his expertise with BPEL.

References

1. G. Alonso, F. Casati, H. Kuno, and V. Machiraju. *Web services: Concepts, Architectures and Applications.* Springer, November 2003.
2. A. Ankolekar, M. Burstein, J. R. Hobbs, O. Lassila, D. McDermott, D. Martin, S. A. McIlraith, S. Narayanan, M. Paolucci, T. Payne, and K. Sycara. DAML-S: Web Service Description for the Semantic Web. In I. Horrocks and J. Hendler, editors, *Proceedings of the 1st International Semantic Web Conference (ISWC2002)*, volume 2342, pages 348–363, Sardinia, Italy, June 2002.

3. D. Berardi, D. Calvanese, G. D. Giacomo, M. Lenzerini, and M. Mecella. Automatic Composition of e-Services that Export their Behavior. In *Proceedings of the 1st International Conference on Service-Oriented Computing (ICSOC 2003)*, volume 2910 of *LNCS*, pages 43–58, Trento, Italy, December 2003. Springer.
4. A. D. Birrel and B. J. Nelson. Implementing remote procedure calls. *ACM Transactions on Computer Systems (TOCS)*, 2(1):39–59, 1984.
5. M. Brambilla, S. Ceri, M. Passamani, and A. Riccio. Managing Asynchronous Web Services Interaction. In *Proceedings of the IEEE International Conference on Web Services (ICWS'04)*, pages 80–88, San Diego, California, June 2004.
6. C. Bussler. Semantic Web services: Reflections on Web Service Mediation and Composition. In *Proceedings of the Fourth International Conference on Web Information Systems Engineering (WISE 2003)*, pages 253–260, Roma, Italy, December 2003.
7. V. De Antonellis, M. Melchiori, B. Pernici, and P. Plebani. A Methodology for e-Service Substitutability in a Virtual District Environment. In *Proceedings of the 15th International Conference on Advanced Information Systems Engineering (CAiSE 2003)*, pages 552–567, Klagenfurt, Austria, 2003.
8. X. Dong, A. Y. Halevy, J. Madhavan, E. Nemes, and J. Zhang. Simlarity Search for Web Services. In *Proceedings of the 30th International Conference on Very Large Data Bases (VLDB'04)*, pages 372–383, Toronto, CA, August 2004.
9. V. Draluk. Discovering Web services: An Overview. In *Proceedings of 27th International Conference on Very Large Data Bases (VLDB 2001)*, pages 637–640, Roma, Italy, 2001.
10. M. Elson. *Concepts of Programming Languages*. Scientific Research Associates, Chicago, 1973.
11. D. Fensel and C. Bussler. The Web Service Modeling Framework WSMF. *Electronic Commerce Research and Applications*, 1(2):113–137, Summer 2002.
12. D. Florescu, A. Gruenhagen, and D. Kossmann. XL: An XML Programming Language for Web Service Specification and Composition. In *Proceedings of the 11th international conference on World Wide Web (WWW'02)*, pages 65–76, Honolulu, Hawaii, USA, 2002.
13. T. Gschwind, M. Jazayeri, and J. Oberleitner. Pervasive Challenges for Software Components. In *Proceedings of the 9th International Workshop on Radical Innovations of Software and Systems Engineering in the Future (RISSEF 2002)*, pages 152–166, Venice, Italy, October 2002.
14. IBM, Microsoft, and BEA Systems. *Business Process Execution Language for Web services (BPEL4WS) 1.0*, August 2002. http://www.ibm.com/developerworks/library/ws-bpel.
15. P. Maes. Concepts and experiments in computational reflection. In *Proceedings of the 2nd Annual Conference on Object-Oriented Programming Systems, Languages and Applications (OOPSLA'87)*, pages 147–155, Orlando, FL, October 1987.
16. D. J. Mandell and S. A. McIlraith. Adapting BPEL4WS for the Semantic Web: The Bottom-Up Approach to Web Service Interoperation. In G. Goos, J. Hartmanis, and J. van Leeuwen, editors, *Proceedings of the Second International Semantic Web Conference (ISWC2003)*, volume 2870 of *LNCS*, pages 227–241, Sanibel Island, Florida, 2003. Springer.
17. L. Melloul and A. Fox. Reusable Functional Composition Patterns for Web Services. In *Proceedings of the Second International Conference on Web Services (ICWS2004)*, pages 498–505, July 2004.
18. D. A. Menascé. Composing Web Services: A QoS View. *IEEE Internet Computing*, 8(6):88–90, November-December 2004.

19. Oasis. *Universal Description, Discovery and Integration of Web services (UDDI) Version 3.0,* 2002. http://uddi.org/pubs/uddi_v3.htm.
20. C. Pautasso.   JOpera: Process Support for more than Web services. http://www.iks.ethz.ch/jopera/download.
21. C. Pautasso. *A Flexible System for Visual Service Composition.* PhD thesis, Diss. ETH Nr. 15608, July 2004.
22. C. Pautasso and G. Alonso. Visual Composition of Web Services. In *Proceedings of the 2003 IEEE International Symposium on Human-Centric Computing Languages and Environments (HCC 2003),* pages 92–99, Auckland, New Zealand, 2003.
23. C. Pautasso and G. Alonso. From Web Service Composition to Megaprogramming. In *Proceedings of the 5th VLDB Workshop on Technologies for E-Services (TES-04),* Toronto, Canada, August 2004.
24. C. Pelzu. Web Services Orchestration and Choreography. *COMPUTER,* 36(10):46–52, October 2003.
25. S. Ran. A framework for discovering Web services with desired quality of services attributes. In *Proc. of the 1st International Conference on Web Services (ICWS 2003),* pages 208–213, Las Vegas, 2003.
26. C. Szyperski. Component technology - what, where, and how? In *Proceedings of the 25th International Conference on Software Engineering,* pages 684–693, Portland, Oregon, USA, 2003.
27. V. Tosic, K. Patel, and B. Pagurek. Reusability Constructs in the Web Service Offerings Language (WSOL). In *Proceedings of the Second International Workshop on Web Services, E-Business and the Semantic Web (WES 2003),* volume 3095 of *LNCS,* pages 105–119. Springer, 2004.
28. W. Tracz. *Confessions of a Used Program Salesman.* Addison-Wesley, 1995.
29. W3C.   Simple   Object   Access   Protocol   *(SOAP)   1.1,*   2000. http://www.w3.org/TR/SOAP.
30. W3C.   *Web   services   Definition   Language   (WSDL)   1.1,*   2001. http://www.w3.org/TR/wsdl.
31. W3C. XML Schema, 2001. http://www.w3.org/TR/xmlschema-0/.
32. W3C.   *Web   Services   Addressing   (WS-Addressing),*   2004. http://www.w3.org/Submission/ws-addressing/.
33. A. M. Zaremski and J. M. Wing. Specification Matching of Software Components. *ACM Transactions on Software Engineering and Methodology (TOSEM),* 6(4):333–369, October 1997.
34. L.-J. Zhang and M. Jeckle. The Next Big Thing: Web services Collaboration. In *Proceedings of the International Conference on Web services (ICWS-Europe 2003),* pages 1–10, Erfurt, Germany, 2003.

Stateful Aspects in JAsCo

Wim Vanderperren, Davy Suvée, María Agustina Cibrán, and Bruno De Fraine

Vrije Universiteit Brussel, Pleinlaan 2, 1050 Brussels, Belgium
{wvdperre, dsuvee, mcibran, bdefrain}@vub.ac.be
http://ssel.vub.ac.be

Abstract. Aspects that trigger on a sequence of join points instead of on a single join point are not explicitly supported in current Aspect-Oriented approaches. Explicit protocols are however frequently employed in Component-Based Software Development and business processes and are as such valid targets for aspect application. In this paper, we propose an extension of the JAsCo aspect-oriented programming language for declaratively specifying a protocol fragment. The proposed pointcut language is equivalent to a finite state machine. Advices can be attached to every transition specified in the pointcut protocol. Furthermore, the complement of a protocol can also be used for triggering aspects. The JAsCo tools support the stateful aspects language and implement it very efficiently by employing the JAsCo run-time weaver. As a validation of the approach, we present a case study in the context of reaction business rules.

1 Introduction

Aspect-Oriented Programming (AOP) [15] is a recent software programming paradigm that aims at providing a better separation of concerns. At its root is the observation that some concerns cannot be cleanly modularized using traditional abstraction mechanisms such as class hierarchies. These so-called *crosscutting* concerns will therefore inevitably appear scattered across different modules of the system, making them difficult to comprehend and maintain. Typical examples of such concerns are tracing, synchronization and transaction management.

In order to enable a clean modularization of crosscutting concerns, AOP techniques such as AspectJ [16] introduce the concept of an *aspect*, in addition to the use of regular classes. An aspect defines a set of *join points* in the target application where *advices* alter the regular execution. The set of joint points is declaratively specified through a *pointcut*. The aspect logic is then automatically *woven* into the target application.

Although AOP research originally focused on a model where aspects are invoked on static locations in the compile-time structure of the program, it was early on argued that the applicability of certain so-called *jumping* aspects [3] can only be expressed in terms of dynamic conditions. Most of the current approaches therefore feature a dynamic join point model, i.e. a model where the join points are run-time events of the program execution. As such, it becomes possible to invoke aspect behavior based on run-time types, call-stack context (e.g. AspectJ's `cflow()` pointcut), dynamically evaluated expressions,...

T. Gschwind, U. Aßmann, and O. Nierstrasz (Eds.): SC 2005, LNCS 3628, pp. 167–181, 2005.

Describing the applicability of aspects in terms of a *sequence* or *protocol* of run-time events however, is generally not supported. With the exception of the cflow() pointcut, the pointcuts of current mainstream AOP languages cannot refer to the history of previously matched pointcuts in their specification. In order to trigger an aspect on a protocol sequence of join points, one is obliged to program code for maintaining a state regarding the occurrence of relevant join points, as such implementing the protocol by hand. Not only is this a cumbersome task, but it is also conceptually undesirable, because it involves mixing the aspect-applicability control-mechanism with the advice code itself.

Explicit protocols are nevertheless frequently encountered in a wide range of fields such as Component-Based Software Development [25,10], data communications [19] and business processes [1]. We therefore believe that protocols are valid targets for aspect application, and argue that it is desirable to support them in the pointcut language itself; delegating the actual control-mechanism implementation to the weaver. This paper proposes an extension of the JAsCo [18] programming language for *stateful aspects* that can declaratively specify a protocol of expected pointcuts.

The paper is structured as follows. Section 2 introduces the JAsCo language and illustrates the need for explicit support of protocols. The JAsCo extension for supporting stateful aspects is discussed in section 3. Section 4 focuses on the implementation details of our approach, while section 5 validates it by presenting a case study. Finally, we discuss related work in section 6 and end up with conclusions in section 7.

2   Introduction to JAsCo

The JAsCo [18] AOP approach is an aspect-oriented extension for Java that allows for a clean modularization of crosscutting concerns. The JAsCo language stays as close as possible to the original Java syntax and concepts and introduces two new entities, namely *Aspect Beans* and *Connectors*. An aspect bean is an extended version of a regular Java Bean that allows describing crosscutting concerns independently of concrete component types and APIs. JAsCo connectors on the other hand are used for deploying one or more reusable aspect beans within a concrete component context and provide support for describing their mutual interactions.

A typical example of a crosscutting concern is the run-time checking of timing contracts [21]. Instead of inserting the logic behind these contracts at various places within the base code, one can modularize this behavior into a single entity by employing a JAsCo aspect bean. Figure 1 illustrates the implementation of the dynamic timer aspect bean.

Typically, an aspect bean contains one or more hook definitions that implement the crosscutting behavior and usually a number of ordinary Java class members which are shared among all hooks. The DynamicTimer aspect bean of figure 1 describes a TimeStamp hook (lines 18-29) and the notification system for its listeners (lines 3-16). The TimeStamp hook is responsible for capturing

```
1   class DynamicTimer {
2
3       private Vector<TimeListener> listeners = new Vector<TimeListener>();
4       private long timestampbefore, timestampafter;
5
6       void addTimeListener(TimeListener aListener) {
7         listeners.add(aListener);
8       }
9       void removeTimeListener(TimeListener aListener) {
10        listeners.remove(aListener);
11      }
12      void notifyTimeListeners(Method method, long time) {
13          for (TimeListener listener : listeners) {
14            listener.timeStampTaken(method,time);
15          }
16      }
17
18      hook TimeStamp {
19        TimeStamp(timedmethod(..args)) {
20            execute(timedmethod);
21        }
22        before {
23            timestampbefore = System.currentTimeMillis();
24        }
25        after {
26            timestampafter = System.currentTimeMillis();
27            notifyListeners(thisJointPoint,timestampafter-timestampbefore);
28        }
29      }
30 }
```

Fig. 1. The JAsCo-aspect for dynamic timing

a timestamp and notifying its listeners whenever some functionality of a component is executed. To this end, the `TimeStamp` hook describes a constructor (lines 19-21), which specifies in an abstract way when the normal execution of a method should be interrupted in order to trigger the aspect behavior. Each constructor receives several abstract method parameters as inputs which are bound to one or more concrete method signatures whenever the hook is explicitly deployed using a connector. The constructor body (line 20) outlines when the behavior of the hook should be triggered. In case of the `TimeStamp` hook, the crosscutting behavior is performed whenever one of the methods bound to the abstract method parameter `timedmethod` is executed. The advices of a hook, namely `before`, `replace`, `after`, `after throwing` and `after returning`, are employed for specifying the various actions a hook needs to perform whenever its behavior is triggered. The implementation of an advice is able to refer to the arguments of the abstract method parameters and accesses the currently visited joinpoint and its reflective information by employing the `thisJoinPoint` keyword. In the aspect bean of figure 1, the before advice describes that a timestamp should be taken prior to the execution of `timedmethod` (lines 22-24). The after advice calculates the time that was required to execute the `timedmethod` method and announces it to all registered listeners (lines 25-28)[1].

---

[1] Notice that the aspect bean implements a very simplistic timestamping mechanism in order to keep the example simple and easy to understand. The provided implementation is not thread-safe and does not work for recursive methods.

```
1  connector TimeConnector {
2    DynamicTimer.TimeStamp timer =
3      new DynamicTimer.TimeStamp (void ComponentX.a());
4    timer.before();
5    timer.after();
6  }
```

Fig. 2. The JAsCo connector for dynamic timing

Abstract and reusable aspect beans are deployed onto a concrete component context by making use of connectors. Each connector allows to explicitly instantiate and initialize one or more logically related hooks. Figure 2 illustrates a connector that instantiates the `TimeStamp` hook of Figure 1 onto the `a()` method of the `ComponentX` component (lines 2-3). As a result, the abstract method parameter `timedmethod` of the `TimeStamp` hook constructor is bound to this given method. Additionally, it is specified that the `before` and `after` advices need to be executed whenever a join point of the newly instantiated hook `timer` is encountered (lines 4-5). To sum up, this connector specifies that whenever the `a()` method of the `ComponentX` component is executed, a timestamp is taken and the corresponding listeners are notified afterwards in order to verify whether the `a()` method satisfies the specified timing contracts.

The `DynamicTimer` aspect bean is suitable to perform time contract verification on a single method. It can however not be reused to verify timing contracts on a full component protocol. Imagine one wants to check whether a particular component protocol `methodA-methodB-methodC` is executed within a predefined time period. These methods can occur in any sequence, so it does not suffice to just add a before advice to methodA and an after advice to methodC in order to time this protocol. One has to explicitly keep track of the protocol. The `ProtocolDynamicTimer` aspect bean, illustrated in figure 3, presents an ad-hoc solution to implement the time contract verification of this particular protocol. It extends the basic `DynamicTimer` aspect bean, this way inheriting the listener notification system. For each step in the protocol, a dedicated hook is introduced, which implements the associated actions. When `methodA` of hook `ProtocolMethodA` is executed (lines 7-9), a timestamp is taken (line 11) and the boolean value `methodAExecuted` associated with that step of the protocol is set (line 12). This `before` advice is only performed the very first time protocol `methodA-methodB-methodC` is executed. This behavior is enforced through the `isApplicable` method (line 14). This additional JAsCo language construct is a method that allows to describe a run-time condition which ensures that the advices of an aspect bean are only performed when its body evaluates to true (similar to the `if` pointcut designator in AspectJ). By employing the `isApplicable` method, the advices associated with hook `ProtocolMethodC` will not be executed as long as the boolean value associated with `ProtocolMethodB` is not set to true (line 36). As such, the three hooks defined within the `ProtocolDynamicTimer` aspect bean ensure that the associated listeners are only notified when a full `methodA-methodB-methodC` protocol is encountered.

Although the aspect bean illustrated in Figure 3 can be used to verify whether the particular component protocol is performed within a specified time period,

```
1   class ProtocolDynamicTimer extends DynamicTimer {
2
3     boolean methodaexecuted, methodbexecuted = false;
4
5     hook ProtocolMethodA {
7       ProtocolMethodA(methodA(..args)) {
8         execute(methodA);
9       }
10      before {
11        timestampbefore = System.currentTimeMillis();
12        methodaexecuted = true;
13      }
14      isApplicable() { return !methodaexecuted; }
15    }
16
17    hook ProtocolMethodB {
18      ProtocolMethodB(methodB(..args)) {
19        execute(methodB);
20      }
21      before {
22        methodbexecuted = true;
23      }
24      isApplicable() { return methodaexecuted; }
25    }
26
27    hook ProtocolMethodC {
28      ProtocolMethodC(methodC(..args)) {
29        execute(methodC);
30      }
31      after {
32        timestampafter = System.currentTimeMillis();
33        notifyListeners(method,timestampafter-timestampbefore);
34        methodaexecuted = false; methodbexecuted = false;
35      }
36      isApplicable() { return methodbexecuted; }
37    }
38
39  }
```

Fig. 3. The JAsCo-aspect for dynamic timing of a component protocol

it requires to explicitly capture each possible state of the protocol in a separate hook. As such, one is obliged to describe and implement the full protocol by hand, as a protocol sequence of join points is not explicitly supported using regular JAsCo and other state-of-the-art aspect-oriented approaches. This also involves tangling the description of the applicability of the aspect with its behavior. In the next section, an extension to the JAsCo language is proposed, which allows to declaratively specify a protocol of expected pointcuts. Advices can be attached to each step of the pointcut protocol, allowing to describe the time contract verification of a component protocol in a more declarative way.

3   Stateful Aspects Language

Mainstream aspect-oriented approaches rarely support protocol history conditions. In many cases, it is only possible to refer to previous join points when they still have an activation record on the stack (i.e. using the cflow() keyword in AspectJ). In order solve this limitation, Douence et al. [6,7] propose a formal model for aspects with general protocol based triggering conditions, named *stateful aspects*. In this section, we illustrate how the JAsCo language is extended with stateful pointcut expressions, based on this formal model.

```
1   class ProtocolDynamicTimer extends DynamicTimer {
2
3     hook StatefulProtocolTimer {
4
5       long timestamp;
6
7       StatefulProtocolTimer(methodA(..args),methodB(..args),methodC(..args)) {
8         ATrans: execute(methodA) > BTrans;
9         BTrans: execute(methodB) > CTrans;
10        CTrans: execute(methodC) > ATrans;
11      }
12
13      before ATrans() {
14        timestamp=System.currentTimeMillis();
15      }
16      after CTrans() {
17        long resultingtime = System.currentTimeMillis();
18        notifyListeners(calledmethod,resultingtime-timestamp);
19      }
20
21    }
22 }
```

Fig. 4. The JAsCo stateful aspect for dynamically checking a timing contract of a component protocol

In figure 3, an ad-hoc solution was presented for implementing time contract verification of a protocol methodA-methodB-methodC. Figure 4 illustrates how the same protocol can be declaratively described by making use of the JAsCo stateful aspect language. The constructor of the hook StatefulProtocolTimer (line 7-11) describes a protocol-based pointcut expression. Every line in the constructor defines a new transition within the protocol. Each transition is labeled with a name (e.g. ATrans), defines a JAsCo compatible pointcut expression (e.g. execute(methodA)) and specifies one or more destination transitions that are matched after the current transition is fired. A transition fires when its pointcut expression evaluates to true. For example, the ATrans transition only fires whenever the concrete method(s) bound to the abstract method parameter methodA are executed. In that case, transition BTrans is activated and will be evaluated for the subsequent join points encountered in the application.

A stateful aspect always starts by evaluating the first defined transition. As a result, a protocol methodA-methodB-methodC is described. In between the fired transitions, other join points can also be encountered. As such, a sequence of events methodA-methodX-methodC-methodB-methodC is also a valid instance for the defined protocol and will trigger the associated transitions. Notice that the JAsCo stateful aspect pointcut does not have to specify the full protocol of the application; a protocol fragment is sufficient.

On every transition defined in the stateful constructor, advices can be attached which are executed whenever the transition is fired. For example, the before ATrans advice (line 13-15) is only triggered whenever the transition

ATrans is fired. In other words, the advice is executed whenever the concrete method(s) bound to the abstract method parameter **methodA** are executed in that state of the stateful aspect. To sum up, the **StatefulProtocolTimer** hook will take a timestamp before the protocol **methodA-methodB-methodC** is executed and will notify all interested listeners after the full protocol is performed.

3.1 Advanced Language Features

In addition to attaching advices on each transition separately, it is also possible to describe global advices that are triggered for all fired transitions. In this case, the advice is specified as usual, but the transition label is omitted. It is also possible to attach a specific **isApplicable** method to a particular transition in the protocol. As such, the transition will only be fired when both the pointcut expression and the **isApplicable** condition evaluate to true. Likewise to advices, a global **isApplicable** condition can be specified which is applied to all transitions. In that case, transitions are only fired when they satisfy their pointcut expression and both the global and local **isApplicable** conditions. The following code fragment shows both a global and local **isApplicable** condition.

```
1  isApplicable() { //global condition for all transitions
2    // returns true if advices should be executed
3  }
4  isApplicable XTrans() { //local condition only relevant for the transition XTrans
5    // returns true if advices should be executed for the XTrans transition
6  }
```

The JAsCo stateful aspects constructor can also specify multiple destination transitions for a given transition. The syntax is illustrated in the code fragment below. After firing the **XTrans** transition, both the **YTrans** and **QTrans** transitions are evaluated for subsequent encountered join points (line 2). Note that the destination transitions are evaluated in the sequence defined in the destination expression. As such, when both the **YTrans** and **QTrans** transitions are applicable for a given join point, only the **YTrans** transition will be fired and only the **YTrans** destination transitions will be evaluated for subsequent encountered join points. This allows to keep the protocol deterministic and efficient to execute. It is also possible to omit a destination transition for a certain transition. In that case, when the transition fires, no more transitions need to be evaluated and the aspect *dies*. This concept is illustrated by the **QTrans** transition (line 3). Also notice that this transition describes a more involved pointcut designator using the **cflow** keyword.

In case the stateful aspect requires to start by evaluating more than one transition, the **start** keyword can be employed. This keyword is followed by a list of starting transitions for matching join points when the aspect is deployed. Multiple start transitions are specified similarly to multiple destination transitions, by using || as delimiters. When no start transition is specified, the first defined transition is used as the starting one.

```
1  start > XTrans || QTrans; //starting with two transitions
2  XTrans: execute(methodA) > YTrans || QTrans; //two destination transitions
3  QTrans: execute(methodB) && !cflow(methodC); //no destination transition
4  YTrans: execute(methodC) > YTrans;
```

The syntax proposed in the previous paragraphs provides a way for specifying powerful protocols but might be tedious in case of simple protocols. Therefore JAsCo also supports a simpler syntax for protocols that do not require multiple destination transitions for a given transition. The following code fragment shows a constructor that is equivalent to the constructor of figure 4. Labeling transitions is still possible in order to be able to attach local advices to specific transitions. Notice that the label start automatically refers to the first transition.

```
1  StatefulProtocolTimer(methodA(..args),methodB(..args),methodC(..args)) {
2    ATrans: execute(methodA) > execute(methodB) > CTrans: execute(methodC) > start;
3  }
```

Normally, aspects are instantiated explicitly in a connector and this instance is used for all encountered join points. In case of protocol checking stateful aspects, it is sometimes desirable to have a unique instance of the stateful aspect for every execution thread in the application as every thread is typically related to a different interaction. JAsCo allows automatically instantiating multiple instances for a single hook instantiation expression by using specialized keywords in front of the instantiation expression in the connector. The following keywords are supported: perobject, perclass, permethod, perall, percflow and perthread. Thus, in order to obtain a unique aspect instance per execution thread, the perthread keyword can be used. The JAsCo run-time system will automatically manage the aspect instances for every thread. This is illustrated by the following code fragment:

```
1  static connector PerThreadConnector {
2    perthread ProtocolDynamicTimer.StatefulProtocolTimer timer =
3      new ProtocolDynamicTimer.StatefulProtocolTimer(void ComponentX.a(),
4        void ComponentX.b(), void ComponentX.c());
5  }
```

3.2   Protocol Complement

The JAsCo stateful aspects language currently supports triggering aspects on a protocol fragment. However, the opposite, namely triggering aspects on every join point besides the defined protocol, can also be useful in many cases. For example, Farias et al. [10] identify that in the context of checking security policies of Enterprise Java Beans (EJBs), explicit protocols are necessary. The current EJB specification only allows to describe that particular methods need to adhere to a given security policy. It is however often required that only the protocol methodA-methodB-methodC on a given component X is allowed for certain users. Farias et al. propose a formal model to specify the allowed protocol of a component, based on finite state machines [12]. As already identified in literature [23], security concerns are typical examples of crosscutting concerns and thus good targets for AOP.

JAsCo supports triggering aspects on the opposite of a protocol using the complement keyword. Figure 5 illustrates a contract checking aspect that makes sure that all invocations on a certain component, besides the defined protocol, are blocked. The stateful aspect defines the same protocol as the one in

```
1   class ProtocolChecker {
2
3     hook StatefulProtocolCheck {
4
5       StatefulProtocolCheck(methodA(..arg),methodB(..arg),methodC(..arg),methodsContext(..arg)) {
6         complement[execute(methodsContext)]:
7           ATrans: execute(methodA) > BTrans;
8           BTrans: execute(methodB) > CTrans;
9           CTrans: execute(methodC) > ATrans;
10      }
11
12      replace complement() {
13        throw new SecurityException(
14          "This protocol on component"+thisJoinPoint.getClassName()+" is not allowed!");
15      }
16    }
17  }
```

Fig. 5. The JAsCo stateful aspect for checking a security contract

figure 4, namely a protocol `methodA-methodB-methodC`. The additional complement definition states that the aspect is interested in the complement of the protocol. The complement expression is also able to specify a JAsCo compatible pointcut designator in order to limit the complement to a certain set of join points. This is often required in the context of checking security contracts of a component. It is not very useful to trigger the aspect on every possible protocol fragment outside the given protocol, because this would also include methods on other components. Therefore, JAsCo allows to limit the set of join points to which the complement of the protocol is computed. For example, the `StatefulProtocolCheck`, illustrated in figure 5, defines that the complement is only triggered when methods bound to `methodsContext` (line 5) are executed and not exactly following the defined protocol. Advices can be attached to the complement of a protocol by specifying the `complement` keyword after the advice name. In this case, a `replace complement` advice is specified (lines 12-15) that replaces the original behavior and throws a security exception instead. Moreover, it is still possible to attach advices to transitions in the allowed protocol by using the syntax introduced before.

Figure 6 illustrates the connector that deploys the security protocol checking aspect bean onto the `a-b-c` protocol of the `componentX` component (lines 3-4). The `methodsContext` abstract method parameter of the aspect bean is bound to all methods of `componentX`. As a result, whenever a method is executed on `componentX` that falls outside the defined protocol `a-b-c`, like for example `a-b-d-c`, a security exception is thrown.

```
1   static connector SecurityConnector {
2
3     ProtocolChecker.StatefulProtocolCheck checker = new ProtocolChecker.StatefulProtocolCheck(
4       void componentX.a(), void componentX.b(), void componentX.c(), void componentX.*());
5   }
```

Fig. 6. Connector for deploying the security protocol contract checking aspect

4   Implementation Discussion

The JAsCo stateful aspects language is equivalent to a Deterministic Final Automaton (DFA) [12] because every expression defines one DFA transition, two DFA states and possibly several connection DFA transitions for the destinations. Therefore, the JAsCo compiler compiles a stateful aspect constructor to a DFA that is interpreted at run-time. Every transition of a DFA contains a representation of the pointcut definition and possibly an `isApplicable` condition. When a join point is encountered, the outgoing transitions of the current state are evaluated with the given join point and when a match is encountered, the state machine moves to the destination state. When this event occurs, all associated advices are executed. Because of this implementation strategy, a stateful aspect can be executed very efficiently. It suffices to check only the transitions of the current state, as JAsCo stateful aspect protocols are regular and can be interpreted by a regular DFA. When non-regular protocols are allowed, a history of all relevant encountered events should be maintained, which is very expensive.

A naive approach for integrating the stateful aspect would be weaving it at all possible join points defined within the protocol. However, this induces a performance overhead at all these join points, while the stateful aspect is only interested in a limited set of join points corresponding to the subsequent transitions that are to be evaluated. JAsCo is a dynamic AOP language and features a genuine run-time weaver that is able to weave and unweave aspects at run-time [20]. The run-time performance of JAsCo is even able to compete with AspectJ's, which is a statically woven AOP approach [13]. Because of this run-time weaver, the JAsCo stateful aspect language induces only a minimal performance overhead. The JAsCo run-time weaver only weaves the stateful aspect at those join points where the aspect is currently interested in. When a transition is fired, the weaver unweaves the aspect at the join points associated with the current transition and weaves it back in at the join points relevant for the subsequent transitions. As such, a real *jumping aspect* is realized. Notice that when the aspect *dies* because no subsequent transitions are defined, it is completely unwoven. As a result, no performance overhead for the aspect is endured any longer.

The weaving process itself does however also require a significant overhead. Therefore, when a given protocol is encountered many times in a short time interval, it might be more efficient to weave the aspect at all possible join points of the protocol instead of weaving and unweaving it on-the-fly. This can be configured in JAsCo by using the novel Java 1.5 annotations (meta-data). When the `@jasco.runtime.aspect.WeaveAll` annotation is supplied to the hook, as illustrated by the code fragment below, the run-time weaver weaves the aspect at all join points and never unweaves it unless the aspect itself is manually removed or dies.

```
1  @jasco.runtime.aspect.WeaveAll
2  hook StatefulHook { ...
```

A proof-of-concept implementation for the JAsCo stateful aspect extension is made available through the regular JAsCo distribution [14].

5   Case Study

To illustrate the usefulness of stateful aspects, an example of reaction business rules is presented. Business rules are volatile and tend to change faster than the core application functionality. Therefore, and due to the crosscutting nature of their integration with the core application [17,5,11], it is recommended to keep them decoupled from the rest of the application. In previous work [4], aspects were successfully employed for integrating business rules that are triggered at single events that denote dynamic points within the core application. In this case study however, business rules that depend on complex behavioral states of the system are considered.

The presented case study is based on an application used in the context of the ADAPSIS[2] (Adaptation of IP Services based on Profiles) project [24]. One of the research topics of this project is the development of an approach that allows to mine end-user profiles, building on existing component-based applications. The main problem is that these applications are generally not designed to allow end-user profile mining. As a concrete research artifact, an e-commerce application is developed that allows customers to buy different products online, such as books, music and movies. This application is an adaptive web application as it incorporates data mining strategies in order to analyze the purchasing behavior of the customers. The Data4s data mining engine is employed to react according to the customer's behavior in an intelligent way. AOP is used to capture all relevant data for the data mining engine and influencing the behavior of the original application depending on the mined information and the user profile. For gathering application events, it is often required to keep track of the history of the user's interactions with the web application. When regular aspects are employed, this historical information results hard-coded in the aspects themselves, making them difficult to comprehend and evolve. With the advent of JAsCo stateful aspects, this problem can be tackled in a more declarative way.

Consider for instance a set of business rules that define a categorization of the customers, depending on their susceptibility to promotions. These rules allow understanding the interests of the different customers to better accommodate to their needs and goals. Promotions can be viewed and purchased from different product-specific web pages as well as from the home page of the shop. Normally, different customers react to the advertisement of promotions in different ways. Some customers for instance tend to browse to the promotions as a first reaction when accessing the shop's home page. Others might prefer to browse the available books, music or videos first and later on decide whether to choose a promotion. The following business rules determine the different degrees of sensitivity to promotions:

1. *High promotion-prone customer*: The customer browses the promotions as his/her first action

---

[2] ADAPSIS is partly funded by the IWT, Flanders (Belgium), partners are the University of Brussels (VUB), Alcatel Belgium and Data4s Future Technologies.

```
1  class MediumPromotionProneCustomerAspect {
2
3    hook MediumPromotionProneCustomerHook {
4
5      MediumPromotionProneCustomerHook(
6        browseProducts(Category category),accessPromotions(CustomerID customer)) {
7          start > browseProdTrans;
8          browseProdTrans : execute(browseProducts) > browseProdTrans || browsePromTrans;
9          browsePromTrans : execute(accessPromotions);
10     }
11
12     after browsePromTrans () {
13       CustomerManager.classifyCustomer(customer, MediumPromotionProneCustomer);
14     }
15 }
```

Fig. 7. Medium promotion-prone customer business rule

2. *Medium promotion-prone customer*: The customer browses first either the books, the music or the videos and only then he/she accesses the promotions
3. *Low promotion-prone customer*: The customer first browses the books and the music and the videos and then he/she accesses the promotions
4. *Promotion-insensitive customer*: The customer never follows the promotions links

In this example a single action, such as the browsing of the promotions, cannot be analyzed in isolation. In order to classify a customer in different categories, it is required to know which actions the customer already performed. In order to keep track of the customer history and trigger the customer classification, stateful aspects are employed. Figure 7 illustrates a stateful aspect implementing the medium promotion-prone customer business rule. In this example, the customer starts by browsing a catalog of products (line 8) and checks out the promotions afterwards (line 9). Figure 8 illustrates how the medium promotion-prone customer business rule is deployed within the e-commerce application.

Stateful aspects can also be employed to implement more complex patterns of behavior such as the following action sequence which could be performed by a customer:

```
1  getPromotions > browseBooks > browseCDs > browseVideos > getPromotions
```

Without stateful aspects, it would not be straightforward to detect this path of execution. We can imagine making the distinction between the place in the system where the promotions and the products are retrieved. However, this change would not be sufficient to distinguish the contextual difference between the first

```
1  static connector MediumPromotionProneCustomerConnector{
2
3    MediumPromotionProneCustomerHook hook1 =
4      new MediumPromotionProneCustomerHook(
5        * ProductManager.browse*(*), * PromotionManager.getPromotions(CustomerID));
6
7  }
```

Fig. 8. Connector for deploying the medium promotion-prone customer business rule

and second invocation of the `getPromotions` and would imply tangling of code to manually keep track of the states. Stateful aspects avoid this problem, allowing the expression of complex contextual scenarios in a natural and non-invasive way.

6 Related Work

Douence et al. propose a model for supporting stateful aspects [6,7,8] as a part of their formal aspect model. The advantage of this formal model is that it allows to automatically deduce possible malicious interactions between aspects. Furthermore, the model supports composition of stateful aspects using well-defined composition operators. A proof of concept implementation of this model is also available [9]. This implementation is however based on static program transformations and as such it requires to advice all possible join points defined within the protocol. The JAsCo implementation improves on this because only a subset of the join points are actually advised.

Walker et al. introduce *declarative event patterns* (DEPs) [22] as a means to specify protocols as patterns of multiple events. They augment AspectJ aspects with special DEP constructs (called *tracecuts*) that can be advised similarly to pointcuts. Their approach is based on context-free grammars, and involves a transformation of the DEP constructs into standard AspectJ aspects containing an event parser, similar to the transformation realized by parser generators in compiler technology. While DEPs can recognize properly nested events and thus possess an even higher degree of declarative expressibility than the JAsCo approach, they only provide for the ability to attach advice code to entire protocols. Separate transitions of the protocol cannot be advised, and several overlapping protocols (realized through several independent event parsers) would have to be employed to mimic this possibility of JAsCo. Furthermore, the fact that DEPs lose their identity in a preprocessing step that reduces them to standard aspects, rules out the possibility for optimizations by a weaver that analyzes the feasible transitions of the protocol. Also, there are some unresolved issues in the current implementation of DEPs regarding optimal conservation of relevant execution traces.

7 Conclusions

In this paper we introduce an extension of the JAsCo language that enables triggering aspects on a sequence of join points. The JAsCo stateful aspects extension allows to declaratively specify a regular protocol. Advices can be attached to each transition in the protocol. JAsCo also allows to trigger aspects on the complement of a protocol given a set of join points. Because of the declarative specification, the stateful aspect is easier to understand and evolve than a manual implementation using singular join points. In addition, the declarative specification allows to optimize the execution of the stateful aspect. By employing dynamic AOP, the stateful aspect behavior is only woven at those join points the aspect is currently interested in.

A limitation of the current approach is that JAsCo stateful aspects can only specify regular protocols. Protocols that require a non-regular language (like for example n times A; B; n times A, where n can be a different number in every occurance of the protocol), cannot be represented. The advantage of keeping the protocols regular is that they can be efficiently evaluated using a DFA. A naive implementation of a non-regular protocol would require to keep the complete history of all encountered join points in memory, which is not very practical. In literature, several domain-specific optimization techniques for interpreting non-regular languages have been proposed [2]. Extending the JAsCo stateful aspects language to non-regular protocols while still allowing an efficient implementation is subject for future work.

Acknowledgements

Davy Suvée and Bruno De Fraine are supported by a doctoral scholarship from the Institute for the promotion of Innovation by Science and Technology in Flanders in the Industry (IWT).

References

1. T. Andrews et al. Business Process Execution Language for Web Services Specification, May 2003. http://www.ibm.com/developerworks/library/ws-bpel/.
2. J. Aycock and N. Horspool. Schrodinger's token. *Software Practice and Experience*, 31(8), 2001.
3. J. Brichau, W. De Meuter, and K. De Volder. Jumping Aspects. In *Workshop on Aspects and Dimensions of Concerns (ECOOP 2000)*, June 2000.
4. M. A. Cibrán, M. D'Hondt, and V. Jonckers. Aspect-Oriented Programming for Connecting Business Rules. In *Proceedings of BIS International Conference*, Colorado Springs, USA, June 2003.
5. C. Date. *What not How: The Business Rules Approach to Application Development*. Addison Wesley, 1st edition, 2000.
6. R. Douence, P. Fradet, and M. Südholt. A framework for the detection and resolution of aspect interactions. In *Proceedings of the ACM SIGPLAN/SIGSOFT Conference on Generative Programming and Component Engineering*, Pittsburgh, USA, October 2002.
7. R. Douence, P. Fradet, and M. Südholt. Composition, Reuse and Interaction Analysis of Stateful Aspects. In *Proceedings of the 3th International Conference on Aspect-Oriented Software Development*, Lancaster, UK, March 2004.
8. R. Douence, P. Fradet, and M. Südholt. Trace-based Aspects. *Aspect-Oriented Software Development*, September 2004.
9. R. Douence and M. Südholt. A model and a tool for event-based aspect-oriented programming (EAOP). Technical Report 02/11/INFO, Ecole des Mines de Nantes, 2002.
10. A. Farias and M. Südholt. On components with explicit protocols satisfying a notion of correctness by construction. In *Distributed Objects and Applications 2002*, Irvine, USA, October 2002.
11. B. Von Halle. *Business Rules Applied*. Wiley, 1st edition, 2001.

12. J.E. Hopcroft, R. Motwani, and J.D. Ullman. *Introduction to Automata Theory.* Addison Wesley, 2st edition, 2001.
13. JAsCo. *JAsCo Run-Time Weaver.* http://ssel.vub.ac.be/jasco/documentation:ruw.
14. JAsCo. *JAsCo website.* http://ssel.vub.ac.be/jasco/.
15. G. Kiczales, E. Hilsdale, J. Hugunin, M. Kersen, J. Palm, and G.W. Griswold. An overview of AspectJ. In *Proceedings European Conference on Object-Oriented Programming*, Budapest, Hungary, June 2001.
16. G. Kiczales, J. Lamping, A. Menhdhekar, C. Maeda, C. Lopes, J-M. Loingtier, and J. Irwin. Aspect-Oriented Programming. In Mehmet Akşit and Satoshi Matsuoka, editors, *Proceedings European Conference on Object-Oriented Programming*, volume 1241, pages 220–242. Springer-Verlag, Berlin, Heidelberg, and New York, 1997.
17. R. G. Ross. *Principles of the Business Rule Approach.* Addison Wesley, 1st edition, 2003.
18. D. Suvée, W. Vanderperren, and V. Jonckers. JAsCo: an Aspect-Oriented approach tailored for Component Based Software Development. In *Proceedings of the 2nd International Conference on Aspect-Oriented Software Development*, Boston, USA, March 2003.
19. A. S. Tanenbaum. *Computer Networks.* Prentice Hall Professional Technical Reference, 4th edition, 2002.
20. W. Vanderperren and D. Suvée. Optimizing JAsCo dynamic AOP through HotSwap and Jutta. In *Proceedings of Dynamic Aspects Workshop*, Lancaster, UK, March 2004.
21. W. Vanderperren, D. Suvée, and V. Jonckers. Combining AOSD and CBSD in PacoSuite through Invasive Composition Adapters and JAsCo. In *Proceedings of Node 2003 International Conference*, Erfurt, Germany, September 2003.
22. R.J. Walker and K. Viggers. Implementing Protocols via Declarative Event Patterns. In *Proceedings of the ACM SIGSOFT International Symposium on Foundations of Software Engineering*, Newport Beach, USA, November 2004.
23. B. De Win, B. Vanhaute, and B. De Decker. How aspect-oriented programming can help to build secure software. *Informatica*, 26(2), 2002.
24. B. Wydaeghe, W. Vanderperren, T. Pijpons, and F. Westerhuis. Adapsis: Adaptation of IP Services Based on Profiles. In *SSEL Technical Report*, May 2002.
25. D. Yellin and R. Strom. Protocol Specifications and Component Adaptors. *ACM Transactions on Programming Languages and Systems*, 19(2):292–333, 1997.

Invasive Configuration of Generic Components

Volker Kuttruff[1] and Thomas Genssler[2]

[1] Forschungszentrum Informatik FZI
kuttruff@fzi.de
[2] CAS Software AG
thomas.genssler@cas.de

Abstract. Prior to being composed to a software system, generic components must be configured according to the requirements imposed by the user and the reuse context. Practice shows that most of these configuration operations are invasive in nature. Thus, modular composition alone cannot solve this problem. This paper presents a methodology for invasive configuration of software systems from generic components. Our approach extends type genericity by allowing in addition to type reference fragments general program fragments and metaoperators as configuration parameters. We will introduce our software adaptation tool called INJECT/J together with the concepts behind it. The tool serves as an infrastructure for the implementation of our approach. We will also present a case study with some preliminary experiences of the practical application of our approach.

1 Introduction

Every mature engineering discipline takes advantage of reusing existing components. Depending upon the engineering discipline, reusable components can be found on different levels of abstraction, e.g. starting from nuts and bolts up to prefabricated building blocks.

In this paper we present our ongoing work on a methodology for feature-driven, invasive configuration of software systems from generic components. In order to be reusable in various contexts, a component has to be generic with respect to certain supported features. Configuring a generic component according to the requirements imposed by the user and the reuse context is the process of binding these features in an appropriate way. In this paper we focus on the technical part of this methodology, which is the invasive configuration of generic components, although the process of mapping features to specifications of concrete configurations of generic components is also part of our methodology. Nevertheless, the case study presented in section 4 gives a first impression on how this part works in our methodology.

Non-invasive configuration fails, because the necessary adaptations required during the configuration of a generic component are usually not local with respect to the used decomposition technique. This is due to the fact that a feature which is to be bound usually cannot be found as a module in the implementation

T. Gschwind, U. Aßmann, and O. Nierstrasz (Eds.): SC 2005, LNCS 3628, pp. 183–197, 2005.

of a reusable component, but in the form of distributed program fragments. This is also true if a decomposition technique other than the object-oriented decomposition is used. This is a direct consequence of the so-called "tyranny" of the primary decomposition [8].

When configuring a generic component, an end-user is interested in the concrete result, and not in how the configuration itself is implemented. Therefore, the specification of a configuration should be *declarative* and oriented at the *application level*. The configuration itself should have *well defined semantics*. This means that a contract guaranteed by the component cannot be broken through an unappropriate configuration of this component. The resulting code should be efficient, i.e. it should be comparable with a manual implementation. Particulary, the resulting component should not contain any unnecessary indirections introduced while configuring the component.

The remainder of this paper is organized as follows. In the next section, we introduce our approach for configuration of generic components by specifying the model and the concepts it is based on. In section 3, we introduce our software adaptation tool INJECT/J, which serves as a technical infrastructure for invasive configuration of generic components. We also sketch which extensions are necessary to fully support our approach. Preliminary experiences of the practical application of our approach are presented in section 4. We give a short overview of related work in section 5 before we conclude in section 6.

2   Approach

The starting point of our approach is type genericity, which is a very basic invasive technique. Type genericity fulfils all the properties postulated in the last section. From a user's point of view, configuration of a generic type is declarative and it has well defined semantics. Unfortunately, it is limited to types, or more exactly, to type reference fragments.

Our approach extends type genericity by not only allowing type reference fragments as configuration parameters, but arbitrary program fragments.

2.1   Generic Program Fragments as Units of Composition

In our model, a software system is the result of a hierarchical composition of different program fragments. From this point of view, configuring a software system means to select and compose program fragments in such a way that the user's requirements are fulfilled. Hierarchical composition is performed at so-called *variation points*, i.e. program fragments of a finer granularity can be composed at these points. In order to be composable, a program fragment must have a composition interface together with a contract specifying the composition conditions. In practice, we do not want to specify program fragments that are particular to one specific configuration, but fragments that can be reused in different configurations. This leads us to the notion of generic fragment types. In our model, a generic fragment type has the following properties:

- A *name* which uniquely identifies this generic fragment type.
- A *super type* denoting that this generic fragment type is a specialization of the stated fragment type. Through this subtype relation together with the name, certain semantics are associated with this new generic fragment type. The top-level types are given by the language metamodel, e.g. class fragments, method fragments etc. For example, a specialization of a general method fragment could be a method fragment computing the maximum of two numbers, thus it has extended semantics.
- A *configuration interface* which specifies the possible parameterization of the generic fragment type, i.e. which other fragments can be plugged into instances of this generic fragment type. The configuration interface consists of two parts:

  1. A list of *typed formal configuration parameters*: They specify which types of fragments can be plugged into instances of this generic fragment type as well as which fragments are provided by this generic fragment type for parameterization of the fragments to be plugged in. Thus, configuration parameters denote a required and a provided interface.
  2. Additional construction constraints which may influence allowed types of formal parameters during (partial) configuration. With these additional constraints, fragment-global constraints can be enforced which cannot be expressed through typed configuration parameters, e.g. dependencies between configuration parameters.

- A *construction plan* that describes how fragments have to be composed based upon given constraints, i.e. how to bind fragments given at the configuration interface to the variation points of this generic fragment type and, in the case of the provided interface, how to bind provided fragments to the required interface of the plugged in fragments. This means that the fragment has control over the composition of its subordinate fragments, thus it can guarantee a correct fragment composition to the extent that is specified in the construction plan.
- A *generic implementation* using declared variation points. This generic implementation can be seen as a fragment template which can be instantiated through configuration.

Generic fragment types can have any arbitrary level of abstraction, starting from simple expressions or statements up to method fragments, class fragments or the whole system. If a generic fragment type has no configuration parameters, it is referred to as a static fragment type.

In our model, a generic component can be regarded as a generic fragment type of a reasonable granularity, since one associates a certain size with the term "component". Examples for a reasonable granularity are method fragments, class fragments or even more coarse grained fragments. Since our model does not distinguish between the different fragment granularities, we will use the term generic fragment type in the remainder of this paper.

2.2 Typed Metaoperators

As stated in section 1, not all features can be implemented by plugging in one program fragment at one predefined variation point. Such features must be implemented by injecting or even removing similar fragments at various variation points. From a programmer's and a maintainability point of view, explicitly declaring all these variation points together with a fragment for each variation point is inconvenient and often not manageable. This is why we introduce the notion of typed metaoperators.

A typed metaoperator consists of a fragment template together with a meta-program specifying how and where these fragment templates have to be instantiated and injected into the resulting code through transformation or generation. Variation points can be explicitly declared or computed based on program analysis results. The latter are also available during instantiation of the fragment template, since this may require context information.

Like generic fragment types, metaoperators have a name and a super type. Thus, a metaoperator defines a new type describing its semantics, i.e. its effects on the program. In particular, a metaoperator can be a subtype of any arbitrary generic fragment type. Being of such a type, together with explicitly specified pre- and postconditions, the metaoperator guarantees that its application has the same effect as composing an instance of the super type or even results in a fragment of the super type in the case of generation. For example, a metaoperator inlining a method fragment has the same effects on the program as composing the corresponding method fragment with a class fragment, provided that certain preconditions hold. As a consequence, metaoperators can be used as parameters for the instantiation of generic fragment types. Given that the type of a metaoperator is compatible to the type of one of the configuration parameters, the metaoperator can be used to bind this configuration parameter.

3 Tool Support

From a technical perspective, our approach is based on INJECT/J[1] [4] [5], a tool for invasive software adaptation[2].

In this section, we first give a brief overview on the concepts of INJECT/J before we introduce the INJECT/J software transformation language. In the following we refer to the program which is to be composed and configured as the *object program*, and the programming language, this program is written in, as the *object language*.

3.1 Inject/J Model

INJECT/J models object programs as collections of program fragments. These fragments are internally represented in the form of an attributed tree, the *adap-*

---

[1] http://sf.net/projects/injectj
[2] INJECT/J itself uses the software transformation engine RECODER, http://sf.net/projects/recoder

tation model. Fragments represent subtrees within this model. The adaptation model captures the syntactical structure and the static semantics of these program fragments and is constructed using standard compiler techniques.

Program fragments are composed at certain designated points in the adaptation model which we call *weaving points*. These weaving points are the technical equivalent to our variation points. As not every syntactical element can be added to, or removed from the program at any place, weaving points can only be bound to fragments of a matching type, i.e. fragments that do not break the syntax of the object language in the given context. Weaving points compare to join points known from ASPECTJ or Assmann's hooks [1].

We distinguish both *implicit* and *declared* weaving points. Implicit weaving points are defined by the syntax of the object language: Every place, where a fragment of a certain type can be added to the program or removed from it, is an implicit weaving point. Declared weaving points are implicit weaving points marked with an additional semantical annotation. The following listing illustrates how this works for JAVA.

```
public class MyClass{

   public /** annotation @name SyncStrategy
                      @type Modifier["synchronized"]
                      @optional true*/
      void criticalMethod(Object o){...}

   public Object nonCriticalMethod(int i){...}
   ...
}
```

The adaptation model is input to the *composition program*. The composition program specifies algorithmically, how a given object program in an object language (e.g. a JAVA-program) will be modified by introducing new program fragments or by removing unnecessary program fragments from the object program.

A composition program typically consists of two tasks. First, it navigates through the adaptation model in order to identify weaving points to introduce new fragments or places where to remove unnecessary program fragments. Second, the actual fragment operations are performed.

To navigate through the adaptation model and to identify program fragments, *model queries* can be used. Model queries are side-effect-free predicates and functions over the adaptation model. They provide structural information, type- and cross-reference information as well as information about qualitative and quantitative properties of program fragments, such as software metrics.

For introducing or removing program fragments, the following operations are defined:

- `insert(<weaving point>, <fragment>)`: Inserts a new program fragment at the specified weaving point. This corresponds to adding a new subtree to the model.
- `oldFragment = replace(<weaving point>, <newFragment>)`: Replaces an existing fragment, currently bound to a weaving point, with another fragment. If $newFragment = \varepsilon$, then the existing fragment is simply removed

from the program. This corresponds to replacing or removing an existing subtree in the model.

These two basic operations are complete as they allow for arbitrary tree modifications. They work, however, solely on a syntactical level. Using them as-is would add considerable complexity to the task of specifying a composition program. Thus, we introduced the concept of *semantic transformations*.

Semantic transformations group semantically connected fragment operations and hide them behind an interface. Semantic transformations guarantee at least correctness with respect to the static syntax and semantics of the object language. Additional fragment operations, such as correcting the syntactical structure when introducing a fragment at a certain weaving point (flattening) or correcting applied occurrences of an identifier when replacing its defining occurrence, are performed automatically

With the help of pre- and post-conditions, additional effects (e.g. semantic effects) can be enforced. Pre- and post-conditions are specified with first-order logic by means of model queries. Beyond that, semantic transformations are atomic: they succeed completely and fulfill their contract or they do not generate any effects. That is, if the pre-condition of a semantic transformation is not fulfilled, the operation is not executed. If the post-condition of the semantic transformation is not fulfilled, the entire transformation is rolled back.

3.2   Inject/J Transformation Language

Composition programs are specified with the help of the INJECT/J *transformation language*. This language is a dynamically typed scripting language which combines declarative elements, e.g. for identifying weaving points, with imperative elements, e.g. for performing the actual transformation.

The following listing shows a very simple example of an INJECT/J script, which introduces a new fragment at method entry by instantiating a *generic implementation* as defined in section 2:

```
script HelloWorld() {
 foreach c in classes do {
  foreach m in c.methods do {
   m.afterEntry(
    ${System.out.println("In method <c.name>.<m.signature>!");}$
   );
  }
 }
}
```

The generic implementation is instantiated by binding variation points within the fragment (parts of a string literal in this example) to appropriate syntactical elements provided by the script.

For navigation through the adaption model, INJECT/J provides a number of mechanisms such as name patterns to match named fragments (e.g. class fragments) by regular patterns over names, or detection patterns, which are arbitrary graph patterns over the program model. These different mechanisms can also be combined. The following listing gives a brief overview:

```
script HelloWorld {
 // detection pattern
 pattern MyPattern(pname):(c) {
  vars m;
  private vars meths;
  init{
    // use a name pattern to match methods with certain parameter types
    meths = method('**.m(java.util.ArrayList , **'));
  }
  conditions {
    (c.package == pname), (m in c.methods), (m in meths), (m.mccabe > 10);
  }
 }

 ...
 // search each occurrence of detection pattern MyPattern in the
 // program model
 foreach p in MyPattern(''mypckg'')(classes) do {
   p.m.afterEntry(${
     System.out.println("Method <p.m.signature> in class <p.c.name>");
   }$);
 }
```

In the above example, only complex methods (McCabe complexity greater than 10) which are defined in classes of a certain package (''mypckg'') and take java.util.ArrayList as first parameter are matched.

INJECT/J comes with an extensive library of semantic transformations which range from refactorings to operations known from AOP.

Additionally, INJECT/J provides a number of built-in types for each type of fragments as well as a number of general-purpose data types (e.g. strings and lists). The language has quantors (i.e., **foreach** and **exists**) and directly supports first-order predicate logic, e.g. for contracts of semantic transformations. Further features include code blocks[3], transactions for isolating transformation sequences with uncertain result, e.g. in case of user interaction, as well as a library concept. For a more detailed description of the INJECT/J language features, we refer you to [4] or the INJECT/J language specification[4].

3.3 Necessary Extensions to Inject/J

To support our approach presented in section 2, the language and the tool IN-JECT/J have to be extended. Basically, there are three extensions which have to be implemented:

1. *A more advanced type system for generic fragment types.* Currently, INJEC-T/J has a static type system, i.e. no new types can be declared. Besides some simple types, INJECT/J supports only the "base" fragment types given by the object language's metamodel.
2. *Support for typed metaoperators.* Metaprograms are currently implemented using scripts or library functions. These scripts do not have a type as required by our approach.

---

[3] similar to closures in SMALLTALK, Syntax: [p|stmt(p);], i.e. p is the parameter which can be used in statement(s) **stmt**

[4] http://prdownloads.sourceforge.net/injectj/Language.pdf?download

3. *Syntactical extensions.* In order to specify generic fragment types efficiently, new syntactical elements have to be introduced to the INJECT/J language, like explicit construction plans. A first impression of how these syntactical elements can look like can be found in the next section.

Currently, we are implementing a prototypical version of INJECT/J which natively supports these new concepts.

4   Case Study

In this section, we present a first case study which demonstrates how generic fragment types can be specified and instantiated by using the extended version of our software adaptation tool INJECT/J as proposed in section 3.3.

4.1   Analysis of the Java Collection Framework

We took the Java Collection Framework (JCF)[5] as a starting point for our case study. The goal was to sketch how to make the JCF more generic by using generic fragment types. First we tried to identify the features implemented by the framework from a user's point of view. Additionally, we took the design decisions[6] presented by the JCF creators into account, especially to find features which were identified during the design of the JCF but which were not implemented for various reasons. Last but not least, we tried to identify features which would additionally be interesting for a user of the JCF. The resulting feature diagram in FODA notation (see [3]) can be found in Fig. 1.

Although the domain of an end user and the domain of the designers of a collection framework usually do not differ very much, since both are programmers, the features are not exactly the same. This is due to the fact that a designer has to consider very technical features. An excerpt of the technical features a designer has to cope with for the domain of collections is presented in Fig. 2.

We used the *Design Spaces* approach [2] to specify the mapping between the user and the producer domain. Design Spaces are basically a more formal notation for feature models than the FODA notation together with a technique based on correlation functions to specify the mapping between features of different Design Spaces. Fig. 3 shows an excerpt of this mapping, where ADS denotes the Application Domain Space (thus, the user's domain) and PDS the Producer Domain Space (the designer's domain). The correlation factor is a value in the continuous range -1.0...1.0, where -1.0 means that if the features and their values in one Design Space are chosen in a way that the feature expression evaluates to *true*, then the features and the feature values of the other Design Space have to be chosen in a way that the corresponding feature expression evaluates to *false*. A correlation factor of 1.0 denotes an implication. Thus, a factor of 0.5 means

---

[5] http://java.sun.com/j2se/1.4.2/docs/guide/collections/

[6] http://java.sun.com/j2se/1.4.2/docs/guide/collections/designfaq.html

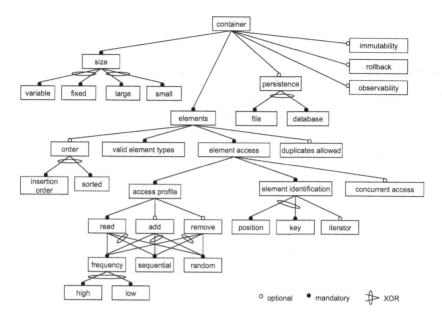

Fig. 1. Collection features from a user perspective

that if one feature is chosen, it is a good idea to choose the other feature as well, but it is not mandatory.

In this case study, we also used the Design Spaces approach to describe the mapping of the implementation Domain Space to a selection of generic fragment types and their parameterization, thus to configuration specifications.

4.2 Implementation with Generic Fragment Types

In the following code samples, we use the proposed extended version of our adaptation language INJECT/J introduced in section 3 to specify generic fragment types and metaoperators. Using this language, a generic fragment type HashSet can be specified as follows:

```
fragment HashSet <
    TypeReferenceFragment Tin, required;
    HashSetPutElementMethodFragment<TypeReferenceFragment Tout,
        Attribute ds> putMethod, optional;
    HashSetRemoveElementMethodFragment<TypeReferenceFragment Tout,
        Attribute ds> removeMethod, optional;
    SynchronizeAttributeAccessOperator<Attribute ds> synchronizer, optional;
    boolean immutable = false, required
> extends ClassFragment,

    conditions { immutable -> putMethod==null && removeMethod==null &&
                    forall a in data.referencingAccesses.filter(
                    [x|return !x.surroundingMethod.isConstructor]):
                        a.isReadAccess; };
{
    // construction plan
    construction {
        // bind provided interface
```

```
    bind HashSet.data -> ds;
    bind Tin -> Tout;

    // bind required interface
    bind put -> putMethod;
    bind remove -> removeMethod;
    bind elemType -> Tin;
    if (putMethod!=null || removeMethod!=null && !immutable)
        execute synchronizer<HashSet.data>;
}

// generic implementation
implementation {
    public class HashSet {
        private @(TypeReferenceFragment elemType)[] data;
        public HashSet() { ... };
        public boolean contains(@(TypeReferenceFragment elemType) element)
        {
            ...
        }

        @(HashSetGetElementMethodFragment put);
        @(HashSetRemoveElementMethodFragment remove);
    }
}
}
```

Fig. 2. Collection features from a technical point of view

```
(ADS.order=yes) -1.0 (PDS.hashtable=yes)
(ADS.concurrentaccess=yes AND NOT ADS.immutability=yes) 1.0 (PDS.synchronisation=yes)
(ADS.concurrentaccess=yes AND ADS.write.frequency.high=yes) 0.5 (PDS.preferwriter=yes)
(ADS.concurrentaccess=yes AND ADS.read.frequency.high=yes) 0.5 (PDS.preferreader=yes)
```

Fig. 3. Mapping between application and producer domain (excerpt)

As stated in section 2, a generic fragment type has a name (HashSet) and a super type (ClassFragment). Thus, in this example a new fragment type is declared, in particular a class fragment type implementing a hash set concept. The configuration interface is given by the formal parameters and the condition part. The formal parameters specify with which fragment types the generic fragment type can be parameterized and whether this parameterization is optional or required. The semantics of what these fragments do is described by their types. It is possible to distinguish formal parameters of the required interface and the formal parameters of the provided interface, i.e. fragments that can be plugged into instances of the generic fragment type and fragments that are provided by instances of the generic fragment type. In this case, the type reference fragment Tin, the method fragments putMethod and removeMethod, the metaoperator synchronizer as well as the boolean value immutable are part of the *required* interface, while the type reference fragment Tout and the attribute ds are part of the *provided* interface. The conditions block specifies constraints which cannot be expressed by the fragment type system.

The construction plan in this example is simple, since the provided fragments are bound in a straightforward way. It is important to note that the generic fragment type itself controls whether and when a fragment is bound or a metaoperator is executed. In this example, synchronization is applied only if a metaoperator is given (otherwise the execute statement does nothing) and if it is necessary to synchronize the access to the data stored in HashSet instances.

The following generic fragment type extends the type HashSetRemoveElementMethodFragment, hence instances can be plugged into instances of the generic fragment type HashSet. It implements the removal of an element in a hash set.

```
fragment DefaultHashSetRemoveElementMethodFragment<
                TypeReferenceFragment T, required;
                Attribute dataAttribute, required>
   extends HashSetRemoveElementMethodFragment<T, dataAttribute>,

   conditions {
     (dataAttribute.type.isArray) &&
     (dataAttribute.componentType.equals(T))
   }
{
   construction {
     bind elemType -> T;
     bind storage -> dataAttribute;
   }
   implementation {
     public boolean remove(@(elemType : TypeReferenceFragment) element) {
       ...
       storage[i] = null;
       ...
     }
   }
}
```

Since in our approach the type of a fragment defines its semantics, it is also possible to plug in a typed metaoperator as a parameter. Being of an appropriate type, the metaoperator guarantees to have the same effects as binding an instance of a "simple" generic fragment type. The following operator is a subtype of HashSetRemoveElementMethodFragment, but instead of providing a concrete method fragment, it inlines the implementation code at all places the remove method is invoked. This also means that the operator has to be executed after the whole system has been composed.

```
operator InliningHashSetRemoveElementOperator<
                TypeReferenceFragment T, required;
                Attribute dataAttribute, required>
   extends HashSetRemoveElementMethodFragment<T, dataAttribute>
{
   dataAttribute.setPublic(true);
```

```
foreach a in this.bindings.referencingAccesses do {
    // Calls to method remove are inlined at all places the method is
    // referenced. The necessary statements are generated and injected by
    // this metaoperator.
    // No implementation of method remove will be inserted in class HashSet.
  }
}
```

The following examples are metaoperators which implement different synchronization strategies sketched in feature diagram Fig. 2. Synchronization is a feature which is not local with respect to the object-oriented decomposition, thus adding this feature to instances of a generic fragment type results in adaptations distributed all over the corresponding fragment or even the whole system. The places where the new synchronization fragments have to be injected is computed by the metaoperator by using suitable program analysis results.

```
operator ExclusiveAttributeAccessOperator<Attribute dataAttribute>
   extends SynchronizeAttributeAccessOperator<dataAttribute>,

   conditions {
      foreach acc in dataAttribute.referencingAccesses:
         acc.surroundingClass == dataAttribute.surroundingClass;
   }

{
   // Synchronizes access the "Java collection way" by adding the
   // modifier "synchronized" to all methods (except constructors).
   meths = []; meths.setUnique;
   foreach acc in dataAttribute.referencingAccesses do {
      if (!acc.surroundingMethod.isConstructor)
         meths.add(acc.surroundingMethod);
   }
   foreach m in meths do { m.setSynchronized(true); }
}

operator SynchronizeAttributeAccessPrioritiseRead<Attribute dataAttribute>
   extends SynchronizeAttributeAccessOperator<dataAttribute>
{ ... }

operator SynchronizeAttributeAccessPrioritiseWrite<Attribute dataAttribute>
   extends SynchronizeAttributeAccessOperator<dataAttribute>
{ ... }
```

Now that we have presented how to specify generic fragment types and typed metaoperators using an extended version of our INJECT/J language, the specification of a concrete configuration, i.e. of generic fragment types instances, is fairly simple. The configuration of a generic fragment type HashSet which can have strings as elements and which allows adding new elements but no removing of elements and that does not support synchronization results in the following specification:

```
HashSet< ${java.lang.String}$;
         DefaultHashSetPutElementMethodFragment,
         null,
         null
         >
```

The same HashSet which additionally supports the features of removing elements and safe concurrent access can be described as follows:

```
HashSet< ${java.lang.String}$;
         DefaultHashSetPutElementMethodFragment,
```

```
InliningHashSetRemoveElementOperator,
  SynchronizeAttributeAccessPrioritiseWrite
>
```

After the desired configuration has been specified, the concrete implementation is built by using the techniques described in section 3, e.g. composing the method fragments and class fragments, binding type reference fragments or applying metaoperators.

4.3 Discussion

Using our approach, we are able to implement an extended, more configurable version of the JCF. Configuring the feature of supported element types has been solved with the introduction of type genericity in JAVA 5, but our approach allows for the configuration of more advanced features, e.g. expressing immutability, functionality like addition or removal of elements or different synchronization strategies. By using invasive techniques, we are able to avoid disadvantages imposed by the JAVA language, e.g. huge numbers of interfaces and implementation classes for expressing features through the language's type system as presented in the Java Collection Framework Design FAQ[7] or unnecessary and even error-prone[8] indirections.

The specification of a concrete configuration can be done in a declarative way, i.e. it is possible to specify *what* is wanted, not *how* it is build. This helps to push the level of abstraction towards the application level. Based on the configuration specification of a generic fragment type, the resulting implementation can be build by an extended version of our tool INJECT/J. This compares to type genericity, where the user specifies what is needed and the compiler internally builds the resulting class or inserts appropriate type casts.

Well defined semantics are introduced by defining a type system for fragments as well as for metaoperators. This allows to guarantee the correctness of a configuration which can be expressed through a type system. By typing metaoperators, their effects on the instances of generic fragment types can be predicted, in contrast to general metaprogramming.

Our case study also showed that in our future work we must take into account that more advanced techniques for identifying concrete binding times and for computing their order are necessary. For example, in our case study, the metaoperator **InliningHashSetRemoveElementOperator** has to be bound (i.e. executed) after the configured (i.e. instantiated) generic fragment type **HashSet** is composed with other fragments to the resulting system at the earliest, while instances of the generic fragment type **DefaultHashSetRemoveElementMethod-Fragment** can be composed with **HashSet** before the latter is composed with

---

[7] http://java.sun.com/j2se/1.4.2/docs/guide/collections/designfaq.html

[8] The JCF provides wrapper implementations which synchronize the access to a collection. However, it is possible to access the collection in an unsynchronized fashion by using the original unwrapped object. This may cause subtle runtime errors, since this unwanted usage cannot be detected by the compiler.

other fragments. Binding order has to be considered because of dependencies between generic fragment types. Some dependencies are declared by the *required* and *provided* interfaces provided by the generic fragment type. Especially in conjunction with metaoperators, the possibility to declare explicit dependencies has to be improved, e.g. the `ExclusiveAttributeAccessOperator` operator is only allowed to be executed after the instance of the generic fragment type `DefaultHashSetPutElementMethodFragment` has been bound, otherwise the `remove` method remains unsynchronized.

5   Related Work

There are several invasive techniques that can be used for configuration and composition purposes. The most visible among them are probably preprocessors like the one found in C or C++. However, preprocessors have no well defined semantics. They are character based and not related to the structure of the programming language, thus no correctness of the resulting implementation can be guaranteed. In addition to preprocessors, another invasive configuration technique found in C++ emerged in the last few years: Template Metaprogramming (TMP, [3]). But TMP also has some drawbacks: It is limited to C++, it is very hard to systematically implement metaprograms and the results are almost unmaintainable for the average programmer.

Traits as described in [7] offer the ability to compose classes from methods, avoiding the problems known from multiple inheritance and mixins. However, the implementation of a feature often affects only parts of a method (i.e., the statement and the expression level). Extracting these statements into trait methods results in an unnatural method decomposition.

A technique which addresses the closed specification of cross-cutting features is aspect-oriented programming (AOP, [6]). The most prominent AOP tool is without doubt ASPECTJ[9]. The main critique is that ASPECTJ only supports fragment composition, but no fragment decomposition or fragment removal, which is necessary in some cases, such as optimization operations.

Invasive software composition as introduced in [1] and implemented by the COMPOST system[10] can be used as an implementation technique for our approach. However, we chose INJECT/J as an implementation base in order to benefit from its expressive script language which can to a large extent be used to specify generic fragment types and metaoperators.

On the process level, which was not the focus of this paper, our approach can be seen as a concrete instance of the generative programming paradigm [3].

6   Conclusion

In this paper we have presented an approach for invasive configuration of program fragments. We introduced the notion of generic fragment types, which

---

[9] http://www.eclipse.org/aspectj

[10] http://www.the-compost-system.org

consist of a configuration interface, a construction plan and the actual generic implementation. In our approach, instances of generic fragment types are the units of hierarchical composition, i.e. a fragment can be plugged into another fragment. The semantics of a fragment is given by its type together with additional constraints. The configuration interface describes which fragments can be composed, while the construction plan determines how the actual composition is executed based on the generic implementations of the involved fragments. As a reaction to crosscutting features, we also introduced typed metaoperators. They consist of a fragment template together with a metaprogram specifying how and where these fragment templates have to be instantiated and injected into the resulting code through transformation or generation. Like generic fragment types, they have a type specifying their semantics. We sketched how an extended version of our software adaptation tool INJECT/J can be used as an implementation base for our approach.

Our future work will be targeted at two directions. On the technical level, we will implement the proposed extensions to INJECT/J. The other direction is to improve our initial process that maps end-user visible features to configuration specifications of generic components.

Acknowledgement

This work was done as part of the project CollaBaWü within the research association PRIMIUM, funded by the Ministry of Science, Research and the Arts of the state of Baden-Württemberg, Germany.

References

1. Uwe Assmann. *Invasive Software Composition*. Springer Verlag, 2003.
2. Lothar Baum, Martin Becker, Lars Geyer, and Georg Molter. Mapping Requirements to Reusable Components Using Design Spaces. In *ICRE*, pages 159–167, 2000.
3. Krzysztof Czarnecki and Ulrich W. Eisenecker. *Generative Programming – Methods, Tools, and Applications*. Addison-Wesley, May 2000.
4. Thomas Genssler. *Werkzeuggestützte Adaption objektorientierter Programme*. PhD thesis, Universität Karlsruhe (TH), Forschungszentrum Informatik Karlsruhe (FZI), 2004.
5. Thomas Genssler and Volker Kuttruff. Source-to-Source Transformation In The Large. In *Proceedings of the Joint Modular Language Conference*, pages 254–265. Springer LNCS, August 2003.
6. G. Kiczales, J. Lamping, A. Mendhekar, C. Maeda, C. V. Lopes, J.-M. Loingtier, and J. Irwin. Aspect-Oriented Programming. In *Proceedings of the European Conference on Object-Oriented Programming (ECOOP)*, LNCS 1241. Springer-Verlag, 1997.
7. Nathanael Schärli, Stéphane Ducasse, Oscar Nierstrasz, and Andrew Black. Traits: Composable units of behavior. In *Proceedings ECOOP 2003 (European Conference on Object-Oriented Programming)*, volume 2743 of *LNCS*. Springer Verlag, 2003.
8. P. Tarr, H. Ossher, W. Harrison, and S.M. Sutton. N Degrees of Separation: Multi-Dimensional Separation of Concerns. In *Proceedings of the International Conference on Software Engineering (ICSE'99)*, 1999.

Author Index

Lecture Notes in Computer Science

For information about Vols. 1–3555

please contact your bookseller or Springer